The *Populus* of Augustine and Jerome

The *Populus* of Augustine and Jerome

A STUDY IN THE PATRISTIC SENSE OF COMMUNITY

BY JEREMY DUQUESNAY ADAMS

NEW HAVEN AND LONDON, YALE UNIVERSITY PRESS, 1971

Published with assistance from
The Mary Cady Tew Memorial Fund.
Library of Congress catalog card number: 70-140521
International standard book number: 0-300-01402-3

Designed by Marvin Howard Simmons
and set in Linotype Granjon type.
Printed in the United States of America by
Vail-Ballou Press, Inc., Binghamton, N.Y.

Distributed in Great Britain, Europe, and Africa by
Yale University Press, Ltd., London; in Canada by
McGill-Queen's University Press, Montreal; in Mexico
by Centro Interamericano de Libros Académicos,
Mexico City; in Central and South America by Kaiman
& Polon, Inc., New York City; in Australasia by
Australia and New Zealand Book Co., Pty., Ltd.,
Artarmon, New South Wales; in India by UBS Publishers'
Distributors Pvt., Ltd., Delhi; in Japan by John
Weatherhill, Inc., Tokyo.

Contents

Preface

This may strike some of its readers as a rather curious book. Structuralist in conception, positivist in development, and yet orthodox humanist in final purpose and allegiance, it offers by way of conclusion a set of hard data relevant to the political and social thought of Augustine and Jerome, rather than a synthetic reinterpretation of certain aspects of that thought. No single salient insight is put forward to serve as the organizing principle for a restructuring of current judgments and well-recognized texts. The data presented here and the study which deals with its derivation are both oriented toward just such an eventual synthesis, which I hope to make public before too very long. Nevertheless, I think that there are adequate reasons for publishing this book at this time and in this state. The results of this study can stand apart from their ultimate relationship to the general theory of patristic group identity which I project; they may well appeal to some readers more than that theory will; and since I have tried assiduously to avoid teleological preoccupations in developing this study, its results can be of genuine and substantial use and interest to readers with long-range concerns other than my own.

I hope (and think) that those results constitute a coherent, nuclear set of information, from which more elaborate conclusions can be developed in a number of directions: the final chapter sketches several such zones of potential radiation. I hope even more fervently that that core possesses properties of inherent interest. It is not simply an arrangement of the raw material of intellectual history, an assemblage of texts subjected to analysis and commentary. It is, instead, a set of refined data, derived from that sort of raw material by a distinctive and substantially new process. I offer both the process and the product to anyone interested.

Approximately two-thirds of this book consists of two-thirds of my Ph.D. dissertation, "Sense of Community in the Early Middle Ages: 'Populus' and Other Sociopolitical Terms in the Works of Jerome, Augustine, and Isidore of Seville" (Harvard, 1966). The newest third of the present work was composed in New Haven and Paris in 1969, thanks in part to the generous and timely support of the Morse Fellowship Fund of Yale University and a Younger Scholars Fellowship from the National Endowment for the Humanities. Throughout its transformations, this project has owed much to Professor Giles Constable of Harvard University, whose rare combination of stringent professional standards, critical rigor, and sympathetic intellectual imagination has exercised unique influence on the shape of the original thesis and its subsequent revisions. I hope that the defects of this final version do not entirely obscure the virtues due to his direction. In its later stages this book has benefited from the constructive advice of Professors William H. Dunham, Jaroslav Pelikan, and Peter Gay of Yale University, Professors Henri-Irénée Marrou, Jacques Fontaine, and Michel Mollat of the University of Paris, and Mlle Marie-Thérèse d'Alverny of the Centre National de la Recherche Scientifique. I am deeply indebted for several kinds of assistance to R. P. Georges Folliet and other members of the staff of *Etudes Augustiniennes* in Paris, and also to Mlles Françoise Chaumais, Marie-Claude Lorrain, and Françoise Sudre of the Centre Universitaire International. I alone am responsible, of course, for the book's deficiencies.

I must express my special gratitude to Mrs. Ruth D. Kaufman and to the imaginative support of Robert L. Zangrando, successive history editors of the Yale University Press during the book's submission and production. Marvin Howard Simmons and Mrs. Sally P. Sullivan handled the numerous problems of design with elegant dispatch. Several other members of the staff, students, and friends read portions of the proof or advised on the index. Finally, without the really Titanic patience and ingenuity of Mrs. Ellen Graham's editorial coordination, this book could not have seen the light of day. It hardly needs to be remarked that my wife's investment of encouragement and endurance in all phases of this undertaking is beyond comparison or adequate acknowledgment.

New Haven, 1971   J. duQ. A.

1 Introduction

Purpose and Assumptions

The purpose of this study is to examine the range of meanings carried by the word *populus* in the Vulgate Bible and in the writings of Augustine and Jerome, or, perhaps more precisely, to report the findings of such an examination. In the course of this examination I have also given consideration to several other words relating to social and political bodies, either because they stand in illuminating contrast to *populus* in the works discussed, or because they serve as satellites. The requisite analysis has been conducted according to a method of selective induction which, if not entirely new, seeks at least to explore a fresh approach to some classic issues of medieval intellectual history.

I hope and expect that this study's method and results will ultimately prove useful to the resolution of a central set of questions: Into which and what sorts of groups was mankind divided in the minds of patristic and early medieval thinkers? To which of those groups did they feel that they, and those to whom they addressed their surviving works, belonged? If they felt a sense of community with several groups or kinds of groups, what did they feel about the proper hierarchy of loyalties in that regard? In view of the magisterial authority exercised by Augustine and Jerome in their own and in subsequent centuries, certifiable answers to such questions should be able to enrich our understanding of a wide range of medieval thought and practice.

This study does not provide a direct or developed set of answers to those questions. I propose in a subsequent study to examine the changing usage of *populus* and some related terms (*plebs, gens, natio,* and *patria*) in the works of Gregory the Great and Isidore of Seville,[1] a comparable pair of near-contemporaries two very different centuries later. The shift in usage undergone by the noun *populus* alone after that troubled lapse of time and, still more, its altered relationship to those other terms are pregnant with consequences for serious students of the political theories constructed then and later with such words. In this volume, however, I have carefully eschewed the broader implications and more exciting theoretical corollaries of the semantic analysis which I have undertaken. I hope the data will speak for itself; I feel that it will do so all the more clearly and be of use to a wider range of readers and interests if it appears uncontaminated by general speculations which must by nature be more subjective than I hope this analysis has been.

The noun *populus* was chosen as the center of this study, the starting point for the larger inquiry which I intend to pursue, because of its evident importance in the political lexicon of Latin antiquity. In most cases it referred to a group of rational beings associated by some form of consent expressed in laws, policy, or public ritual. The consent involved was usually conscious and at least potentially subject to alteration; predetermining factors such as ethnic or linguistic affiliation were not closely or normally associated with it. On the other hand, *populus* was not a narrowly political term of strictly technical employment: it was usually applied to a fully articulated community with a wide range of activities and several levels of self-consciousness, and it appears quite frequently in the surviving literature.[2] It was a word full of meaning and resonance, quite different from the diffuse and broadly polysemic *people* which is less its heir than its descendant. I have assumed that any major and sustained shift in the usage of such a word indicates, or at least strongly suggests, a significant change of attitude and habits on the part of the users. The task of the present study has been to establish that word's meaning (or meanings) in two patristic literary corpora of important volume and authority, to serve as a standard for assessing the usage of their own and later generations.

I have assumed further that a close look at the exact language which men use when speaking or writing about certain kinds of groups is the best procedure we have for arriving at an approximation of their sense of social or political community. It seems to me that such an examination brings us closer to the ways in which men like Augustine and Jerome formulated their feelings than the scraps of outright theorizing on the subject which we find scattered throughout their diverse works. Some of the most powerful and persistent of human convictions operate just beneath the level of formula construction, and in patterns interestingly different from statements held up for public exhibit. It is not uncommon to find such prejudices (to use Burke's neutral and honorable term for this kind of sentiment about the right shape of things) pervading the writings of even an accomplished author far more consistently and vividly than do his formal ideas on related topics, and thereby affecting both the prejudices and the ideas of later readers who depend on his categories of language to formulate their own thought.

Because of this assumption, this study may appear to concentrate on Augustine's and Jerome's less than fully self-conscious use of political and social terms rather than on the deployment of these terms in finished theory. In a sense it tries to trap those authors in their own words, assembled as cumulative evidence from over the years, rather than in the more intense and *perhaps* purer intentions of single statements. If such an emphasis appears unbalanced, I can only plead that the less traditional side of this inquiry and its less familiar techniques needed more attention.

This study is in large part an attempt to develop a rather novel type of semantic analysis which should assist the historical sociologist as well as the intellectual or political historian in refining or resolving a number of interesting issues. It seems to me that the modern intellectual historian can ask the great thinkers of the past two general types of questions: those they posed themselves, and those they did not but which we must. Treatment of the first sort of question (e.g., "What was Augustine's teaching concerning the two natures of Christ?") is an indispensable step toward the elucidation of a great man's thought, especially if his categories of expression are not precisely our own. There is, fortunately, no acute shortage of this kind of work in the field of Latin patristics.

The latter kind of question can produce conclusions both more risky and more original, and from one point of view more inter-

esting. Such inquiry can, of course, be cast in terms so anachro-
nistic as to be absurd ("What would Augustine the African bishop
have thought about racial segregation in twentieth-century America?"), but that is not an inevitable failing. How much (if any)
legitimacy Augustine attributed to secular society is a question
that rises quickly and spontaneously in the minds of most serious
readers of *The City of God,* and one to which the author supplies
no outright answer. Arquillière has shown how several distorted
answers to that question became lively sources of propaganda and
even of policy inspiration in the period of the Investiture Controversy. Within our own century that problem has once more attracted the attention of intellectuals, some of whom have spent no
little store of ingenuity in their attempts to solve it.

In this one particular not too distant from their medieval predecessors, modern scholars have usually relied on a method of
analysis proceeding from the selection of a few key texts, to a
subtle dissection or reconciliation of them, and then to a deductive
application of the interpretation thereby derived to the rest of the
author's work or "mind." It should be no surprise that this critical
technique has produced results as irreconcilable as they are bril-
liant.

Although such disagreement is undoubtedly an exhilarating
contribution to the endless dialectic which has long been one of
the most evident characteristics of the history of ideas, it leaves
something to be desired. In this study I have attempted to reverse
the method, selecting a series of questions which would not, I
think, have seemed incomprehensible or irrelevant to the authors
concerned, and then trying to arrive at answers through the collection and classification of inductive evidence.[3] Most of my questions
are very modest in scope ("What did *A* mean by *x* and/or *y*?");
however, Appendix A proposes a solution to the dispute about
Augustine's respect for secular society, and Appendix D offers new
evidence on Latin translations of the Acts of the Apostles which
can either complement or refute the arguments of a type of biblical
criticism relying on stylistic analyses derived from general literary
principles. I hope that readers with still other interests will find
this book a similarly useful critical tool, or at least a suggestive
exercise.

The choice of Augustine and Jerome as initial samples for a

semantic investigation of the medieval sense of community hardly needs justification. Few other Latin authors in any Christian century have written works of such diversity in both genre and inspiration; few if any wielded equal influence on the millennium that followed. I think that neither of these points needs much further elaboration in the case of Augustine, incomparably the master of reflective Western thinkers for nearly a millennium after his death, and author of those epochal generic novelties, the *Confessions* and *The City of God,* as well as of conventional dialogues and treatises, several varieties of scriptural commentary, and hundreds of letters and sermons.

Jerome's influence on the later thought and language of Latin Christendom may seem at first glance simply a by-product of his translation of the Vulgate, and so comparable in neither regard to Augustine's contribution. It is perfectly true that Jerome was in no sense a creative thinker. Obsessed by a dread of heterodoxy, he was by instinct a votary of the literary text, whether secular or sacred, and his only novelties were those of a scholar committed to critical purity. In his most striking departure from the Christian intellectual consensus of his age, his steadily mounting distrust of allegorical exegesis, he showed once again his fidelity to traditions already established.

Jerome's impact on later ages should not be discounted, however. His translation was no passive rendering of formulations unaffected by the transfer; as I shall argue in detail in chapter 3, Jerome dressed the content of Scripture in a very distinctive language, the vocabulary of which he chose according to sweeping interpretative judgments of his own. Furthermore, his ten dozen letters, each the product of acute literary self-consciousness, served as models of elevated expression for several Christian renaissances. Can such an influence on the language of the intellectual classes be devoid of influence on their thought? It may be an indirect contribution of semantic habit rather than a direct gift of specific propositions, but I find it impossible to deny the weightiness of such a legacy. Jerome's role in shaping the reflective language of the Christian West was different from Augustine's, but the difference itself is interesting, and provides a worthy basis for thoughtful comparison.

The fact that Augustine and Jerome were nearly exact contemporaries, products of the same class and of very similar educations in quite different provinces of the Roman Empire, makes the comparison all the more alluring. Each was the intellectually precocious son of a family of decurion status in a small town with little past and less future—Illyrian Stridon has disappeared today, and Numidian Tagaste is nearly unrecognizable under the name of Souk Ahras. Costly educational ambitions soon led both from home, Jerome going to Rome in his early adolescence and Augustine to Madaura and then Carthage in his unforgettably reported fifteenth and seventeenth years. Each went on to greater capitals in later stages of educational formation: Jerome to Constantinople and Antioch, Augustine to Rome and Milan. Each spent brief but decisive periods in the northern metropoles of an Italy whose most up-to-date concerns looked to the east and to the northern frontiers: Augustine in Milan and Jerome in Aquileia (as well as Trier, its Gallic counterpart). Moving in the orbit of the high senatorial aristocracy to which they did not belong, both men sought high career advancement in those cities and, more persistently, in Rome: Jerome in the secretariat of Pope Damasus, Augustine in rhetorical appointments apparently in the gift of Symmachus's party. Disappointed or disenchanted with their ambitions for such metropolitan success, both retired to the edge of the desert for a mode of life which promised a blend of spiritual contemplation and personal recollection but turned into something more like semimonastic intellectual factories.

Both acknowledged Cicero as their supreme master. In love with his rhetoric, they came late to know each other through the epistolary conventions which were his second most important generic legacy to letters. Jerome studied directly under Donatus, who came from the African school tradition native to Augustine, and under Marius Victorinus, whose conversion to Christianity put Augustine's religious sincerity decisively on the spot. Each was baptized in a major Italian cathedral basilica during the Easter Vigil, the supreme annual ritual of Christian citizenship.

The differences between the two men give a comparison wider general value, as well as saving it from monotony. Jerome studied language and the history of texts, Augustine philosophy and Christian doctrine. Augustine, who never names his teachers, had that rare talent for creating new ideas and literary forms, and felt little but impatience with Jerome's extraordinary critical acumen. Jerome traveled more widely than Augustine, but Augustine had a wider experience of life. Each had a close and uneasy relationship with women, but their early encounters and adult dealings with the other sex were disparate indeed: we know nothing about Jerome's mother, hear no hint of any mistress, and find that women were almost the only friends of his later years, while Augustine the bishop, a master of easy masculine friendship, avoided any private interview with members of the sex that he had known all too well before. Jerome knew the Jews better and probably liked them less. Compulsively orthodox, he ended up as usual on the wrong side of local ecclesiastical authority, whereas Augustine died organizing the defense of his episcopal city, which he had been steadily purging of Donatists with the help of the imperial police.

Perhaps most importantly for the purposes of this study, both men belonged to that generation which spent its childhood in the last decades of relative external tranquillity, and died after the Roman peace had been forever shattered, the urban symbol of its intactness burned and pillaged. Jerome, in letters that needed no artifice to convey his anguish, simply could not comprehend the violation of the city which he loved above all others; Augustine, who professed contempt for the Roman mission but could not imagine the empire's being replaced by another form of secular order, was irritated into composing his greatest and most comprehensive masterpiece. I do not contend that these two men define, exhaust, or in any other way express the "mind" of the whole literate generation that experienced in its maturity the sack of Rome—or even the Christian side of that historically pivotal generation. However, I can think of no other pair of Latin authors more essential to consider for anyone attempting such a definition.[4]

In assessing the value of a word in its various and varying appearances within the literary output of these two men, I have not assumed a constant rate of seriousness, self-consciousness, or semantic care on either author's part. I have, on the contrary, assumed a good deal of variation in the way each author used his vocabulary. It is precisely by paying close attention to the value of a word in a number of different literary genres and contexts, and at different times and in different situations of the author's life, that I have tried to see if the word had any more or less constant range of meanings for him. If so, I have tried to describe the variant as well as to isolate the constant elements of the word's meaning. All of my investigation has proceeded on the general assumption that a man of fair intelligence and appropriate training, reading the work of another man in whom he is interested, can get from that work some sense of the author's habits and intended meanings.

In order to do so, I began my research with hundreds of instances of usage gathered at random, attempted to classify them purely on the basis of their significance in context, and then tried to point out inconsistencies between definitions and usage rather than to resolve them. Any "definitions" of usage which I offer myself seek to be descriptive and as inclusive as possible; I hope that they contain no terms which are not the product of inductive processing of the examples. I consider examination of the concrete context of composition or delivery extremely important to the proper analysis of any example (whether or not later medieval readers shared this concern). Finally, I have tried to counterbalance the natural and widespread tendency to concentrate attention on single and rather special works like *The City of God*.

The Problem of Consistency

It may be advisable at this point to clarify my understanding of semantic consistency. I do not consider this understanding one of this study's primary epistemological assumptions, but it figures importantly in the results and may well be misunderstood. In order to avoid extremely technical formulations, I propose as a valid standard the following definition of *consistency* from *Webster's Third New International Dictionary*:

> 3a: agreement or harmony of parts, traits, or features: uniformity among a number of things . . . *specif.*: the characteristic of two or more propositions and derivatively of properties and propositional functions in logic that appertains if their conjunction does not result in contradiction.

In posing the question, "What does it mean to say that an author uses a word consistently?", we must make a few distinctions:

1. We must distinguish between internal and external consistency. In discussing the word's discernible content, the declared or apparent meaning or meanings conveyed by the written sign for which we search in an authors' writings, we may question the logical coherence of the elements of meaning conveyed. Such coherence may be termed internal consistency, although some linguists would object to that phraseology. However labeled, this relationship is a valid object of evaluative study for philosophy or theoretical linguistics, and may become so for political theorists or historians of ideas, especially if they encounter one of those extended metaphors so dear to classical political theory: for example, if an author speaks of the realm of England as a family of which the king is father, what does he really mean by *family* (and *father*)? Can such extended meanings claim any internal consistency? What, therefore, are we to think of policy recommendations drawn from such usages? This sort of evaluative criticism is not, however, an object of primary concern for this study, which tries to describe the range of meanings conveyed by the chosen words, rich as they may be in potential for such extended application.

2. External consistency can be of three types: (a) between the definition of a word and one or more patterns of usage; (b) between two or more patterns of usage; (c) among "parts, traits, or features" of a composite definition or usage, either within one combination of attributes or by substitution with attributes in another combination (presumably varying rather than totally different). As should be evident, this is not identical with the question of internal consistency or coherence. An attempt to solve question 2c seeks a descriptive answer rather than an evaluative assessment on the order of higher truth.

I hope that the following chapters will not make the reader need reassurance about my concern for properly careful treatment of questions 1, 2a, or 2b. It is about question 2c that I have felt most nagging concern.

If we observe a definition or pattern of usage consisting of attributes (perhaps *features* would be a more attractive, less "philosophical" term) A, B, C, and D, and another usage unmistakably referring to feature A and in no way ruling out implication of B, C, and D, we may surely declare the latter usage consistent with the definition or former usage. I think we may validly make the same judgment about a usage referring to any of those four features (let us say A) and either stating or (because of context) implying a fifth (E) which does not in logic, common current usage, or paraphrasable mood contradict any of the other three (B, C, or D).

But what if we discern the following situation: *Usage 1:* A, B, C, D; *Usage 2:* A, B, E, F (contradicting D)? Then it becomes necessary to make a decision about the relative importance of D and F to each pattern of usage and to one another. If either or both seem a relatively minor feature, or if F seems to offer no essential contradiction to a more important feature (such as A), then I do not think we are required to declare Usages 1 and 2 essentially inconsistent. I fully recognize that a geometrician would declare otherwise, that a legal theorist might prefer to, and that strict linguistic theorists would probably be unhappy with the form in which this discussion has been cast. Most of them would prefer simply to measure the relative polysemy of the various usages examined, reserving the question of consistency for the relation of such usages to a formal definition.[5]

Perhaps a hypothetical analogy drawn from the realm of literary criticism will make my assumptions and intent in this matter more concrete. It may cloud whatever logical clarity is left in the preceding statement, but that tends to be the way of literary language and indeed of human speech.

Consider the noun *epic,* defined either as "A poem celebrating in stately verse the achievements of heros or of demigods; a heroic poem" (*Funk & Wagnalls Standard College Dictionary,* New York, 1943), or as "1: A long narrative poem recounting the deeds of a legendary or historical hero; a: . . . having a serious theme developed in a coherent and unified manner, written in a dignified style, and marked by certain formal characteristics . . ." (*Webster's Third New International Dictionary*). Most literate men would consent to the application of that term to the *Iliad* and to *Paradise Lost.* They might reasonably feel uncomfortable about applying the term *drama* to those poems, but be willing to admit the validity of a reference to the *tragic* aspect of *Paradise Lost.* In the last case, it would be important for a student of their terminology to determine, if possible, whether the critic in question assigned *Paradise Lost* to the same literary genre as *Antigone* and *Macbeth,* or simply referred to one important common trait: the saddening but grandeur-struck fall of a central character due to some internal flaw. In other words, did the critic intend a full definitional identification (of individual *Paradise Lost* with species *tragedy* of the genus *drama*) or was he simply employing metonymy? If the latter is true, then I think we can say that the author is not confusing epic and dramatic forms, that he does not mean that *Paradise Lost* is a tragedy (or even drama) *rather than* an epic, and that he is not using his literary terminology in an inconsistent manner.

To carry this analogy a bit further and also in a somewhat different direction, let us imagine three critics who differ somewhat in their employment of the word *epic.* Critic 1 defines the term according to both of the definitions given above. He uses it to refer to the *Iliad, Paradise Lost,* and James Joyce's *Ulysses,* but in the last of these cases he clearly enjoys the striking effect of his metonymy and the chance it gives him to raise such questions as the real differences between poetry and prose. He also calls *Paradise Lost* a tragedy on occasion. Critic 2 does not define epic form, despite great literary sensitivity. He generally mirrors Critic 1's habits of classification, except that he goes further, applying the word *epic* (perhaps as an adjective) to the *Confessions* of St. Augustine, thereby drawing attention to its frequent allusions to the *Aeneid* and emphasizing certain of its authentic attributes not usually noticed. Similarly, he calls *The Yellow Submarine* a visual epic. At times he points out the tragic dimensions of the *Iliad* as well as of *Paradise Lost*—but not of the *Odyssey.* Critic 3 goes to great pains to define epic form, and does so more fastidiously and conservatively than Critic 1. We notice that in the full range of his writings he applies the term *epic* to the *Iliad, Paradise Lost, Ulysses,* the *Confessions, The Yellow Submarine* (he respects antecedent authority), and also to Agatha Christie murder mysteries, P. G. Wodehouse stories, Pope's *Essay on Criticism,* and

Tintern Abbey (making *epic* mean, in effect, any literary production of wide reputation).

It seems clear to me that no one could reasonably deny that Critic 1 used the term *epic* in an essentially consistent manner; I think that only an extreme rigorist would deny that virtue to Critic 2, and only an extreme laxist claim it for Critic 3. To anticipate some of my conclusions through the medium of this admittedly crude device, I think that in their usage of *populus* Augustine resembles Critic 1, Jerome Critic 2, and Isidore of Seville Critic 3. Including Isidore in this quasi-Homeric simile may be a bit unfair, since the proof of my contentions concerning him lies beyond the scope of the present volume. Unfortunately, his loosely scattered usage of *populus*—or, to speak with more technical precision, his broadly polysemic usage of *populus*—emphasizes the startling tightness (or "consistency") of the two earlier authors' usage as no other example can.

Method

The research for this study was undertaken in three stages. First, I made a random search through the primary material, using indexes when they were available but otherwise avoiding secondary literature as completely as possible. Next, I undertook a more thorough examination of patterns of usage in a few individual works of the author under consideration; this step required the guidance of some secondary critical literature, but an effort was made to hold that influence to a minimum. Last, after preliminary conclusions had been reached and recorded, a broad survey of the secondary literature was undertaken, to see how far those conclusions agreed with, paralleled, superseded, or differed from other work in the field.

The first of these stages needs little comment, aside from my surprised discovery that the Maurist indexes to Augustine's complete works were the only indexes of consistent utility, although they make no pretensions to completeness. Individual works were selected for more careful investigation in the second stage according to some of the following criteria:

1. Special concern with political or social issues, as in *The City of God* and the Acts of the Apostles.

2. No special concern with such issues, or their appearance in an evidently subordinate or apparently subconscious guise; for example, sermons or passages of scriptural exegesis of which the main point is individual salvation, the godlessness of the theater, etc. Documentation was sought from this sort of context in order to get a balanced view of the full range of each author's usage, but such cases were not collected nor are they put forward as copiously as the examples of outright political relevance.

3. Some opportunity for isolating the personal, strictly individual vocabulary of the author under consideration. Exegetical paraphrases of the words of Scripture provided several revealing instances of personal preference.

4. The popularity in decisive later contexts of individual works, or the interesting contrary. For example, in chapter 3 I have paid considerable attention to the relationship between the Latin side of *Codex Laudianus* and the Vulgate Acts of the Apostles (see Appendix D). I was not as much concerned with the question of Jerome's immediate "models" as with the chance to explore some of the differences between his translation and the version of the Acts preferred and commented upon by Bede, otherwise one of the chief promoters of the Vulgate in his time.

The third stage, a survey of the secondary literature related to my inquiry, has had a limited effect on the conclusions and arguments derived from the two previous stages. Some new loci were suggested, analysis of which was then incorporated in the revised text. Unfortunately, most of the existing literature seemed relevant only negatively or tangentially to the specific questions posed and the method followed in this study. Some of the footnotes which serve as compressed bibliographical essays on such material attempt to give a selective impression of the range of current and still instructive older scholarship.

Parallel Studies

In the course of surveying the secondary literature, I came upon four studies in connection with which my own results and method may be interestingly compared. The first of these chronologically is R. T. Marshall's doctoral dissertation, *Studies in the Political and Socio-Religious Terminology of the "De Civitate Dei"* (Patristic Studies, vol. 86). Marshall set out primarily to establish the intellectual content of the term *civitas* in Augustine's magnum opus, although he considers a few examples from elsewhere. In order to give broader perspective to that inquiry, he discusses also (although much more briefly) the meanings of the less important terms *populus, regnum, gens, societas, ecclesia,* and *res publica.* His line of investigation is essentially deductive: first he analyzes Augustine's formal definitions of the term in question; then he collects a considerable number of representative examples of that term's use, presents them in a series of tables, and discusses some of them as further demonstrations of the definition already established or suggested; finally, if there are any contradictions among definitions or between definitions and examples, Marshall tries with great subtlety to effect a logical reconciliation.

Marshall's ultimate goal seems to be the establishing of a terminological vocabulary of contemporary as well as patristic relevance, and of wider than historical utility. He is constantly concerned to classify each term (or, at any rate, each major variety of its application) as either "political" or "socio-religious." He wishes, for example, to establish that *civitas Dei* is a "socio-religious" entity, and *populus Romanus* a "political" body; it is also clear that the latter kind of term interests him less than the former.[6]

Two years after Marshall's dissertation, a lengthy article entitled "La equivalencia de *civitas* en el 'De civitate Dei'" appeared in the special number of *La Ciudad de Dios* commemorating Augustine's fifteen-hundredth birthday. It was the joint effort of Juan José R. Rosado and Gabriel del Estal. They paid close attention to Marshall's study, supplementing it in several ways. First, Rosado produced a 31-page tabulation of every appearance of *civitas, populus, gens, regnum, saeculum, ecclesia, res publica, imperium, societas, urbs, Ierusalem, patria,* and *Babylon* in *The City of God,* thus correcting and expanding Marshall's quantitative estimates,[7] and providing later researchers with a splendidly useful statistical resource. I have relied heavily on it in compiling the frequency table in Appendix B. Second, the article offers a lengthy sketch of civic theory and practice in the Greco-Roman world. Third, it relates the whole discussion to current traditions of translating the title *civitas Dei* and to the analytical categories of classical German sociology (the influence of Tönnies' *Gemeinschaft-Gesellschaft* model is dominant, but Max Weber's insights are also present). The actual discussion of Augustine's use of *civitas* and of the lesser terms departs little from Marshall's in method or conclusion, although it is both more compressed and stylistically more refined. Consequently, this exercise in synthesis seems to me to go even further in the direction of abstract, deductive categorization than Marshall's thesis. Some of my specific disagreements are touched on briefly in notes 24 and 30 to chapter 2.

Very different from these two studies are the relevant portions of two German monographs: Josef Ratzinger's *Volk und Haus Gottes in Augustins Lehre von der Kirche* and Wolfgang Seyfarth's *Soziale Fragen der spätrömischen Kaiserzeit im Spiegel des Theodosianus*. Neither book is primarily concerned with the investigation of terminology, but each devotes a significant part of one chapter to considering such problems [8] before moving on to more central questions. Both of these treatments have achieved terminological analyses of persuasive subtlety, thanks to the close attention they pay to historical context and to their reliance on an easily communicable variety of common-sense logic for categories of reference. Neither study makes the most of terminology-analysis, however. I must disagree with Ratzinger's conclusion about the difference in meaning between *populus* and *populi* or *plebes*.[9] Its formulation suggests an atypical and damaging over-ingenuity, and is based on an inadequate collection of examples. Similarly, Seyfarth would have done well to take some of the language of the sermons and letters of Augustine into account when he set out to explore the social context and effects of the Theodosian Code. I feel sure that further evidence derived from such a source would have enriched and in places modified his conclusions.

I must express my particular admiration for a recent synthetic study, Herbert Deane's *The Political and Social Ideas of St. Augustine*. It bears eloquent witness to the value of building conclusions upon wide, free, and sensitive citation from all aspects and phases of an author's work. Unfortunately, the scope of Deane's inquiry did not permit him to examine very deeply the terms fundamental to his argument. I hope that it is not too presumptuous to volunteer this study in the service of that tradition of Augustinian scholarship, besides offering it to students of Jerome and still other patristic and medieval authors as something at least of a methodological novelty.

2 *Populus* in Augustine

Definitions in The City of God

To Augustine, bishop of Hippo Regius, the word *populus* conveyed a definite, sophisticated, and important set of concepts—or, to be more exact, two variations of a central political insight. In the second of his *Twenty-two Books on the City of God*,[1] struggling with the problem of justice in society and of the consequent validity of secular society itself, he turned for inspiration and authority to the doctrine of Cicero's dialogue *On the Commonwealth*. Recapitulating at some length much of the second and third books of that late republican treatise, he reminded his readers of the venerable Scipio's insistence that any profitable discussion of civil society must proceed from a definition of the essential term *res publica,* which is, in a form both more simple and more exact, a *res populi.*[2]

[Scipio] specifies, however, that by *populus* he means, not every gathering of a multitude, but a gathering united in fellowship by a common sense of right and a community of interest. Then he explains the great advantage of definition in debate, and he concludes from those particular definitions that a *res publica,* that is, the *res* of a *populus,* exists when there is a good and lawful government, whether in the hands of a monarch, or of few nobles, or of the whole *populus.* When, however, the monarch is unjust—he used the usual Greek term "tyrant" for such a monarch—or the nobles are unjust—he called their mutual agreement a faction—or the populus itself is unjust—for this he found no current term if he were not to call it too a tyrant—

then the *res publica* is no longer merely defective, as had been argued the day before, but, as a chain of reasoning from the foregoing definitions would have made plain, does not exist at all. For there was no *res* of a *populus,* he said, when a tyrant or a faction took over the *res publica,* nor was the *populus* itself any longer a *populus,* if it was unjust, since in that case it was not a multitude united in a fellowship by a common sense of right and a community of interest, as a *populus* had been defined.[3]

The definition is as famous as Augustine's resulting condemnation: a "common sense of right" (*consensus juris*) cannot exist without *justitia,* of which the essential principle is rendering to each his own; by failing to render God the adoration due Him, pagan Rome failed to qualify as a genuine commonwealth. However, Augustine knew perfectly well that that criticism did not exhaust the question of the validity of earthly society, and promised to hande it more properly later on, "according to more probable definitions." [4]

Seventeen books and about ten years later,[5] Augustine kept that promise. When he wrote book XIX, he was evidently in a different frame of mind, possibly more tolerant, certainly more original. No longer primarily concerned to debunk Roman claims to a superhuman historical mission,[6] he was concentrating his apologetic energies on the intellectual reputations of pagan philosophers and especially on Varro and Porphyry, whose authority he felt must always be taken to account and whose following he was at some pains to convert. Creative speculation suited this more amicable rhetorical purpose better than paradoxical refutation or frontal assault, both aimed at well-known and crystallized positions of authority. Besides, as he slowly neared the announced end of this work which kept growing "beyond all bounds," Augustine was raising his sights at the promptings of his own interests.

In the first twenty chapters of book XIX, Augustine discussed the various goals and forms of happiness proper to the earthly and heavenly Cities. When in chapter 21 he returned as promised to Cicero's definition of *res publica* and hence of *populus* through the persona of Scipio, he did so in order to emphasize that a human polity ignorant of God can never attain that ultimate justice without which any society must fail to achieve its full potential. Although the categorical condemnations of both republic and pagan empire from book II are echoed with essential fidelity, the earlier harshness seems muted.

The next, short chapter (22), a summary declaration of faith in the identity of the Christian God with the God imperfectly perceived by Varro and Porphyry, engaged Augustine in an extended defense of the Christian mandate against Porphyry's doubts and aspersions. At the end of this digression (chapter 23) on a subject close to his heart,[7] Augustine restated that ingenious Ciceronian critique of Roman polity, and with the opening words of the following chapter (24) went much further than he had before.

> But if a *populus* be defined not in this but in some other manner, for example, in this way: "A *populus* is a gathering of a multitude of rational beings united in fellowship by their agreement about the objects of their love," then surely, in order to perceive the character of each *populus,* we must inspect the objects of its love. . . . According to this definition of ours, the Roman *populus* is a *populus,* and its *res* is without doubt a *res publica.* But what this *populus* loved in its early and in subsequent times, and by what moral decline it passed into bloody sedition and then into social and civil warfare, and disrupted and corrupted that very concord which is, so to speak, the health (*salus*) of a *populus,* history bears witness, and I have dealt with it at length in the preceding books. And yet I shall not on this account say either that there is no *populus* or that its *res* is not a *res publica,* so long as there remains, however slight, a gathering of a multitude of rational beings united in fellowship by a common agreement about the objects of its love. But what I have said about this *populus* and about this *res publica* let me be understood to have said and meant about those of the Athenians, those of any other Greeks, of the Egyptians, of that earlier Babylon of the Assyrians and of any other *gens* whatsoever, when they maintained in their commonwealths an imperial sway, whether small or great.[8]

Three things seem especially noteworthy about these extended definitions. First, they are neither opposed nor mutually exclusive.

The latter, depending on a general consensus of desire, is broader than and can include the former, for which the essential consensus is one of legal order and pragmatic interest, themselves specific objects of social desire. The latter definition is capable of wider applicability, not only in terms of analytical description, but also along a scale of moral values, since it can suit both the City of God (of which it gives a more sublime description than the former definition) and earthly societies intent merely on decadent gratifications or even on self-destruction. So the two definitions are ultimately one, the Ciceronian statement becoming simply one dimension of Augustine's more original insight—perhaps simply being absorbed by it.

There are, to be sure, some important shifts of emphasis between these two definitional formulas. In the latter, Augustine's attention is centered on love, the attractive force (one is tempted to say the specific gravity) of everything in the universe—mute beings as well as sentient and social life—a general ordering principle of pervasive dynamism despite the cosmic balance which it ultimately guarantees. The former definition, by contrast, is dominated by a concern for the final verdict of justice, a standard tending to hierarchical evaluations, if not always or necessarily to fixed sentences. The *populus* of the earlier definition is brought together and determined by a *consensus* about law and a *communio* of interest, both cooler states of agreement than the *concors communio* about "the things which it loves" of the more spontaneous *populus* in the second definition, at once simpler and more capable of exaltation. The shift in rhetorical purpose from polemic devastation to more speculative persuasion has already been remarked.

Nevertheless, these significant differences in spirit, tone, and potential for subsequent extrapolation should not obscure the ease with which these two definitions can be logically reconciled on the level of literal formula. Aside from the fact that "justice" and "law" are normal objects of social desire, those two final terms of the former definition pertain to the latter by virtue of a logical and psychological implication which is hard to escape, given the context in which Augustine proposes and formulates the second definition.[9]

The second point especially worthy of notice is that Augustine seems to have been quite aware of the dangers of semantic confusion attending the formulation of such elaborate definitions. This is evident from his conclusion to the chapter in which Cicero's statement first appears.

> True justice, however, exists only in that *res publica* whose founder and ruler is Christ, if you please to call it too a *res publica,* since we cannot deny that it is the *res* of a *populus*. But even if this name, which is current with other associations and meanings, is perhaps too far removed from common usage, the fact remains that true justice resides in that *civitas* of which the holy Scriptures say, "Glorious things are said of thee, O city of God." [10]

The master rhetorician knew how wide a range of meanings a common word could convey in ordinary speech.[11] He set himself on guard against too much such diversity in this instance, and so invited his readers to expect fairly rigorous usage on his part. This impression of his intent is at least reinforced by statistical evidence. The word *populus* appears in XIX, 21, 23–24 thirty times, a higher frequency than in any other three topically unified chapters of *The City of God;* II, 19–22 constitute one of the two comparable chapter-sets with the second highest frequency of *populus* appearances (seventeen) in that huge work. Quantity seems to reflect the self-conscious quality of his employment of this word in this pair of definitions to which it is the stated key.

The third especially noteworthy point about these definitions is the tone of authority which one can hardly help sensing throughout the careful argument. Cicero exercised an immense and avowed influence on Augustine's literary style and habits of philosophical formulation, whatever reservations Augustine had about his character.[12] Vergil is probably Cicero's only pagan rival in this regard.[13] It is true that Augustine depended heavily on Plotinus for formal philosophical notions and felt a great (if distant) reverence for Plato,[14] but his youthful antipathy for the Greek tongue [15] necessarily left Cicero and Vergil preeminent among his non-Christian intellectual forebears. However overwhelming his theological and personal spiritual debt to the Scriptures,[16] however great the aesthetic and ethical impression made on him by Vergil, Augustine was too long a professional rhetorician and then too exclusively dedicated in his literary production to sermons, letters, and prose treatises and dialogues not to be profoundly dependent on Cicero in his basic habits of language. A definition based on a direct appeal to Cicero—and through him to the solemn reputation of Scipio in his prophetic last days [17]—must have acquired greater solidity thereby in its author's own mind, as well as in the eyes of his contemporaries. The fact that the discussion ultimately went deeper and farther than that source, but did not really abandon it, could only add more force to Augustine's somewhat audacious originality.[18]

General Usage

A great deal of *The City of God* undoubtedly remained beyond the ken of many of its readers in subsequent centuries. The dialectical subtlety of the categories involved in this pair of definitions underwent, in fact, considerable distortion in the course of the millennium that followed. However, Augustine wrote many books of more accessible size and character, throughout which his use of the word *populus* is quite consistent with his formal definitions of it and with his employment of it elsewhere in *The City of God*. This consensus is very striking, particularly in view of the great volume and variety of his writings, and the diversity of styles which he utilized in the forty-four years (386-430) of his attested literary activity.[19] His hundreds of sermons were to become models of the *sermo humilis* in the service of the Christian ministry, balancing carefully between the demands of maximum popular communication on the one hand and of established grammatical standards on the other.[20] *The City of God* is a monument of the *sermo sublimis* in its nonnarrative sections, and its narrative is developed in full fidelity to the most elevated stylistic canons of traditional pagan literature.[21] Somewhere between these two major modes is the highly individual style of the *Confessions,* destined in its turn to become a standard of "Christian cultural Latin." [22] One would expect this heterogeneity of style to be reflected in some disparity of vocabulary values, especially for the more common words. But in the case of *populus* the contrary tendency is dominant.[23]

A consideration of examples taken from several of his works should suffice both to show that consistency and, more importantly, to indicate the range of properties, applications, and nuances which are involved in his usage of the important word *populus*.[24] All taken together, they permit us to see that that noun represents in Augustine's writings a fairly coherent notion, which the socio-political terminology of this century would describe as a legitimate polity, unified by an essentially conscious agreement.

In order to establish this descriptive definition, I shall explore three distinctions in the negative order, and proceed thereafter to an examination of four positive attributes and applications of the term. Finally, I shall raise the question whether Augustine conceived of a plurality of connected *populi*—overlapping or mutually inclusive on several levels—a question which springs with logical inevitability from Augustine's language, a problem which underlies many of the later attempts to claim him as an authority for irreconcilable political theories, but to which his own language seems to offer no clear answer.

The first distinction which needs to be established is that between *populus* and *civitas*. It is not an easy one to make, and any attempt to make it too neatly will do violence to the range and flexibility of Augustine's lexicon. As the two great definitions suggest, *populus* is very closely related to *civitas* in Augustine's mind. However, though their meanings often overlap, they are not really identical. Sometimes they are logically indistinguishable, as in a letter of 412 to the imperial commissioner Marcellinus, a close friend with whom he seems to have felt a high degree of intellectual rapport.

For what is a *res publica*, if not the *res* of a *populus*? A *res* in common, therefore, and certainly the *res* of a *civitas*. But what is a *civitas*, if not a multitude of men gathered together by some bond of concord? One reads in the works [of Cicero and other ancient authors]: "Through a brief concord the scattered and aimless multitude had become a *civitas*." But what further precepts of concord did they ever consider worth reading in their temples? For those unhappy men were forced to wonder how they could worship their discordant gods without offending some of them; and if they wished to imitate their discord, the *civitas* would collapse, since its bond of concord would have been shattered . . .[25]

Here one can see not only the clear equation of *populus* with *civitas* (primarily as a function of the common term *concord*), but the unmistakable germ of several chapters of books II and XIX of *The City of God*. Little wonder, since Augustine began its composition in the following year, as a fuller answer to Marcellinus's appeal for apologetical assistance against the pagan proconsul Volusianus.[26]

About four years earlier, in a letter to the pagan gentleman Nectarius, Augustine had made it clear that he considered a *civitas* a moral as well as a physical entity.[27] In a sermon to the people of Hippo about the sack of Rome he went further along this line.

Do you think that a *civitas* should be thought of as something made of walls? A *civitas* consists of its citizens, not its walls. . . . Would not God have spared the *civitas* [of Sodom] if the *civitas* had migrated, and escaped the destruction of that fire?

In a less ingenious and allusive sentence of the same speech, Augustine referred to the imperial city on the Tiber as the *civitas Romana;* it is hard to see how his saying *populus Romanus* would have made much difference in that context.[28]

Nevertheless, a *civitas* is some things for Augustine that a *populus* is not. Sometimes he equates the *civitas Romana* with the *regnum Romanum,* which was not the same entity in standard legal language,[29] and certainly does not seem to have been so in Augustine's usage either.[30] Far more central to his thought is the triad of *civitates*—*Dei, diaboli,* and *terrena*—to which no comparably schematic triad of *populi* seems to correspond. The term *populus Dei* abounds in his works, as do many strictly earthly and even impious *populi,* but *populus terrenus* is a rather rare term, and I have so far failed to find a *populus diaboli* neatly so formulated.[31] Perhaps this divergence indicates that *populus* was a word less charged with transcendent associations for Augustine than *civitas*—that it was, in short, a more neutral, simply descriptive term.

Even when these two words seem practically synonymous, a close examination reveals important differences of tone. About 411, some dozen years after one of the more unsettling and widely reported earthquakes in Constantinople's long seismic history, Augustine preached a sermon comparing that trial to the older capital's ordeal during the very recent Visigothic sack.

Is it not true that a few years ago, when Arcadius was emperor at Constantinople (it may be that several of you who are now hearing this story already know it; indeed, there are some among this *populus* who were there), God, wishing to terrify the *civitas* and by terrifying it to emend, convert, cleanse, and change it, came in a vision to a faithful servant of His? The man was, as the story goes, a soldier. God told him that the *civitas* was about to be destroyed by fire from heaven, and warned him to tell the bishop. The report was delivered; the bishop did not scorn it, and addressed the *populus;* the *civitas* was converting to mourning and penance, as once was that ancient Ninive.[32]

A fiery cloud advanced over the *"civitas* . . . until the whole *urbs* was terribly threatened." Many ran to church, seeking baptism and forgiveness, and the cloud shrank somewhat. "The *populus,* having become a little more secure, then heard that evacuation was absolutely necessary, because on the next sabbath the *civitas* would be destroyed. The whole *civitas* went forth with the Emperor"; after an emotional march of several miles, "that great multitude" saw the cloud pass over their homes, but returned to find nothing damaged, thanks to their piety.[33]

It seems clear that the *populus* here is a human group listening to a bishop or someone similar, whether in Hippo or Constantinople. The *civitas,* on the other hand, is less distinctively and exclusively a gathering of attentive persons. It can be physically destroyed or overshadowed by a cloud, just like an *urbs,* almost as if it were just a group of buildings (despite the preacher's earlier remark in that same sermon about citizens and walls). When it acts morally, in conversion of spirit and then in mass migration with its ruler, it does so as a rather faceless mass collectivity. This looseness of usage is a bit strange for a word which Augustine applies much more readily than *populus* to such awesome, significance-fraught bodies as the Roman Empire and the Society of the Elect; however, it accords well with the differences between Augustine's definitions of those two common nouns. According to those formulations, a *civitas* (a multitude "gathered together by some bond of concord") is a body capable of wider generalization than a *populus* (a multitude "united in fellowship by their agreement about the objects of their love"). So Augustine may not just be varying his vocabulary when in this sermon he makes a *populus* appear to be a body more intensely conscious and more coherent on the local level than a *civitas*.

A variation of this relationship between *civitas* and *populus* appears in an *Enarratio* (or exegetical sermon) on Psalm 61, which Augustine also delivered to his flock in Hippo. That psalm does not strike modern eyes as particularly rich in political or social coloration, but Augustine made several of its verses serve as starting points for digressions which contain some of the most vivid evocations of the Two Cities outside the magnum opus itself. Commenting on verse 4, Augustine observed:

> For this common *res publica* (as it were) of ours, each of us pays what he owes, and for the possession of his bodily powers incurs, as it were, a fixed minimum charge of passions. . . . But do not think, my brothers, that any of the just who suffered the persecution of wicked men, including those who came before the Lord's coming, do not belong among the members of Christ. Heaven forbid that he not be a member of Christ, who belongs to that *civitas* which has Christ for its king. For there is one heavenly Jerusalem, a holy *civitas;* and that one *civitas* has one king.[34]

A little further on, discussing the attempt of Christ's enemies to "drive away his honor" (a reference to the first clause of verse 5), Augustine asked:

> But all those diverse errors hostile to Christ, are they to be described only as numerous, and not also as unified? I dare to affirm openly that they are all together one error, for there is one *civitas* and one other *civitas,* one *populus* and one other *populus,* a king and another king. What does that mean: one *civitas* and

one other *civitas?* One Babylon; one Jerusalem. Whatever other mystic names they may be called, they remain nevertheless one *civitas* opposed to the other *civitas,* the king of one being the devil, the king of the other, Christ.[35]

And Augustine went on from there to a lengthy development of his vision of the great duality that decisively divides mankind.

The author's interest here is so clearly in establishing parallelism that, even though *populus* is not actually synonymous with *civitas,* the similarities between the two terms are more important than the differences. *Civitas* is also much more in evidence here than *populus.* The second passage quoted from this *Enarratio* continues as an exposition of the natures and proper attributes of the two *civitates* and their *reges,* in which *populus* appears no more. It appeared once between the two passages here quoted, in an allegorical aside concerning the "excellence of the first (i.e., Jewish) people"; [36] but that was neither a central nor a lengthy point, and the *"res publica* (as it were)" with which this section opened was presented explicitly as a figure of speech.

However, as the sermon progresses, *populus* comes in for more frequent use, and the distinction between its meaning and that of *civitas* becomes progressively easier to see. For illustrations of the fact that the *cives* of one of the two transcendental Cities often administer the *res publica* of the other, Augustine urges his audience to turn to biblical history: "Therefore, look at that first *populus,* whose mission was also to prefigure the later (i.e., Christian) *populus."* [37] Commenting in this vein on the next clause of verse 5, *"Cucurri in siti,"* Augustine calls attention to Moses' melting down the head of the golden calf and plunging the molten mass into the water which he gave the people to drink (Exod. 32:20). This allegorically linked incident, he says, is a *"magnum sacramentum."*

The calf's head was the body of the impious, in the likeness of a grass-eating calf because the impious seek after earthly things, and "all flesh is grass." . . . Moses in anger put it into the fire, reduced it, doused it in the water, and so gave it to the *populus* to drink; and the prophet's anger thus became an instrument of prophecy. For that body is put into the fire of tribulation, and reduced by the word of God. Little by little men drop away from the unity of that body: like a garment, it is eaten away in time. Each person who becomes a Christian is separated from that *populus,* and takes part in the reduction of the whole. . . . And what could be more evident than that through baptism men were to be brought over to the body of the *civitas* Jerusalem, whose image was the *populus* of Israel? On that account it was doused in water, before being proffered as a drink. Thus far unto the end He thirsts; He runs thirsting. He has drunk many, but never will He be without thirst. Thus comes that request: "I thirst, woman; give me to drink." . . . For what, after all, art Thou thirsty? Why art Thou thirsty? Will so many *populi* not slake Thy thirst? [38]

Putting together the *civitas*-dominated and the *populus*-filled sections of this sermon, one can hardly escape the conclusion that *populus* represents in most instances either the strictly historical aspect or a specific embodiment of the more mystical, eternal, universal *civitas.* That "body of the *civitas* Jerusalem, whose image was the *populus* of Israel": a classic metaphoric formulation, central to Augustine's usage in the sermon, and perhaps to his general usage as well.

The second major distinction to make regarding Augustine's general usage of the word *populus* involves the class content of that term. For him a *populus* was a group embracing several social classes, or at least cutting across several class lines. Only very rarely did he use the word as a label for what modern English calls "the common people," that is, the "lower classes," for which the proper term was *plebs.* Augustine makes this distinction, which his master Cicero did not always bother to observe, quite early in *The City of God.*

Troy herself, the mother of the Roman *populus,* was, as I said, quite unable to afford, in the areas consecrated to her gods, any protection for her own citizens from the fire and steel of the Greeks, who themselves worshipped those same gods. Nay, even
 . . . in the sanctuary of Juno
 Phoenix and dread Ulysses, chosen guards, were
 Watching over the booty . . .

. . . Compare now that asylum, not an asylum of any god of the herd or of the *turba plebis,* but the asylum of the sister and wife of Jupiter himself and queen of all the gods, with the memorial shrines of our apostles,[39]

which were spared by Alaric's Arian army.

One of Augustine's sermons, delivered in the midst of the dog days, on the feast of St. Laurence the martyr around the year 400, contains a curious admonition to the *populus* of Hippo which has been interpreted as a reproof of mob turbulence. That was undoubtedly part of his intent, but larger issues were involved as well, and the preacher's use of the crucial word itself is cogent evidence that *populus* in his mind meant the whole adult body politic of Hippo Regius, not merely its lowest social stratum or some lower-class interest group within it.

The sermon's argument runs roughly as follows. An oppressive official has been lynched as a result of his corrupt behavior, which may have involved his exploiting the struggle then taking place between the pagan and Christian elements of the Numidian population. Some of the lynchers sought ecclesiastical asylum, which was denied, even though the Catholic community had been implicated in the crime of some of its members; at the very least, a largely Catholic crowd had cheered the assassins on. Augustine's main point is that the bishop must castigate such bloody bypassing of due process, whatever the apparent provocation, however popular that recourse to violence may have been.[40]

It would perhaps be better, Augustine says, to reprove the guilty in a discreet fashion, but "who can admonish the *populus* in part? Who can lead the *populus* aside, and admonish it without anyone else's knowing?" So he does his duty openly, in public. Having refuted various excuses for complicity in the crime, he insists that individual regret about it will not keep the *populus* from getting so dangerously out of hand again.

But it is not enough, as I have said, it is not enough not to do such a thing, not enough to bewail it, unless you also resist what lies within the power of the *populus* with your own strength. I do not say, my brothers, that any single one of you can go out and resist the *populus;* neither can we succeed in that.

However, each man can start to exercise his proper authority within his own household. And let him do so without petulance or delay.

> My brothers, I fear the anger of God. God does not fear mobs (*turbas*). How often one hears the saying, "What the *populus* has done, it will have done; who can punish the *populus?*" Who, indeed, but God? Did God fear the whole world when He loosed the Flood? Did He fear the *civitates* of Sodom and Gomorrha when he wiped them out with fire from heaven? [41]

And remember that He often makes no external distinction between innocent and guilty individuals in such visitations.

Augustine clearly felt that the lynching tainted many members of his congregation, at least verbally and in sympathy. It had generated collective guilt and individual duty to avoid collective retribution. Augustine's word for the guilty collectivity is *populus*, and his use of it in this sermon of the most direct contemporary relevance carries no hint of social stratification.

Augustine's occasional use of the plural form *populi* for a single collectivity can carry pejorative overtones, but the downgrading implied is usually moral rather than social.[42] One clear instance of this tendency occurs in a sermon which he preached on Low Sunday in 416 or 417, presumably in Hippo. Beginning his address with an allegory about spiritual light and darkness in the souls of men, he then turned to the newly baptized, white-robed members of his congregation.

> And for that reason I address you, who are one daylight altogether, who were ill-born children of Adam, and have been well reborn in Christ. Recognize that you are daylight, and that the Lord has made you. He has sent the sinful darkness flying from your hearts, he has renewed your life. Today you are to be integrated into the ranks of the *populi:* choose whom you will imitate. Do not choose those who are lost, with whom you may perish.

A long list of the vices dear to the so-called "faithful" follows, ending with this exhortation.

You are called faithful, so live faithfully. Keep faith with your
Lord in heart and behavior. Do not mingle with evil behavior
in the *turba* of bad Christians.[43]

Augustine does not seem to have used the noun *plebs* and its
derivatives very much.[44] In contemporary reference, he employed
plebs to designate the Christian community or some element
thereof, and the "common people," usually under the aspect of
some class solidarity. Examples of his use of *plebs* for the laity or
the whole Christian people will be cited later in this chapter. An
interesting instance of the more purely temporal, class reference of
plebs can be found in a sermon which Augustine preached at
Bulla Regia at the request of its bishop. This sermon is a particularly good source for his usage of *plebs* because in it Augustine
applied that word also to the Christian community at Carthage
and to the laity of the Church at large.[45] Besides, Bulla provides
an almost perfect context for examining the normal resonance of
such a word in the world of Augustine's active ministry.

Bulla Regia, nearly home territory for Augustine, lay slightly
more than fifty miles down the valley of the river Bagradas (Med-
jerda today) from his native Tagaste, and about the same distance
from Madaura, where he had gone to school around 369 and had
begun to experience a larger and more exciting world than he had
been raised to know.[46] The most direct route to Carthage from
either of those towns went through Bulla, as did the shortest road
from Hippo, seventy-five miles to the northwest. Bulla was no
sleepy provincial crossroads, however. Like Hippo Regius, it seems
to have been a favorite of the Numidian kings, and the contents of
Augustine's sermon indicate that five centuries later it was still
a wide-open community, the reputation of whose theaters and
other pleasures traveled across the sea-lanes of the Mediterranean.[47]
Consequently, one might reasonably expect a preacher as conscious
of his audience as Augustine to employ on such an occasion language of general currency at least in the North African segment of
the western empire. Even if he exaggerated the extent of Bulla's
worldliness—as visiting preachers are wont to do—it would not lie
beyond likelihood that remembered impressions of earlier and
rather different visits contributed to that impulse.

The sermon was delivered between 397 and 400, on the feast commemorating the birth of the Macchabees—probably the first of August. Augustine began with some exegesis, in the course of which he declared that every class and occupation of mankind is called to belief and to its consequences, as was demonstrated by the early Christians after the first Pentecost.

> Not only the plebeians, not only some artisans, not just the poor, the indigent, or those of middle station gave up their all with the onset of persecution; so also did many rich men, senators, and most distinguished ladies . . .[48]

Turning from this (possibly anti-Donatist) comment on sacred history to contemporary moral exhortation, Augustine held up a shining example: "I will be so bold as to say, 'Imitate your neighboring *civitas,* imitate the neighboring *civitas* of Simittu.'" That town fifteen miles up the valley, still quite Punic if we may hazard such a guess from the form of its name, would have nothing to do with theatrical spectacles.

> An official wanted to have that sort of turpitude performed. No member of the leading class, no plebeian attended; no Jew attended. And are they not a respectable community? Is not that *civitas,* is not that *colonia* all the more respectable for lacking such things?

The special, limited reference of those two *plebs*-derived substantives is emphasized by contrast with the two appearances of *populus* in this sermon: once it is used in reference to the size of the whole population of Bulla, and once for that people for whom Christ will render judgment at the end.[49]

The third major distinction to make concerning Augustine's general use of *populus* has to do with birth. Except in the providential case of the historical Israel, he did not consider that membership in a *populus* had much to do with birth. In one sermon he speaks of a *"populus* born for the anger of God," but there he is referring to the *populus infidelium,* those predestined to damnation,[50] and is clearly using birth as a metaphor made all the more exceptional by providential nuances. The same metaphor occurs

frequently and less dramatically in connection with admission into
the visible Church, a society more identifiable if not less mystical.
Augustine remarked in one Low Sunday sermon that "all those
reborn through Christ's baptism should celebrate with special devotion the solemnity of the octave which throughout the *orbis
terrarum* has subjected *gentes* to the salvation of His name."
After explaining the significance of the white robes of candidacy
which the newly baptized would now put away, he said: "But
since we solemnly celebrate the fact that you are crossing the bar-
riers behind which in spiritual infancy you were separated from
others, since now you will mingle with the *populus,* be sure to
adhere to the good." [51]

The theme of spiritual rebirth is much more fully developed
in another, very brief Low Sunday sermon which Augustine
preached in the Leontian basilica in Hippo.

> So as to avoid delay in the midst of a full schedule, those who
> have been reborn in baptism and today are to mingle with the
> *populus* deserve a short though serious sermon. You who have
> been baptized and complete today the sacrament of your octave,
> consider briefly the thought that the circumcision of the flesh
> has been symbolically transferred to circumcision of the heart.
> According to the Old Law, one's flesh was circumcised on the
> eighth day: this was a prefiguring of Christ our Lord, who
> after a day of sevenfold sabbaths arose on the eighth and lordly
> day. It was commanded that circumcision be performed with
> stone knives; but Christ is the Rock. You are called infants be-
> cause you have been born again and have entered upon a new
> life; you have been reborn for eternal life, if that which in you
> is reborn be not suffocated by evil living. You are to be re-
> turned to the *populi,* mixed in among the *plebs* of the faithful:
> beware lest you imitate evil believers, nay, false believers, who
> are faithful in profession but unfaithful in the evil of their
> lives.[52]

A list of popular infidelities follows, beginning with incontinence.
The utilization of *plebs* and *populi,* both for stylistic variety and at
the point of transition from edifying exegesis to stern admonition,
strengthens the reader's (if not the hearer's) awareness that *popu-*

lus is the normal and morally neutral term for the Christian community.[53] It is not inconceivable that Augustine developed the paradox of rebirth more forcefully in this sermon than in the previous example because the society to which the neophytes were gaining admission was here described through the metaphors of Jewish rather than of Roman citizenship, and Israel was more notoriously a brotherhood of descent than was the Roman people.

Augustine's notion that membership in a *populus* did not depend on physical birth was applicable to historical as well as to mystical societies. Citizenship in Mediterranean societies was normally acquired by some sort of inheritance, but Augustine never seems to stress this point,[54] and places all the emphasis on consent in his definition of *populus*. Even in the "carnal Israel" birth was not the final criterion of membership. His final editorial comments on *The City of God* include a revision which makes his understanding of this issue perfectly clear.

> In the seventeenth book what is said about Samuel, "He was not of the sons of Aaron," should rather have been put: "He was not the son of a priest." It was, of course, preferred legal custom for sons of priests to succeed priests; for the father of Samuel appears among the sons of Aaron, but he was not a priest, nor was he among the sons in the sense that Aaron begot him, but in the same sense in which all who belong to the *populus* Israel are called sons of Israel.[55]

As will be shown later in this chapter, the predominant *populus* of book XVII of *The City of God* is Israel, directed toward its destiny by God's prophetic emissaries. Divine election has more to do with that group's character than with the choices of individual "sons of Israel," who seem to belong to that group simply by virtue of birth; however, that sort of heredity does not appear to be a major issue in that book. These sentences of corrective afterthought from the *Retractations* serve as confirmation that birth is beside the point, that mature participation in a *populus* as well as in the priestly profession remained for Augustine a consequence of personal election, at least in noteworthy cases.

Several of the positive attributes of a normal *populus* are expressed quite clearly in several genres of Augustine's literary corpus, sometimes explicitly.

Not surprisingly, that philosophical heir of Plotinus stated at various times that a *populus* must possess unity simply in order to exist. One of the most striking examples of this affirmation occurs in a sermon on Martha and Mary. Mary's superiority to her well-intentioned sister consisted in her concentration on "the one thing necessary" (Luke 10:42). The moral is that we must not let ourselves be distracted from the goal of our pilgrimage here.

> Be single-minded, my brothers, and see if in that multitude [of earthly distractions] anything delights you, beside the one thing necessary. Behold how numerous you are, thanks to the kindness of God; who could bear you, if you were not of one mind? Where else would your tranquillity come from, amid such diversity? Grant a point of unity, and a *populus* exists; take that unity away, and it is a mob (*turba*). For what is a mob except a confused multitude? [56]

Having Augustine's definitions in mind, we are tempted by such passages from other works to begin elaborating the definitions through the medium of expanding paraphrase. A *populus* must be first of all a multitude (as we have seen, one including several social classes); since it is a group of such size and diversity, it needs a central focus or it will cease to be itself. Since it is a human multitude, its unity must be rational, and that inevitably raises the question of assent.

Much the same notion, more thoroughly developed and more generally applied, occurs in a purely classical context in the treatise *On Order* which Augustine composed in his Italian retreat at Cassiciacum in November 386, five years at least before he preached his first African sermon. Having discussed at some length the general value of harmony (inseparable from the notion of justice in Stoic social theory),[57] Augustine proceeds to the corollary proposition that unity is essential to the existence, not to say survival, of stones, trees, and any kind of body. He continues:

What else do friends strive for, but to be one? And the more they are one, the more they are friends. A *populus* is a *civitas* to which dissension is perilous; but what is dissension, if not a failure to be of one mind? From many soldiers one army comes into being: is it not true that any multitude is less easily conquered, the more it comes together toward unity? [58]

As we search for the word *populus* through the wide range of Augustine's writing, we must keep track of the specific historical groups to which he applied that idea-laden term. Many of those applications help us to perceive further properties of concrete *populi,* or further nuances of the attributes already noted. At the very least, they put the whole discussion into sharper historical perspective.

Even a cursory skimming of Augustine's works indicates that he used the noun *populus* to designate three main classes of historical groups: Israel, the Church, and a broad cluster of civil societies less marked by divine favor—Rome in particular, but many others besides.

The *populus Israel* held a very special place in Augustine's mind. "The God of the Hebrews, then, gave to this Hebrew *populus* the law, written in the Hebrew language, and not obscure or unknown, but now celebrated among all *gentes,* in which it is written: 'He who sacrifices to other gods, save to the Lord only, shall be uprooted.' " [59] Nor was this only a mystical *populus;* it was a very visible people, uniquely chosen by God to be His witness in a world gone wayward, but not necessarily including all the elect born before Christ.

Wherefore if there has come or shall come to our knowledge any alien, that is, one not born of the line of Israel and not admitted by that *populus* to the canon of the sacred Scriptures, who has written prophecy concerning Christ, he can be cited by us as a crowning authority. . . . Nor do I think that the Jews dare to maintain that no one has belonged to God who was not an Israelite, from the time when Israel began his line after his elder brother was rejected. To be sure, there was no other *populus* especially called the *populus Dei;* nevertheless, they cannot deny that among other *gentes* too there have been certain men who belonged not by earthly but by heavenly fellowship to the company of true Israelites who are citizens of the *patria* that is above. For if they deny it, they are very easily refuted by citing the holy and wonderful man Job, who was neither a native-born Israelite nor a proselyte (that is, a stranger received among the *populus* of Israel), but one who sprang from the *gens* of Edom, was born in the land of Edom and died there.[60]

Satisfying both definitions of *populus*,[61] Israel remained one legitimately even when Moses had to coerce it for its deviations,[62] and even though it could never be more than a *populus carnalis* by comparison with the New Israel of the Church.[63] Augustine strove to make this privileged but eventually secondary status very clear in a lengthy and intricate letter of 418 to his fellow bishop Asellicus. Starting with the statement that "the Apostle Paul teaches that it is not fitting for Christians, especially those coming from among the Gentiles, to Judaize," [64] he discusses the proper attitude of contemporary Christians toward the Mosaic Law, accuses Pelagius of doctrinal Judaizing, and declares:

> Again, the race of Edomites belongs according to carnal origin to Esau, who is called Edom; while the race of Jews belongs to Jacob, who is also called Israel. But according to a spiritual mystery, the Jews belong to Esau, and the Christians to Israel. Thus is fulfilled what is written: "the elder shall serve the younger"; that is, the Jewish *populus* of earlier birth shall serve the later-born Christian *populus*. Behold in what manner we are Israel: glorying in divine adoption, not human kinship; not in the open, but in hidden significance; not by the letter but in the spirit; Jews by circumcision of the heart, not of the flesh.[65]

Augustine saw Israel in its various stages of providential development as a social, political, and religious entity both complex and prophetic. Several common nouns refer to it. *Populus* and *gens* seem, reasonably enough, to be the most frequent; *plebs, regnum, tribus,* and the like occur both with less frequency and with less general applicability, usually denoting specific and distinct aspects of that polity's experience. When Augustine used *populus* instead of *gens* for the group as a whole, he usually did so because he was interested at the moment in certain of its dominant features, and not just because of random vocabulary variation.

This purposeful tendency can be discerned in two discussions of salvation history separated by more than a quarter-century of Augustine's experience and reflection. The first of these occurs in book 1 of his commentary *On Genesis against the Manichees,* written at Tagaste about 389, before he became a priest. The second sweeps through books xv–xviii of *The City of God,* which were composed in Hippo sometime between 415 and 425.[66]

Let us examine first the lay theologian's exegetical commentary. In the course of explaining, by resort to his favorite apologetic technique of allegorization, why God rested on the seventh day, Augustine urges on his Christian and Manichean audience an explanation of the six preceding days of creation as representations of the ages of the world and the life of individual men. Chapters 23 and 24 of book 1 are given over to this exposition.

The first age is that of the emergence of the human race (*genus humanum*), stretching from Adam to Noah through ten generations. It is also the period of individual infancy, which is likewise "obliterated as though by a flood of oblivion." [67]

The second age, that of boyhood, stretched through another ten generations from Noah to Abraham: "its evening is the confusion of tongues among those who built the tower, and the next morning begins from Abraham. But neither did this age beget the *populus Dei,* for neither is boyhood an apt age for begetting." [68] Little in the preceding chapters or in the discussion of the first age has prepared the reader for this sudden irruption of interest in the *populus Dei,* which from this point on dominates chapter 23.

Of the third age, Augustine says:

> The next morning, then, begins from Abraham, and the third age, like adolescence, gets under way. It is fittingly compared to the third day, on which the dry land was separated from the water. For the error of the *gentes,* unstable and volatile as all the manifold winds in its idolatrous doctrines, is well signified under the name of the sea; and so from this vanity of the *gentes* and from the unsteady billows of this world the *populus*

of God was separated by Abraham like the land when it first
appeared, thirsting for the heavenly rain of the divine commandments. Through its cultivation of the One God, this *populus,*
like an irrigated field, was granted the holy Scriptures and the
prophets, so as to bear useful fruit.

This age was able to beget a *populus* to God, for the third
age of human adolescence can have sons. And therefore was it
said to Abraham:

"I have made you father of many *gentes,* and I will increase
you very greatly, and I will make you into *gentes,* and your
issue shall be kings. I will establish a covenant between Myself and you and with your seed after you, generation after
generation, a covenant in perpetuity, to be your God and the
God of your seed after you. I will give to you and to your
seed after you the land you are living in, the whole land of
Canaan, to own in perpetuity, and I will be their God." (Gen.
17:5-8)

This age stretches from Abraham to David in fourteen generations. Its evening comes with the sins of the *populus,* in
which they transgressed the divine commandments, up through
the misdeeds of that most evil king Saul.[69]

The personal character of Augustine's employment of *populus* in
this passage is heightened by its complete absence from the scriptural text which he inserted as the climax of his exposition.

The fourth age is that of the kingdom of Israel, a time like
youth. The word *regnum* appears four times in a passage less than
half as long as the preceding quotation; *plebs* appears once
("What could more clearly signify the splendor of the kingdom
than the sun's supremacy? The moon's splendor represents the
plebs obedient to the kingdom."); and *gens* once ("Its evening
came as it were with the sins of the kings, on whose account that
gens merited captivity and servitude"). *Populus* is entirely absent.[70]

The fifth age began with the chastening dawn of the migration
to Babylon, "in which captivity the *populus* was slowly recollected
through the inactivity of its wandering (*in peregrino otio*)." This
age lasted until the coming of Christ, and was for Israel the decline

from youth to old age, marked by a division and dispersion of powers and purpose. *Populus* appears three times in this passage of average length, once in the formula *populus Judaeorum*. *Gens* appears three times also, once as the *gens Judaeorum* being multiplied like the animals and the birds of heaven and the great sea beasts ("better suited for domination amid the billows of this world than for serving in captivity") and twice as the Gentiles.[71]

The sixth age, that of the old age of the old man, dawned with the preaching of the Gospel. The carnal *regnum* of Israel falls into decrepitude, as does "that *gens* insofar as its kingdom's vigor is concerned." *Gens* appears twice more in this extended terminal passage of chapter 23, but in those cases it designates the Gentiles. This passage contains three *populi:* that of Israel serving the Law surrounded by the sea of the Gentiles; a later stage of Israel, serving along with the Gentiles as a source of the Church; and finally the Church itself, "that *populus* [which] is spiritually fed by the nourishment of the holy Scriptures and the divine Law: partly in order to be capable of fertile conception of ideas and speech (*rationum atque sermonum*)—as though on a diet of seed-bearing plants; partly so as to learn behavior appropriate to human social intercourse—as though feeding on fruit-bearing trees; . . ."[72]

In the slightly more than 1000 words of chapter 23, *populus* appears eleven times, *gens* ten times, *regnum* seven times, and *plebs* once. *Regnum* appears only in remarks about Israel's experience of a certain type of government. Before and after Israel had a king, it was no *regnum*. *Plebs* appears as a term for the body of the monarchy's subjects, tranquilly reflecting its glory. *Gens* designates Israel three times, and the Gentiles seven times. Israel as a *gens* is closely related to the *regnum*, first as the group deserving captivity because of its kings' sins, and then sinking into decrepitude with the enfeeblement of the restored monarchy. In its sole appearance as the fully labeled *gens Judaeorum*, it is actively multiplying itself in dispersion: a context sufficiently genetic to satisfy the most etymologically inclined of critics.

When is Israel a *populus?* When begotten by Abraham like dry land at last amid the flux of the sea (Age 2); when sinning so consequentially against God's law as to incur as penalties first "that most evil king Saul" (Age 3) and then (when the kingdom was finally extinct) a blindness incapable of recognizing the Lord (Age 5); when recollecting itself in the purgative experience of exile (Age 5); and finally, as the membership of the Church, Israel's true continuation (Age 6).

In most of these appearances, this continuous *populus* is intimately linked to its distinctive law, whether in fidelity or disobedience: the connection is stated outright five times (Ages 3 and 6), and can be inferred without strain twice more. Surprisingly enough, this highly political *populus* has an allergy to monarchy. It is absent (or perhaps demoted *vice synonymatis* to a *plebs*) in the passage extolling the quite legitimate splendor of the Davidic kingdom, and only reemerges with the Babylonian exile. Augustine is not usually so chastely republican in his usage of *populus,* but this instance of selective employment is a striking example of his consistent tendency to associate it with a group distinguished for its conscious awareness of legal responsibility. Nowhere in this chapter is the essential character of that attribute more evident than in the final appearance of *populus* as the Good Shepherd's flock, deriving the energy for rational contemplation and socially responsible action from the nourishment of the Scriptures and the Law.

Books xv–xviii of *The City of God* trace the progress of the Two Cities from the Fall to the age of the Christian martyrs. In them we see again, although in vastly grander development, most of the themes which Augustine presented in neat capsules in book I, chapter 23 of *On Genesis against the Manichees.* We can see that several important changes have occurred in his thought: the chronological framework is constructed both more cautiously and more subtly, and the sense of providential direction throughout is so much more profound as to be almost a new idea. Nevertheless, on an intermediate level somewhere between basic questions of chronology and the higher reaches of historical theology, we can observe Augustine using *populus* very much as he had in his apologetical Genesis commentary of a quarter-century before.

He prefers to use that noun for Israel than for any other group, and so uses it (in formulas like *populus Dei, populus Israel, populus Israeliticus*) with steadily rising frequency. Yet more striking is the fact that Augustine uses *gens* more frequently than *populus* in those four books, but much less frequently for Israel, and the percentage of times that he calls Israel a *gens* declines fairly steadily. To put it somewhat differently, Israel is more a *populus* than a *gens,* and progressively more so, as it evolves first toward political maturity and then toward prophetic awareness of its mission.

Populus is an important word in this massive sample if only because of its high frequency therein. Forty-two percent of its appearances in *The City of God* come from these four books, which, long as they are, account for no more than 24 percent of the whole work. Augustine applies that noun to the community of Israel 104 times in the course of these four books, nearly three and a half times as often as he so designates any other collectivity, although these books hardly lack other historical polities of solemn stature.[73] The following summary of the range of the twenty-seven Gentile applications in that sample should indicate both the relative rarity of that usage in this context and its essential consistency with his general usage elsewhere.

Two unmistakably reprobate *populi* (both in the plural number) appear in xvi, 4 and xviii, 12. In the former chapter, Augustine concludes that the Tower of Babel was built at the instigation of the devil:

> He with his *populi,* therefore, erected this tower against the Lord, and so gave expression to their impious pride; and justly was their wicked intention punished by God, even though it was unsuccessful. But what was the nature of the punishment? As the tongue is the instrument of domination, in it pride was punished; so that man, who would not understand God when He issued His commands, should be misunderstood when he himself gave orders.

Augustine's use of *populi* here, atypical in these books of *The City of God,* stands out in this context because he usually considers that a *gens* is defined by its language as well as by its descent; a few lines later, he summarizes the chapter: ". . . and the *gentes* were divided according to their languages (*linguae*), and scattered over the earth as seemed good to God, who accomplished this in ways hidden from and incomprehensible to us." [74]

In xviii, 12, an attack on the games and plays instituted in honor of the false gods by early kings of Greece, Augustine remarks that intelligent pagans knew perfectly well that Europa had been abducted by Xanthus, king of Crete, rather than by Jupiter, and regarded the Jovian attribution of that exploit, "which the poets sing, the theatres applaud, and the *populi* celebrate, as empty fable got up as a reason for games to appease the deities." [75]

The latter use of *populi* recalls similar phraseology in other attacks on pagan religious festivals in *The City of God* and elsewhere. If it suggests little in the way of specifically political action on the part of the groups to which this brief allusion is made, it certainly evokes their vocal participation in public celebrations of a character both civic and religious as well as festive, celebrations which seemed to Augustine particularly vivid proof that their societies were incapable of attaining true justice in the social and political order.[76] The former of these two uses of *populi* is much more clearly related to a decisive act of communal responsibility, a conscious collective effort dooming all subsequent earthly dominion to inevitable frustration of purpose. In that instance Augustine draws from the Hebrew revelation rather than the Greco-Roman mythological tradition a vivid illustration of the same basic point, one of the dominant themes of *The City of God*.

Gentile *populi* of a less articulate but still political character appear elsewhere in these books. In xvi, 10, six chapters after his discussion of the Tower of Babel, Augustine remarks that the Scriptures give a satisfying explanation of the extraordinary proliferation of the stock of Sem, so that we may "understand . . . how regions and kingdoms so vast could be filled by the descendants (*genus*) of Sem; especially the kingdom of the Assyrians, from which Ninus, that tamer of Orientals, ruled in all directions in a huge prosperity of *populi,* and bequeathed to his descendants (*posteri*) a vast but thoroughly consolidated empire (*regnum*), which held together for many centuries." [77]

Two books later, in xviii, 2, Augustine returns to the subject *populi* of the Assyrian Empire, which seemed to him the military prototype of Rome's dominion, much as Babylon was its prototype in spiritual motivation. In that chapter he also refers to the *populus* of the primitive Romans, but only by citing the title of Varro's *De gente populi Romani,* which he mentions similarly, in connection with the Trojan War, eleven chapters later. After the Trojan War Augustine surveys other civic fables of antiquity. In three eloquent chapters (19-21), he rises from fable to history: Aeneas's predestined wanderings, the foundation of Rome with its line of Latin kings, the end of the Athenian monarchy and the foundation of its republic, and the establishment of the Davidic kingdom of Israel pass in summary review, without the intervention of a single *populus.*

Right after that epic procession, Augustine gives a succinct statement of the progressive typological connection between Assyria and Rome.

> To be brief, the *civitas Roma* was founded, like another Babylon, and as it were the daughter of the former Babylon, by which God was pleased to conquer the whole world, and subdue it far and wide by bringing it into one fellowship of government and laws (*in unam societatem rei publicae legumque*). For there were already powerful and brave *populi* and *gentes* trained to arms, who did not easily yield, and whose subjugation necessarily involved great danger and destruction as well as great and horrible labor. For when the *regnum* of the Assyrians subdued almost all Asia, although this was done by fighting, yet the wars could not be very fierce or difficult, because the *gentes* were as yet untrained to resist, and neither so many nor so great as afterward; forasmuch as, after that greatest and indeed universal flood, when only eight men escaped in Noah's ark, not much more than a thousand years had passed when Ninus subdued all Asia with the exception of India. But Rome did not with the same quickness and facility wholly subdue all those *gentes* of the east and west which we see brought under the Roman *imperium,* because, in its gradual increase, in whatever direction it was extended, it found them strong and warlike.[78]

Whereas both the Assyrian *regnum* and the Roman *civitas-imperium* had subdued *gentes,* only the Romans had conquered *populi* as well, and their latter-day conquests were more substantial as well as tougher, and effected for a larger purpose.

Why did Augustine use *populus* at all for those Gentile groups? The rest of xviii, 22, offers a striking demonstration of Israel's near-monopoly of that noun: Israel is twice a *populus*, and simply and fully that, in five concluding sentences about half as long as the passage just quoted. Perhaps in this case Augustine was simply varying his vocabulary. The contrary alternative, that he was implying some definite point about the groups designated by that noun, seems more likely, however.

The key to that point occurs early in this grand historical sequence, in xv, 8, a discussion of Cain's ability to build a *civitas* so early in the race's history. Genesis 4:17 informs us that "Cain knew his wife, and she conceived and bore Enoch, and he built a city and called the name of the city after the name of his son Enoch." [79] Must we suppose that Enoch was Cain's first son, and hence that his building a *civitas* for three inhabitants was rather absurd—and hence that the sacred history is absurd, too? By no means.

> For it is quite possible that though he had other sons, yet for some reason the father loved him more than the rest. Judah was not the first-born, though he gave his name to Judaea and the Jews. But even if Enoch was the first-born of the founder of the *civitas*, that is no reason for supposing that the father named the *civitas* after him as soon as he was born; for at that time he, being a solitary man, could not have founded a civic community, *which is nothing else than a multitude of men bound together by some associating tie.* But when his family increased to such numbers that he had quite a population (*iam populi quantitatem*), then it became possible for him both to build a *civitas*, and give it, when founded, the name of his son. For so long was the life of those antediluvians . . .[80]

The formulaic definition of a *civitas* italicized in the preceding quotation has drawn the attention of several modern commentators. Not unworthy of notice is the *populi quantitas* which functions as the minor premise in this syllogism about man's first city-planning project: we have already encountered Augustine's notion that a *populus* is a certain kind of *multitudo*, which must be fairly numerous before it can take on attributes of a higher order. Our sense of those other attributes is sharpened by a look at the contexts in which Israel qualifies for the designation *populus* in these four books of *The City of God*.

For a representative sample, typical of Augustine's usage and of the meaning which it conveys, we need go no further than xv, 8, the source of the passage just cited. In that chapter's final sentence, which describes the growth of the *gens Hebraea* into the *populus Israel* by virtue of becoming so numerous as to muster a force of 600,000 warriors during the Exodus, we can discern clearly enough once more Augustine's sense that sufficient quantity is one essential attribute of a *populus*.[81] We also see that mere size is not enough, from one clause of that final sentence in which Augustine caps his argument about general demographic expansion since the Flood by remarking that he will not even mention "the *gens* of the Edomites which did not belong to the *populus* of Israel, although sprung from his brother Esau, who was also a grandson of Abraham, and the other *gentes* which were of the seed of the same Abraham, though not through his wife Sarah." [82] Do we see here, in the midst of this deprecatory Ciceronian device, just another instance of vocabulary variation without further significance? I think not, since this selective reservation of *populus* for Abraham's legitimate offspring accords well with Augustine's statement of the scriptural author's purpose in the third sentence of this same chapter.

> The design of that writer (who in this matter was the instrument of the Holy Spirit) was to descend to Abraham through the succession of ascertained generations propagated from one man, and then to pass from Abraham's seed to the *populus Dei,* in whom, separated as they were from the other *gentes,* was prefigured and predicted all that relates to the *civitas* whose reign is eternal, and to its king and founder Christ, which things were foreseen in the Spirit as yet to come; yet neither is this object so effected as that nothing is said of the other society (*societas*) of men which we call the earthly *civitas,* but mention is made of it so far as seemed needful to enhance the glory of the heavenly *civitas* by contrast to its opposite.[83]

Another cluster of the relevant group terms, large enough and significant enough to be useful for analyzing thought-revealing usage, occurs in the last chapter of book XVI. It starts out looking like just another assertion of Israel's growth from a *gens* to a *populus* because of an increase in size, but soon indicates the presence of another, more distinctive feature of the transformed group: its sense of solidarity achieved through its historical pilgrimage across the earth and through several types of political regimes.

Jacob being dead, and Joseph also, during the remaining hundred and forty-four years until they went out of the land of Egypt, that *gens* increased to an incredible degree, even though wasted by so great persecutions, that at one time the male children were murdered at their birth, because the wondering Egyptians were terrified at the too-great increase of that *populus*. Then Moses . . . became so great a man that he—yea, rather God, who had promised this to Abraham, by him—drew that *gens,* so wonderfully multiplied, out of the yoke of hardest and most grievous servitude it had borne there. . . . Then, when the Egyptians would not let God's *populus* go, ten memorable plagues were brought by Him upon them. . . . Then for forty years the *populus Dei* went through the desert, under the leadership of Moses, when the tabernacle of destiny was dedicated, in which God was worshipped by sacrifices prophetic of things to come, and that was after the law had been very terribly given on the mount, for its divinity was most plainly attested by wonderful signs and voices. This took place soon after the exodus from Egypt, *when the populus had entered the desert,* on the fiftieth day after the Passover was celebrated. . . .

On the death of Moses, Joshua the son of Nun ruled the *populus,* and led them into the land of promise, and divided it among them. By these two wonderful leaders wars were also carried on most prosperously and wonderfully, God calling to witness that they had got those victories not so much on account of the merit of the *populus Hebraeus* as on account of the sins of the *gentes* they subdued. And after these leaders there were judges, when the *populus* was settled in the land of promise, so that, in the meantime, the first promise made to Abraham began to be fulfilled about the one *gens,* that is, the

Hebrew, and about the land of Canaan; but not as yet the promise about all *gentes* and the whole wide world, for that was yet to be fulfilled, not by the observance of the Old Law, but by the advent of Christ in the flesh, and by the faith of the gospel. And it was to prefigure this that it was not Moses, who received the law for the *populus* on Mount Sinai, that led the *populus* into the land of promise, but Joshua, whose name also was changed at God's command. . . . But in the times of the judges prosperity alternated with adversity in war, according as the sins of the *populus* and the mercy of God were displayed.

We come next to the times of the kings. . . . David . . . was made a kind of starting-point and beginning of the advanced youth of the *populus Dei,* who had passed a kind of age of puberty from Abraham to this David. . . . For from the age of puberty man begins to be capable of generation; therefore [the evangelist Matthew] starts the list of generations from Abraham, who was also made the father of many *gentes* when he got his name changed. So that previously the *populus Dei* was as though in this type of boyhood, from Noah to Abraham; and for that reason the first language was learned, that is, the Hebrew . . .[84]

Not the least interesting feature of this historical summary is its reference to the analogy with the ages of human life which had served in cruder, brasher form as the framework of *On Genesis against the Manichees* 1, 23. In some of the sentences of this summary, at once subtler and more ambitious than that earlier piece of exegesis, *gens* and *populus* stand synonymously for Israel. In each of those cases, however, the synonyms are neatly paired, and *populus* is the later member of the pair. By the end of the summary, Israel is a *populus* only. A close inspection of the context rather than mere frequency shows that while both the *gens* and the *populus* are involved in demographic change, it is the *populus* which is led out of Egypt through the desert to the promised land, which in the course of that long journey receives a law (what a Law!), a set of rituals, and a destiny, and which thereafter wages wars and undergoes political organization and the experience of territorial settlement. No translation can project the strictly grammatical undertones of the clause italicized above: *et in deserto populus esse coepit.*

Was this only a momentary choice of vocabulary for Augustine? The other passages we have examined suggest the contrary conclusion, as does a look at his recapitulation of this notional and semantic scheme in the first two chapters of the following book, devoted to the age of the prophets. Chapter 1 opens (not only from this study's point of view) with a *gens Israelitica* begotten by Abraham in the flesh and foreshadowing all those nations (*omnes gentes*) which will become his seed through faith. Then comes a brief résumé of Israel's experience with monarchy: its *regnum* established by David, its captivity as a kingless *populus* in Babylon, and the more significant fact that Israel had had prophets all the while, from the time that "kings began to appear *in Dei populo.*" Chapter 2 recapitulates the divine promise of a special territory. In this discussion of a property which he does not normally attribute to a *populus,* Augustine used *gens* more frequently than *populus*—7 times (plus one scriptural citation) to 5—but while 3 of those uses of *gens* refer to Israel, 4 refer to the Gentiles, and all 5 *populi* have to do with Israel, 4 of them with that group's destiny-conscious journey to the promised land and beyond it.

There is no need to weary the reader further with this sort of small-scale statistical breakdown, especially not in connection with book XVII of *The City of God.* In that book *populus* appears 47 times in Augustine's own phrasing, and another 17 times in quotations from Scripture, for a total of 64 appearances, the highest frequency in any book of *The City of God.* In 46 of those 64 instances—34 pure Augustine, 12 scriptural—*populus* designates Israel, and another 8 times (all pure Augustine) it refers to a *populus Dei* which is more than historical, an Israel writ large. The remaining 10 occurrences of *populus* are evenly divided between the Gentiles (2 Augustine, 3 Scripture) and the Christian Church.[85]

Gens, usually more frequent in these books than *populus,* appears only 36 times, 28 times among Augustine's own words, and 8 times in scriptural citations. Ten of these 36 instances refer to

Israel, 2 to the Jews after the coming of Christ, and 24 to the Gentiles (6 times via Scripture, 18 times in Augustine's extensions of that model). The Christian Church appears only in overlapping implications. Considering only Augustine's own wording, we see that *gens* refers to the historical Israel 32 percent of the time, while *populus* is so used 72 percent of the time.

Yet more significant than the statistical evidence just summarized, Augustine's application of *populus* to Israel corresponds 18 times to a reference to that group's prophetic destiny. He uses scriptural citations 8 times to make this association, and all 8 references to the metahistorical *populus Dei* make it as well. In other words, in 34 of its 64 appearances in book xvii (or 53 percent of the time, spread quite evenly), *populus* connects the historical Israel or its transcendent descendant with the providential mission that gave historical and theological meaning to both groups, the destiny that in the largest sense "defined" them.

The efficient, intellectually coherent exploitation of *populus* in this book is entirely consistent with its theme, the new clarity and singleness of purpose with which God spoke to mankind from the time of Samuel, who chose the first David to be king and prophet and proclaimed the coming of a Son of David who would be king, prophet, priest, and more. Before then, God had revealed His purposes through spectacular but enigmatic events like the Flood (the boundary between books xv and xvi). With Samuel's oracular and political vocation, He began to teach by public utterance as well as deeds, and not only to one chosen group of worshipers. Israel's predicted bursts of inattention and bad behavior would symbolize for all to see that the frontiers dividing the City of God from the other City are spiritual and interior; even Israel's monopoly of the original language of mankind would not prevent the message of the Hebrew books from invading the consciousness of Gentile philosophers. That message was essentially simple: the advent of the universal Savior, whose sacrifice would involve all nations and terminate the significant history of the Two Cities.

With book xviii Augustine returned, perhaps after a certain lapse of time, to that tangled double history. It is one of the longest books of *The City of God*, and in some ways one of the least compelling. Augustine was deeply concerned to demonstrate in it the nonmythical, historically authentic character of Israel's election; to insert that people's history into the recognized chronology of the great pagan empires, he relied heavily and uncreatively on three main sources: Varro's *Antiquities,* Josephus's *Jewish War,* and Eusebius's *Chronicle* in Jerome's Latin translation. They were authorities of the highest current respectability, which Augustine had no reason to scrutinize skeptically; nevertheless, the modern reader may be justified if he misses the personal rapport and critical intimacy that distinguish Augustine's use of Varro in books vi and xix, for example.[86] Not surprisingly, his usage of *populus* is less careful as well as less frequent than in book xvii, and much less susceptible of clear statistical correlation with the main themes. On the other hand, the very complexity of the relationship between the thematic content and the employment of *populus* within it indicates once again the value of that chosen word as an index to the author's state of mind.

Despite the comparative confusion of that unit of thought and literary composition, we can still discern in book xviii a special relationship between *populus* and the Israel which adds to size and solidarity a third characteristic acquisition: an increasingly sophisticated consciousness of its law and its mission.

In chapter 8, the reader is reminded that "When Saphrus reigned as fourteenth king of Assyria, and Orthopolis as the twelfth of Sicyon, and Criasus as the fifth of Argos, Moses was born in Egypt, by whom the *populus Dei* was liberated from the Egyptian slavery, in which they behoved to be thus tried that they might desire the help of their Creator. . . ." The contemporary Gentiles were also beginning to realize the possibilities of their own, perverted form of religious self-consciousness: ". . . yet, down to Cecrops king of Athens, in whose reign that city (*civitas*) received its name, and in whose reign God brought His *populus* out of Egypt by Moses, only a few dead heroes are reported to have been deified according to the vain superstition of the Greeks." [87]

In chapter 25, a sudden escalation of sophistication in such matters is reported, in the form of a reappraisal-provoking political reversal for Israel and an intellectual awakening among the Gentiles.

When Zedekiah reigned over the Hebrews, and Tarquinius
Priscus, the successor of Ancus Martius, over the Romans, the
populus Judaeorum was led captive into Babylon, Jerusalem and
the temple built by Solomon being overthrown. For the prophets, in chiding them for their iniquity and impiety, predicted
that these things should come to pass, especially Jeremiah, who
even stated the number of years. Pittacus of Mitylene . . . is
reported to have lived at that time. And Eusebius writes that,
while the *populus Dei* was held captive in Babylon, the five
other sages lived, who must be added to Thales . . . and Pittacus, to make up the seven. These are Solon of Athens, Chilo
of Lacedaemon, Periander of Corinth, Cleobulus of Lindus, and
Bias of Priene.[88]

Two chapters later, Augustine explains the symbolic reason for
the apparent historical accident that the *populus* of Israel began
to record its prophets' utterances at the same time that Assyria's
empire began to shrink and the modest Roman dominion began
to grow.

> . . . these fountains of prophecy, as I may call them, burst
> forth at once during those times when the Assyrian *regnum*
> failed and the Roman began; so that, just as in the first period
> of the Assyrian kingdom Abraham arose, to whom the most
> distinct promises were made that all *gentes* should be blessed in
> his seed, so at the beginning of the western Babylon, in the time
> of whose governance (*qua . . . imperante*) Christ was to come
> in whom these promises were to be fulfilled, the oracles of the
> prophets were given not only in spoken but in written words,
> for a testimony that so great a thing should come to pass. For
> although the *populus* Israel hardly ever lacked prophets from
> the time when they began to have kings, these were only for
> their own use, not for that of the *gentes*. But when the more
> manifestly prophetic Scripture began to be formed, which was
> to benefit the *gentes,* too, it was fitting that it should begin when
> this city was founded which was to rule the *gentes*.[89]

The affinity of *populus* for a religiously mature Israel, discernible
in book xviii as well as elsewhere, is attested even in a later pas-

sage of that book (chapter 45), which seems at first to contain an instance of the relatively featureless synonymity of *populus* with *gens*.

The *gens Judaea* indubitably became worse after it ceased to have prophets, just at the very time when, on the rebuilding of the temple after the captivity in Babylon, it hoped to become better. For so, indeed, did that carnal *populus* understand what was foretold by Haggai the prophet, saying, "The glory of this latter house shall be greater than that of the former." Now, that this is said of the new testament, he showed a little above, where he says, evidently promising Christ, "And I will move all *gentes*, and the desired One will come to all *gentes*." In this passage the Septuagint translators, giving another sense more suitable to the body than the head, that is, to the Church than to Christ, have said by prophetic authority, "The things shall come that are chosen of the Lord from all *gentes*," that is, *men*, of whom Jesus says in the Gospel, "Many are called, but few are chosen." For from such chosen ones of the *gentes* there is built, through the new testament, with living stones, a house of God far more glorious than that temple which was constructed by king Solomon, and rebuilt after the captivity. For this reason, then, that *gens* had no prophets from that time, but was afflicted with many plagues by kings of alien race (*alienigenis regibus*), and by the Romans themselves, lest they should fancy that this prophecy of Haggai was fulfilled by that rebuilding of the temple.[90]

From all the rest that we have seen, we can conclude that Augustine was not merely varying his vocabulary when he put that one *populus* among all those *gentes*, Jewish as well as Gentile. Sophistication is no guarantee of wisdom, and even this uniquely chosen people was about to miss its rendezvous with its proper destiny. A *populus carnalis*, unified by race but not by higher attributes, is an anomalous sort of *populus*, almost a figure of speech. It is exactly a *gens* without prophets, which would very soon be left with no political liberty and only a stubborn parody of its law.

One community which has little trouble qualifying for the title of *populus* in Augustine's writings is the Church, in both its universal and its local dimensions. In a recently discovered letter to the Carthaginian priest Firmus, he expresses his hope that the forthcoming *City of God* will be useful to those of Firmus's friends who desire instruction, "whether they be among the Christian *populus* or are still held by some superstition." [91] The second book of that promised magnum opus attributes true justice only to Christ's commonwealth, undeniably (as will be remembered) a *res populi*.[92] In his treatise *On Catechizing the Uncultured*, composed for the African deacon Deogratias around the year 400, Augustine gives a classic definition of the Church as *populus*.

> All things written before the Lord's coming which we read in the holy Scriptures were written for no other reason than to announce His coming and to prefigure the future Church, that is, the *populus Dei* throughout all *gentes,* which is His body. With it are joined and numbered also all the holy ones who lived in this world before His coming, believing that He would come just as we believe that He has.[93]

Augustine constantly refers to the Church as a *populus* when he is considering it in a more concrete, local context. The very title of his *Sermones ad populum* shows that was normal,[94] as do numerous passages within those sermons. Even more conclusive is a description of Christian congregations listening to such sermons, which we find in his correspondence with Marcellinus. The great pagan authors, he says, urge that one forget injuries to oneself, and are praised as encouragers of civic virtue.

> But when one reads on the teaching authority of God that evil must not be rendered for evil, when this extremely healthy admonition resounds from a high place in the congregations of *populi,* as though in public schools for each sex and all ages and ranks, religion is condemned as an enemy of the commonwealth! [95]

More intimate and concrete are Augustine's references to his own congregation, as exemplified in a tropological question posed for their benefit at the end of an explanation of the double catch of fish in John 21:1–12 (the second catch, amounting to 153 fish, symbolized the election of those who will be saved).

And all those, how many will they be? One hundred and fifty-three? Far be it from me to say that among this *populus* which stands here before me, there will be so few in the kingdom of heaven, where John saw thousands, innumerable thousands, dressed in white robes.[96]

Possidius's *Life of Saint Augustine* preserves a similar employment of the word in one of those anecdotes which are probably the best sources we have for making surmises about the tone of Augustine's everyday conversation.

I know also, and not only I but also my brethren and fellow-servants who were at that time living together with the holy man in the church at Hippo, that when we were seated at the table he said,

"Did you notice my sermon in church today, and the fact that both the beginning and the end worked out contrary to my usual custom? For I did not bring to its conclusion the subject which I proposed, but left it hanging."

To which we replied, "Yes, we know it and remember that we wondered about it at the time."

Then he said, "I suppose that perhaps the Lord wished some wanderer among the *populus* to be taught and healed by our forgetful wandering; for in His hands are we and all our speech."

Needless to say, "a certain merchant, Firmus by name," was so moved by that digression that he renounced his Manicheism and subsequently became a priest.[97] Augustine's *populus* could include auditors whose membership was only potential.

The *Confessions* depict very vividly the solidarity and communal fervor which could animate a great metropolitan church. In book IX, Augustine recalls the impact made on him before his baptism, in February 386, by the sung liturgy which Ambrose had recently introduced.

The Church in Milan (*ecclesia Mediolanensis*) had not long begun this kind of consolation and exhortation, in which the voices and hearts of the brethren joined in zealous harmony. It was about a year, or not much more, since Justina, the mother of the boy emperor Valentinian, persecuted thy servant Ambrose, as a result of the heresy into which she had been seduced by the Arians. The faithful *plebs* stayed night and day in the church (*ecclesia*), prepared to die with their bishop, Thy servant. My mother, Thy handmaid, was one of the leaders in these cares and vigils, living on prayers. We ourselves, as yet unheated by the warmth of Thy Spirit, began to feel the *civitas*-wide emotion and unrest. At that time, the practice of singing hymns and psalms, according to the custom of the East, was established so that the *populus* would not become weak as a result of the boredom of sorrow. It has been retained from that day to this; many—in fact, nearly all Thy flocks (*greges*)—now do likewise, throughout the rest of the world.

Four swift months later, Ambrose was shown in a dream the resting place of the martyrs Gervase and Protase, whose relics were transferred to the episcopal basilica amid scenes of intense enthusiasm. Not only were demoniacs healed, "but also a certain man who had been blind for many years, a very well-known *civis* of the *civitas,* asked and was told the reason for the tumultuous joy of the *populus.* He jumped up and begged his guide to bring him thither." His eyesight was restored, "and though the mind of the hostile Justina was not brought to the sanity of belief, at least it was restrained from the insanity of persecution." [98]

Worth noting in this specimen of heightened style is the variety of terms applied to the Christian community. The group is first called an *ecclesia,* lest any mistake be made about its identity; however, that obvious appellation is also so neutral that within two sentences it applies with equal aptness to a building. The generic name for the group's collective membership is *populus.* Once, probably for the sake of stylistic flexibility, it is called a *plebs,* and further relief from monotony is provided for the hallowed metaphor of the *grex.* But the congregation of this *ecclesia* is ordinarily a *populus,* active within but not coterminous with its *civitas.*

The last book of *The City of God,* written perhaps twenty-six years after the *Confessions* and a full forty years after the prodigy reported in the passage just analyzed, contains a long chapter about contemporary miracles which gives us a picture of urban and rural Christian *populi* that is in some ways even more vivid. The differences between these two chapters—*Confessions* IX, 7 and *City of God* XXII, 8—should command the attention of students of Augustine's psychology and style, as well as church historians interested in the issues they touch. The most interesting development from this study's point of view is that undergone by the noun *populus:* its usage in the latter chapter is entirely consistent with that of the earlier chapter, but it has become so standard a term for the Christian community, that it takes precedence ahead of *ecclesia* in frequency, resonance, and stylistic position.

City of God XXII, 8 begins with a reference to the previous chapter's discussion of Cicero's skeptical attitude toward the "resurrection" of Romulus—his mythical ascension, under the new name of Quirinus, to the company of the gods—and the contrast between that fable and the resurrection and ascension of Christ, which now command wide (though still incomplete) assent. What a striking contrast, considering the lessened credulity, the generally increased rationality of the "more enlightened present time." This progressive skepticism—evidently commendable in most cases—is one reason why the numerous miracles which continue to attest the truth and power of Christ's resurrection get so little publicity, so much less attention than those of biblical times. Another, supplementary reason is that

> the canon of the sacred Scripture, which behoved to be closed, causes those to be everywhere recited, and to sink into the memory of all the *populi;* but these modern miracles are scarcely known to the whole *civitas* or even to the neighborhood (*quocumque commanentium loco*) in the midst of which they are wrought. For frequently they are known only to a very few persons, while all the rest are ignorant of them, especially if the *civitas* is a large one; and when they are reported to other persons in other localities, there is no sufficient authority to give them prompt and unwavering credence, although they are reported to the faithful by the faithful.

The miracle which was wrought at Milan when I was there, and by which a blind man was restored to sight, could come to the knowledge of many; for not only is the *civitas* a large one, but also the emperor was there at the time and the occurrence was witnessed by an immense concourse of people (*inmenso populo teste*) that had gathered to the bodies of the martyrs Protasius and Gervasius . . .[99]

Once more we see a *populus* active within but not coterminous with its *civitas,* and we may well feel that the "neighborhoods," the *loci commanentium,* which are ill-defined units but which hear and are capable of judging reports, have as much conscious personality as the *civitates* of which they are either parts or rural counterparts. We see, in fact, what may seem to modern eyes two kinds of active *populi:* the Christian congregation and the whole population of a *civitas.* Were they so distinct in the mind of Augustine the aging bishop?

Throughout this chapter, which in subject matter and in tone (though not in style) seems more akin to the *Sermons* than to the rest of *The City of God, populus* is used for variations of one group. In twelve of its thirteen appearances it stands quite clearly for Christian congregations of an exceptionally alert character, for which no other noun is used (except for one appearance of the official *ecclesia Carthaginensis, ecclesia* stands for a building). In the perhaps exceptional instance cited above, it designates an "immense" Milanese *populus* witnessing and bearing witness to a miracle that entailed numerous consequences, political as well as religious. In that context, that *populus* also seems overwhelmingly Christian, thanks to its literary surroundings as well as according to imperial policy and probable historical fact.

This chapter ends with one of the most vivid narratives Augustine ever wrote—the account of a brother and sister from Cappadocia who were cured of palsy during Easter week at the memorial chapel of the martyr Stephen in Hippo, and then became the object of tumultuous acclaim in Augustine's cathedral church and the subject of four sermons delivered there.[100] The *populus* of Hippo Regius appears six times in that narrative, always in the cathedral basilica, always highly conscious, either paying silent attention or (more often) in bursts of intense enthusiasm, and thoroughly unified in a fairly active state of rational participation. The Vandals seem very far away—or then no more of a threat than the civilized Arians.

The Church obviously suits both the strict and the broad definitions of *populus;* societies of an exclusively secular and even rather vicious nature can meet the requirements of the broad, second definition. Its statement in chapter 24 of book xix of *The City of God* mentions Athenians, Egyptians, and Assyrians as specific examples. Two chapters later, speaking more generally, Augustine says: "Wretched therefore is the *populus* alienated from [the true] God." [101] In the fourteenth of his *Tractates on the Gospel of John,* he says that "there is a *populus* prepared for the anger of God, to be damned with the devil; no one of its members receives the testimony of Christ." Here he is evidently referring to an eternal, transcendent society, the opposite number of the *civitas Dei,* which he calls *"illum populum distinctum"* a few lines farther on.[102]

One of Augustine's most famous stigmatizations of the false values of contemporary pagans (in book ii, chapter 20 of *The City of God,* and hence something of a prelude to the first definition of *populus*) contains these sentences:

> Let the *populi* applaud, not those who have their interests at heart, but those who are lavish with pleasures. . . . Let those be considered true gods who saw to it that the *populi* should win the occasion of such bliss and preserved it when won.[103]

Attacking the "demons" whose cults countenanced such decadence, he says:

> To prevent the destruction of the Roman Republic the protecting gods ought to have made rules of life and conduct their first gift to the *populus* that worshipped them in all those temples, with all those priests and varieties of sacrifice, all those frequent and varied ceremonials, all those anniversary feasts and all those celebrations of those important games.[104]

It is unlikely that the plural form *populi* in the first of these two passages should be taken to mean simply "crowds" or "the mob," especially in view of the singular, Roman *populus* in the second passage which summarizes the point made by the first, and seems to point at least one moral of the great Ciceronian *excursus* which is the chapter in between. More probably, the plural form denotes the numerous distinct *populi* of the ancient world. Even if not, the *populi* of the first passage are a crowd remarkably united in values, purpose, and action (or reaction).

One further implication appears in these citations: however objectively illusory and earthly the evil objects of its love may be, there is something inescapably religious about the consensus which produces a *populus*. A "secular state" in the modern sense, or even a "secular" set of political or social values, utterly neutral toward religion, seems to have been beyond the reach of Augustine's imagination—at least beyond that zone of it revealed through his vocabulary.

This ultimate subjection of all aspects of human society to the law of Providence comes out very clearly in book 1 of Augustine's dialogue *On Free Will*, which he began in Rome in 387 or 388, may have continued at his monastery at Tagaste, and completed in Hippo around 395. Chapters 5 and 6 of that book are centered on a distinction first drawn by Evodius between "that law which is written for the governance of a *populus*" and "a certain law, more stringent and very secret" which both speakers call divine providence. The *populus* for which and from which this distinction is developed is civil society, consisting of *cives*, making use of *ministri* subject *"iure atque ordine"* to various forms of authority, in order to promote the public interest and control evil-doing. In regard to such concerns the *populus* of this conversation seems entirely secular, but both Evodius and Augustine agree that it is a moral entity, which if *modestus, moderatus,* and *gravis* should have the power of choosing its own magistrates, but if *levis, depravatus, corruptus,* or *dissolutus* should have that power transferred to "one good man who can do more." [105] It is this essential and essentially ethical element which puts the *populus* finally under the jurisdiction of transcendent values.[106]

Perhaps of some significance is the fact that Augustine has the very conventional Evodius, a soldier and civil official before his conversion by Ambrose, use no term but *populus* (once in the combination *populi civitatesque*) for the forms of society under discussion. Augustine casts himself in the role of trying to elevate and generalize the discussion, and so occasionally uses other terms as well: *civitas* appears twice in his remarks, and *populus* appears once in the combination *homines et populi;* three chapters earlier he remarks that adultery should be considered evil *"omnibus gentibus atque populis."* [107] However, the author of the dialogue does not forget that he and Evodius had been childhood playmates and schoolmates in Tagaste; despite his somewhat more flexible vocabulary, he puts *populus* in his own mouth [108] eight times in chapters 5 and 6 as the sole label for civil society.[109]

The Problem of Plurality

Did Augustine conceive of a plurality of *populi* within a community which was also called a *populus?* It is a logical consequence of what has gone before that the *populus Dei* and its opposite number coexist on earth, their members belonging also to many local, mortal *populi*. But what is the functional relationship between either or both of those transcendent societies and any temporal one? What about the same problem among the different levels of temporal society? As soon as the question is posed in this way, and placed in any specific context, the answer is in doubt. Obviously, it seems to us, Augustine must have felt that a unity such as the *populus Hipponensis* consisted of rational persons who belonged also (and on much higher levels) to the *populus Romanus* and the *populus Christianus*. The fact that this research has failed to find any texts which say that in so many words need not trouble us unduly. The author may have felt himself that so necessary a corollary to his major doctrines did not require statement. Sometimes Augustine took pains to elaborate the obvious, but usually only when some object more worthy of persuasion justified the exercise.

On the other hand, it should also be clear from what has gone before that, when Augustine uses *populus* in a local reference without a modifier indicating otherwise, he tends to mean either a group of active citizens or the Christian community.[110] When he addresses the *populus* from his preacher's throne, he includes women, children, and slaves in that appellation. But he certainly does not refer directly to those three classes of human beings when he mentions some *populus* engaged in strictly political or military activity. Conversely, that *populus* in church of which and to which he so frequently speaks could not possibly include Jews who hold Roman citizenship. Are there several concrete *populi* in Hippo Regius, or one? Logically there must be at least two,[111] but the distinctions immediately following upon that conclusion do not appear in Augustine's own language. Hippo, like Constantinople, appears to have a single *populus* of its own, within whose simple sphere occur most of its members' most important actions. If so, what is its unifying consensus? How composite can it afford to be and still retain that constituent unity? This is one of those cases in which semantic consistency seems not to equal logical consistency (substitute "coherence" for "consistency," if desired), especially if we demand those virtues from propositions or verbal formulas which we criticize from the viewpoint of their consequences or corollaries. Beyond that problem, this is a case in which questions important to the political theorist encounter questions that appear natural to the grammarian—perhaps we moderns should say "linguist"—and the result is the reverse of Augustine's remark about the Tower of Babel in *The City of God* xvi, 4: [112] the language is the same (whether his Latin or our English), but the dominant interests are different.

Unfortunately, the historian of ideas cannot leave it at that. If it seems that men can validly be citizens of two (or more) true *populi* at the same time, then a way of thinking not too distant from modern theories of the separation of church and state can develop without too much ideological shock. Some modern scholars claim that Augustine started just such a process by constructing his triad of overlapping *civitates;* [113] if that is true, it would be both interesting and reassuring to detect a comparable sense of plural allegiance or structural overlap in Augustine's usage of *populus*. This study has already argued that *populus* seems to have been for Augustine a more modest, more neutral group label than *civitas*, so we might well expect to find it describing or referring to some such pragmatically overlapping citizenship.

On the other hand, if Augustine's normal usage of his normal word for sociopolitical groups to which men belonged primarily by virtue of some sort of consent seems to shrink from such a bifurcation of membership, then we may be well advised to look elsewhere for the grandfather of pluralism. But to resolve this question of intellectual history, we must (in this study, at least) return to the lexical level, to the plane of grammatical order, and there we find ourselves facing a dilemma.

Two passages of Augustine's scriptual exegesis seem at first to ease the dilemma. His *Enarratio* on Psalm 47 runs into real difficulty with verse 10: *"Suscepimus, Deus, misericordiam tuam in medio populi tui."* How to understand these last four words, "as though there are some who have received it, and others in the midst of whom they have done so?" Such a notion, not terribly troublesome to modern sensibilities, is evidently contrary to some of Augustine's assumptions about *populi*. A subtle solution is offered, however.

> Now, to be sure, all those who bear His sacraments are on the census lists of God's *populus,* but not all . . . belong to His mercy. All receiving the sacrament of baptism are indeed called Christians, but not all live worthily of that sacrament. . . . Nevertheless, on account of that appearance of piety they are named among the *populus* of God, just as the chaff belongs to the threshing-floor along with the grain, as long as threshing-time lasts. But surely it does not belong to the granary? And so here in the midst of an evil *populus* there is a good *populus,* which has received God's mercy.[114]

We are obviously on the threshold of the distinction between the Visible and the Invisible Church,[115] but Augustine refrains from entering so arcane a region, perhaps sensing yet worse contradictions ahead—for the last few lines might require that he characterize the Visible Church as distinctively reprobate (if it equals the chaff), or at the very least morally neutral (if it equals the threshing floor; and then what about the inherent spiritual value of the granary?). The "evil *populus*" can hardly be the world, since the whole psalm and his commentary on it are set "in the *civitas* of God, in His holy mountain."

So we do not get much help after all, particularly since Augustine makes no effort to disguise the special ingenuity required here. It is a fitting irony that the whole embarrassment would have disappeared if the Bishop of Hippo had been less stubborn in his refusal to follow the priest Jerome in the matter of scriptural translation.[116] The so-called Gallican Psalter, Jerome's compromise between the Septuagint and the Hebrew versions, which he composed about 387 after comparing the Septuagint with Origen's *Hexaplar,* renders the troublesome phrase as *"in medio templi tui,"* thus correcting the λαοῦ of the Septuagint tradition to ναοῦ.[117]

A less dubious exercise in relevant exegesis occurs in a long sermon on Jacob and Esau which Augustine delivered for the feast of the martyr Vincent (January 22), sometime between 410 and 419:

> [Esau] comes late, and brings what his father ordered; and he finds his brother blessed in his stead, and is not blessed with another blessing. Now those two men were *populi,* while the single blessing signifies the unity of the Church. But although they are two *populi,* Jacob is both. However, the two *populi* belonging to Jacob can be understood in another way as well. For our Lord Jesus Christ, who came to the Jews and the Gentiles, was repudiated by the Jews, who belonged to the elder son. Nevertheless, he chose some who belonged to the younger son, who began spiritually to desire and understand the Lord's promises, not receiving according to the flesh that land which they had been desiring. Rather they desired that *civitas* where no one is born in a fleshly manner, for no one dies there either carnally or spiritually.

The themes are familiar, if not overly lucid. Here we have the *civitas Dei,* the Church (whether visible or invisible) as the *populus Dei,* and the historical Jews, especially the remnant rejecting Christ. But even that involved scheme, it soon develops, is too simple.

> Those two *populi,* coming as though from different regions, are also signified by the two walls. For the Church of the Jews came from the circumcision, and the Church of the Gentiles from the foreskin. . . . Therefore the two kids are those two *populi;* so also are the two sheepfolds, the two walls, the two

blind men who sat by the road, the two boats in which the fish were drawn up. In many places in Scripture we can recognize the two *populi:* but they are one in Jacob.[118]

This reassertion of the unity of all those things in Jacob is extremely frustrating to anyone seeking in this passage a resolution of Augustine's apparent confusion about the potential plurality of *populi* in a given geographical context. One of the advantages of paradox is its exemption from most of the usual regulations, and a paradox erected on a mound of allegorical equivalencies is safely beyond the reach of pedestrian grammatical logic. We are left with our dilemma.

A much clearer and more useful set of distinctions appears when Augustine leaves the mystical regions of the psalms and patriarchs to deal with the problem of overlapping groups in the world of places like Bulla Regia. The sermon which he preached there on the feast of the Macchabees in the course of a journey to Carthage has already been cited in another connection; several other passages are relevant to the present question. After a lively description of Bulla's bad reputation among its *vicinae civitates,* Augustine says:

> But perhaps you will say, "We are just like Carthage. There is a holy and religious *plebs* here just as at Carthage, but the *turba* is so great in that great *civitas,* that everyone excuses himself on account of others. 'Pagans do it, Jews do it,' they can say at Carthage; here, whoever does it *has* to be a Christian!" . . . But we say to Your Charity: we know your *civitas,* too, in God's name! as well as those neighboring you; we know just how large a *multitudo* is here, how large a *populus.* Can any of you help but be known to the man [i.e., the bishop] who dispenses unto you the Word and the sacraments? Who will excuse you, then, from your disgrace?
>
> Perhaps you will say, "Fine! You who are clerics, you who are bishops, may abstain from the theaters, but not we laymen." Does that sentiment really strike you as just? For what are we, if you perish? What we are on our own account is one thing; what we are on your account is another. We are Christians on our own account, clergy and bishops for no other reason than on account of you. The Apostle was not speaking to clergy, to

bishops and priests, when he said, "But you are the members of Christ." He was speaking to the *plebes,* he was speaking to the faithful, he was speaking to Christians. . . . I fear very greatly lest Christ say to us in His judgment: "Evil servants, you gladly accepted the praise of my *populus,* but you kept silence on the subject of their imminent death." [119]

In this passage Augustine uses *populus* for two groups. First, it stands for the whole population of a *civitas.* Is that collective body a *populus* (as well as a *multitudo*) at Bulla, but a *turba* at Carthage, because the former city was unified in its superficial Christianity? Unfortunately, the text does not seem to warrant so subtle an interpretation. The point seems rather to be that the size and the religious composition of a *populus* like Bulla or Carthage are irrelevant to the moral duty of the Christian community there; the most exact term for that community in this passage is *plebs.* Augustine probably felt that *turba* was particularly apt for Carthage because of the dense crowds of humanity which any traveler from Bulla would be likely to encounter (and remember) in the metropolis of Africa, especially in its commercial and theatrical districts.

In its second and final appearance in this sermon, *populus* stands for the People of Christ, including lost members. Is it possible that this second *populus* refers only to the damned (and, presumably, the saved) among the laity? If so, why exclude the clergy with whom Christ is presented as being angry? Clergy and laity seem to share a common range of guilt and reward as Christ judges what He is made to call "My people." Such a distinction of ranks seems unnecessarily strained. The word for the laity of the whole Church in this passage is *plebes,* and the singular form of that noun is used either for the laity of the Church of Carthage or for its whole membership.[120] Consequently, it seems most reasonable to conclude that *populus* in this extemporaneous sermon stands for relatively large, inclusive, morally responsible groups, subdivisions or more particular aspects of which may be called *plebes* (as well as other things), especially if the context has to do with Christian church organization.

This sermon simply shows us that, when discussing the concrete

confusion of differing groups within a community, Augustine
knew how to clarify the situation by varying his vocabulary just
enough for the less than grammatical interests of his audience.
From such a context it is not fair to expect the resolution of questions of political theory or semantic precision. The dilemma remains unsolved.

The answer to this problem of plurality is probably that Augustine was guilty of a certain amount of logical inconsistency, but
of no more semantic inconsistency than that of most intellectuals
deeply and articulately involved in public affairs. Caracalla's edict
of 212, giving Roman citizenship to all free men in the empire,
must have done much by Augustine's time to obliterate any practical sense of the difference between citizenship in the universal
Roman *populus* and that in the local one of Hippo.[121] Since Constantine's successors (with the rule-proving exception of Julian),
and certainly since Theodosius, the Roman *populus* was supposed
to be or to become Christian as well. Prohibitions of public pagan
worship, such as those of 399, 407, and 408, won Augustine's
enthusiastic support. The drift of imperial and episcopal policies
in Africa for the greater part of a century had been in the direction
of cooperation and unity.[122] Fine distinctions about the composition of society usually lead to some questioning of actual authority,
and in Augustine's immediate set of circumstances that could only
have helped the Donatists.[123]

Some modern critics may instinctively reject this disappointing
reflection of the status quo in the most subtle of the Latin Fathers.
It is important to remember, however, that despite all those
philosophical dialogues Augustine was a rhetorician rather than a
dialectician, a man of high literary talent professionally as well as
personally bent toward concrete persuasion; few of his most loyal
modern disciples maintain that his undoubted genius was particularly sympathetic to pure abstraction or the construction of purely
speculative models. In regard to the present question, my own
suspicion is that Augustine was not a pluralist by instinct. That
position is easy to maintain by an examination of his public policy
as bishop; I think it reveals itself also in those reflexes, those
"prejudices" about human groups which we can discern in his

astonishingly precise vocabulary. If the consequences of his most original ideas would lead distant disciples to other and contrary positions, that would be their own problem.

Summary Redefinition

Even if we take into account all the distinctions and exceptions treated earlier in this chapter, it seems fairly clear that the noun *populis* normally represented for Augustine a fairly definite, fairly coherent cluster of concepts, which may be described in twentieth-century terminology as a legitimate, unified polity, whether earthly or heavenly, temporal or eternal, formed and sustained by an associative consent belonging ultimately to the order of conscious ethics.

This descriptive definition is cast in frankly modern language which may strike some readers as an incongruous vehicle for the verbal association-schemes of one of the richest minds of Christian antiquity. I hope that this definition's attempt to translate, not only Augustine's outright definitions of a *populus,* but that word's normal value throughout the whole range of his works, will illuminate for us that word's meaning to him by setting it in the sort of perspective which can only be drawn if we fully recognize that twentieth-century speakers of English employ a language more distant from that of fourth-century Romans than a standard Latin-English lexicon would make immediately obvious.

The claim that Augustine normally used the word *populus* in accordance with the modern definition here proposed may appear to many readers most unlikely, in view of the complexity, elusiveness, and frequently contradictory richness which we usually encounter in Augustine's thought, which indeed we associate with it almost by reflex. When that fecund and digressive intelligence spoke and wrote about grace and predestination, the illumination of the human intellect, or the protean value of Roman civic pride, the result was very often a set of statements which, taken all together, impress us by their mutual discordance almost as much as by their vividness. The peculiar opulence of Augustine's mode of expression often seems to depend on an accumulation of utterances which, if not overtly inconsistent with one another, usually fail to fit together with neat congruence. For all his fascination with the single-valued purity of numbers, Augustine was no geometrician in argument. How then could he have used a word like *populus,* so well endowed with associative potential, as narrowly as I contend?

I must confess that I was initially as startled by this emerging contention as I expect many readers to be. In planning this study, I expected to find in Augustine's works a wide range of usages for this respectable word, and hoped to find suggestive correlations between that variation of usages and some variations in the date, genre, and context of the *populus*-bearing passages. The results of my research simply did not fit those expectations, and so I am compelled to offer the reader the spare, rather bland conclusion here presented.

Should it be so startling, after all? For a large part of his adult life Augustine's craft was the manipulation of words, and during his late childhood and adolescence he had received deep training in a grammatical tradition which considered most individual words true signs of discrete things, objects worthy of respect and exact understanding. To produce full arguments or discrete statements marked by alluring and commanding variety and nuance of phrasing is one thing; to make equally variable the individual words of which those propositions are composed is quite another. I suspect that the comptrollers of late Roman grammar and rhetoric felt most secure when dealing with statements based on a standard and tightly regulated vocabulary: if those statements' component parts, the individual substantive words, were not of recognized and unvarying coinage, who could certify what they all added up to? A certain type of literary taste, current in the twentieth as well as in other centuries, prefers the excitement of gambling on the tables of lexical money-changers; how many of Augustine's models or contemporaries shared that taste? [124]

Perhaps some of the richness of Augustine's style of argument on complex theological, philosophical, and political issues is due to the rigor and precision with which he handled the individual units of his vocabulary. If from time to time he was careless about the ultimate logical consequences of his polemical or speculative utterances, he was not careless with the words of which he constructed them. In that contrast of treatment may lie much of the compelling, even paradoxical tension of his thought.

3 *Populus* in Jerome

For Jerome, the word *populus* seems to have possessed essentially the same content and value that it had for Augustine. There are, to be sure, some significant differences between the ways in which they handled it. Jerome never defined *populus* as precisely as Augustine did, nor did he speculate about the grammatical implications of its meaning or the consequences of its employment as a dialectical term. These differences, however, have to do with varying degrees of thoroughness in attention to the word, rather than with substantive disagreement about its content, and are entirely consistent with the differences between the intellectual concerns and temperaments of the two men. Both admired variety and richness of style in the Ciceronian manner, and both were conscious of the advantages of exact terminology, but for all Jerome's critical interest in precise wording, despite the nearly constant involvement with comparative linguistics that characterized the last forty-five years of his life, Jerome's intelligence remained to the end more loosely encyclopedic and less probing than Augustine's. By no stretch of the pious imagination can Jerome be called a philosopher.[1] Nevertheless, it seems clear that for these two immensely influential Fathers of the Church who were also the greatest Latin rhetoricians of their generation, *populus* was the term denoting a group whose specific characteristic was one of unity deriving from law or some sort of political responsibility.

Jerome's literary output was of two kinds: his translations, especially of the Bible; and his "own" compositions. His 120 collected letters, composed between 369 and the year of his death, comprise the bulk of this latter group, besides being his most personal productions and, according to Jean Leclercq, the chief agent of his influence on the consciousness of medieval monastic culture. Of his short treatises, critical, theological, and hagiographical, *De Viris Illustribus* possesses peculiar value for this study.[2] Composed at Bethlehem in 392 in response to a suggestion of Jerome's friend the praetorian prefect Dexter, this pioneer essay in Christian literary history allows the reader to observe a distilled combination of Jerome's literary and biographical interests, his ecclesiastical and regional prejudices, his close dependence at times on such authorities as Eusebius, and his areas of independent opinion and truly original composition. Examination of the word *populus* in the *Letters* and in *De Viris Illustribus* reveals a clear meaning and a fair degree of consistency in its employment throughout the fifty years of Jerome's literary activity.

Personal Usage

Before exploring Jerome's central and most frequent usage pattern, we must take note of two minor and peripheral usages which appear more frequently in Jerome's works than in Augustine's: *populus* as a featureless group and as the lower classes.

At times *populus* may be nearly interchangeable with *gens* and *natio,* hardly more than a synonym employed for the sake of stylistic variety. About 389, Jerome wrote an artful letter for the Roman aristocrat Paula and her daughter Eustochium, urging their friend Marcella to come join them in their monastic establishment at Bethlehem.

. . . Nor do we say this so as to deny that the kingdom of God is within us or that holy men dwell also in other regions, but simply as an assertion of fact that especially those who are of the first rank in the whole world congregate here. We ourselves came to this place not as belonging to the first rank, but as belonging to the lowest, so that we might behold the first of all *gentes,* here. . . . Whoever has been among the first in Gaul hastens here. If a Briton, divided from our world, advances in the practices of religion, he leaves behind the setting sun and seeks this place so well known by reputation and the accounts of the Scriptures. What shall we report of the Armenians, what of the Persians, what of the *populi* of India and Ethiopia and of Egypt herself, rich in monks, Pontus and Cappadocia, Hollow Syria and Mesopotamia and all the swarms of the Orient? [3]

Perhaps seven years later Jerome undertook the sad duty of composing a eulogy for the young priest Nepotian, nephew of an old friend from student days in Rome, from his sojourn afterward in Aquileia, and from that interlude "sweeter than light" at Evagrius's villa near Antioch. Some comfort for the premature death of this promising young man could be found, he urged, in the universal triumph of the Cross, to the ministry of which he had dedicated himself.

Where [before Christ] were the inhabitants of the whole world from India to Britain, from the ice-bound northern zone to the burning heat of the Atlantic Ocean? Where were its countless *populi* and such great *gentium multitudines,*

'In dress and arms as varied as in speech'?

They were but packed together like fishes and locusts, flies and gnats; for without knowledge of his Creator every man is but a brute. But today the voices and the writings of all *gentes* proclaim the passion and the resurrection of Christ. I say nothing of the Hebrews, the Greeks, and the Latins, *nationes* whom the Lord dedicated to His faith by the inscription of His cross. . . . The savage Bessians and their *turba* of skin-clad *populi,* who used to offer human sacrifice to the dead, have now dissolved their rough discord into the sweet music of the Cross, and the whole world with one voice cries out, 'Christ.' [4]

However, such easygoing usage is unusual. Jerome's more common tendency was to use *populus* in a much more restricted sense, conveying one of several rather exact meanings.

Populus can also mean "the crowd," "the masses," "the common people." A little after his arrival in the desert of Chalcis—probably in 375, therefore—Jerome wrote to three friends in Aquileia a letter concerned primarily with family matters. The new ascetic was in no mood to speak kindly of the bishop of his native Stridon, one Lupicinus, who seems not to have been enthusiastic about the monastic currents then sweeping through the Latin Church. As for my own *patria,* it is enslaved to barbarism, and men's family god is their belly. One lives there only for the day, and the richer you are the more saintly you are held to be. Furthermore, to use a well-worn saying of the *populus,* the cover there is worthy of the dish; for Lupicinus is their priest.[5]

Ten years later, in an even more caustic mood as what he considered worldly hostility was driving him to seek monastic refuge in the East for the second time, Jerome wrote to the Roman patrician Asella a letter castigating those who had vilified him and his ascetic friends.

Had they frequented fashionable watering-places and used their own particular scent, had they employed their wealth and widow's freedom as opportunities for extravagance and self-indulgence, they would have been called 'Madam,' and 'saint.' As it is they wish to appear beautiful in sackcloth and ashes, and to go down to the fires of hell with fastings and filth. Oh, plainly they are not allowed to perish amid the applause of the *populus* along with the *turbae!* [6]

When Jerome used *populus* in so slighting a fashion, he tended to use it in a plural form, even though the group so described was a collective unit. Two years after the sack of Rome, Jerome wrote to the lady Principia a eulogy of his confidante and adviser Marcella, who had been among the first in Rome to take up the monastic life, despite the fact that what little was then known of it had given it "a degrading name among the *populi*" ("*vile in populis nomen*").[7] A short while after that eulogy, in a verbose panegyric to the aristocratic virgin Demetrias, he recommended the example of "holy virgins who keep their feet at home on feast days because of the press of the *populi,* and do not go out at times when greater caution than usual is to be observed, and the public (*publicum*) very much to be avoided." [8] This use of *populi* to describe a crowd appears also in a nonpejorative context in Jerome's eulogy of Paula, written very soon after her funeral in

Bethlehem on 28 January 404. Endowed with the pilgrim's (and the historian's) love for the concrete, she had delighted in beholding such places as "the wilderness in which many thousands of the *populi* were satisfied by a few loaves, from the leavings of which were filled the baskets of the twelve tribes of Israel." [9]

The adjective *popularis* seems always to have carried pejorative overtones for Jerome. In a letter of exhortation written from Bethlehem to the deacon Julianus, he made quite clear his opinion of the standard classical philosopher—"glory's creature and vile slave to the breath of popular approval." [10] In the panegyric to Demetrias already mentioned, he castigated the pursuit of Greek letters and rhetoric as being likewise "an affected gravity seeking after glory and the breath of popular approval." [11]

It is surprising to find that Jerome used *plebs* sparingly in his letters, and not at all in *De Viris Illustribus*. In one of his earliest letters, written to the still very dear Rufinus in the autumn of 374, Jerome mentioned "an Alexandrian monk, whom the pious devotion of the *plebs* had sent over to the Egyptian confessors—in will they are already martyrs. . . ." [12] Twenty years later, in a letter of vocational advice to the newly ordained Nepotian, Jerome attributed to Gregory Nazianzen the edifying opinion that there was little honor in overawing the *plebicula* from the preacher's throne.[13] In neither instance does *plebs* seem to have been a word of much resonance for Jerome; in any case, these instances are too sparse to permit conclusions of any validity.

Jerome used *populus* frequently in referring to what we would call "the congregation," "the laity," or "the churches." Such seems to have been his intention in a letter written from Antioch in 374 to Florentinus, whose friendship Jerome wished to cultivate, partly in the hope that he would persuade Heliodorus to join Jerome in his projected retreat to Chalcis. It begins, "How much Your Grace's name is mentioned in the conversation of diverse *populi*, you may judge from the fact that I begin to love you before I know you." [14] *Populi* are much more clearly "churches" in a letter written two years later from Jerome's cave in Chalcis to Pope Damasus. The hermit asked for doctrinal guidance.

Inasmuch as the Orient, set at variance by the inveterate rage of its *populi* against each other, has torn to pieces, little by little, the seamless robe of our Lord that was woven from the top throughout, and the foxes are destroying the vines, so that amid the broken cisterns that can hold no water it is hard to discover where the fountain sealed and the garden enclosed is, therefore I have decided that I must consult the chair of Peter and the faith that was praised by the lips of the Apostle. I now crave food for my soul from that source whence I originally obtained the vestments of Christ.[15]

It was largely a semantic problem, Jerome realized, but some persons of genuinely heretical intent were using the current confusion to extract Arianizing professions of faith at least externally in conflict with the Nicene Creed: "Far be it from our Roman faith. Let not the pious hearts of the *populi* imbibe so great a sacrilege." [16] Things did not work out according to Jerome's expectations, and relations with his largely Syrian neighbor-hermits began to deteriorate. In the following year, he wrote a querulous appeal to Mark, a priest with some jurisdiction in Chalcis. After complaining about local barbarism, he apostrophized some heretical interlocutor: "You are evidently afraid that I, a most eloquent man in the Syrian tongue or in Greek, may go about to the churches (*ecclesias*), seduce the *populi*, bring about a schism." [17] Fifteen years later Jerome employed the same usage in *De Viris Illustribus*, describing two great Greek bishops who had flourished during the reign of Marcus Aurelius.

27. Dionysus, bishop of the church of the Corinthians, was of such great eloquence and industry that by his letters he instructed the *populi* not only of his own *civitas* and province, but also those of other provinces and *urbes*. . . .

28. Pinytus the Cretan wrote to Dionysus, bishop of the Corinthians, a most elegant letter, in which he teaches that the *populi* should be nourished not always on milk, . . . but should also eat solid food so as to advance toward spiritual maturity.[18]

Two years later the same usage appeared in the letter of advice to Nepotian. In this extremely clear instance *populus* is singular.

When you are preaching in church (*ecclesia*) try to evoke not the applause of the *populus* but lamentation. Let the tears of your audience be your glory. A presbyter's discourse should be seasoned by his reading of Scripture. Be not a declaimer nor a ranter nor a gabbler, but show yourself skilled in God's mysteries and well acquainted with the secret meaning of His words. Only ignorant men like to roll out phrases and to excite the admiration of the unlettered *vulgus* by the quickness of their utterance. Effrontery often tries to explain things of which it knows nothing, and having persuaded others claims knowledge for itself. My former teacher, Gregory of Nazianzus, when I asked him to explain the meaning of St. Luke's phrase δευτερόπρωτον, that is, 'second first' sabbath, wittily evaded my request. 'I will tell you about that in church,' he said, 'and there, when all the *populus* applauds me, you will be compelled against your wish to know what you do not know, or else, if you alone remain silent, you will undoubtedly be put down by everyone as a fool.' There is nothing so easy as to deceive a *vilis plebicula* or an ignorant *contio* by voluble talk; anything such people do not understand they admire all the more. Listen to Cicero, . . .[19]

In each of the five preceding passages *populus* denotes a mass of men, usually in some sort of subordinate relationship to a bishop or preaching priest. However, these instances are not merely examples of the former usage of *populus*—that is, the lower orders, or at best, the common run of citizens—transferred to an ecclesiastical setting.[20]

The group referred to is presented as something more coherent than a mob, more limited and specific than the *canaille;* in the last example the *populus* is quite clearly not identical with the various kinds of vulgar gathering in general which Jerome labels as *vulgus, plebicula,* and *contio.* Even in that extremely visual evocation of Gregory Nazianzen in a Constantinopolitan church, no mention is made of any intermediate element between the preacher and the laity, such as the other clergy probably present. The *populus* is the whole Christian assembly, all-inclusive except on those occasions when there is some special reference to a pastoral figure.

Jerome also used *populus* to denote secular groups possessing a coherence and personality similar to those of Christian congregations. However, he seems to have been rather discriminating in deciding what sort of groups qualified for that label. One suggestive piece of evidence appears in a letter which he wrote from Chalcis to Niceas, a subdeacon of Aquileia. Mentioning primitive Italian tribes which Ennius reports as using wooden books, Jerome significantly modified his source, a procedure which he by no means always scrupled to follow. Ennius had called them *"prisci casci populi . . . Latini";* Jerome referred to them more fastidiously as "those crude men of Italy, whom Ennius calls Casci." [21] Naturally enough, their politically more sophisticated successors frequently merited the description of *populus* in Jerome's mind.

The *populus Romanus* appears fairly often in his writings, and with special poignancy after the sack of Rome. Jerome's admiration for that city and its imperial sway was considerably stronger than Augustine's, or at any rate less mixed. During the greater part of his life, this sentiment existed on the level of an enthusiastic patriotism, rather naive and capable occasionally of chauvinistic arrogance. [22]

The question of his family's ethnic origins is insoluble; in any case, it is irrelevant, since he grew up in a thoroughly Latinized province, embraced the Ciceronic and Vergilian culture of the schools with eagerness, and was only too delighted to go to the city itself for higher studies. There he encountered Donatus firsthand, idolized Marius Victorinus, and spent eight vividly conscious adolescent years amid the monuments of both secular and Christian heroism. Baptized there, probably in the Lateran basilica, during the Easter Vigil of 366, Jerome enjoyed calling himself *"homo Romanus"* during his doctrinal quarrel with the "barbarous" Syriac monks of Chalcis. Although his ordination to the priesthood around 378 took place in Antioch, his loyalty there was to a splinter church as strictly Western in its alliances as it was intransigently Eustathian in doctrine. His and Paula's monasteries in Bethlehem were outposts of Latin culture and sentiment that never really got along with the local Greek hierarchy—certainly not as successfully as did the Latin monastery of Melanie and Rufinus, for example. When a raid made on his monastery by a band of Pelagian monks, acting in full knowledge of Bishop John, marked the low point of Jerome's relationship with the Palestinian authorities, his natural (and successful) appeal was to Pope Innocent I.[23] He underwent, to be sure, a period of lessened fervor for the city of Rome after his expulsion therefrom in 385. Shortly thereafter, in the preface to his translation of Didymus's treatise on the Holy Spirit, he even called his old favorite Babylon the "scarlet woman," and so on, alluded slightingly to Romulus's hut and the Lupercal, and declared that the homeland of Christ was more venerable than that of the fratricide.[24] But it was a brief disenchantment, after all, and Jerome was swift to forget rancors as new clouds gathered over the city. When she fell to Alaric, Jerome's grief was at least as intense as Augustine's and found frequent literary expression.

It is worth noting that in all periods of his literary production, Jerome preferred to speak of Rome as a *civitas*, an *urbs*, or an *imperium* [25] than as a *populus*, and when he did evoke the *populus Romanus*, it tended to appear in strictly political, and often slightly archaic, dress. Two clear examples of this tendency date from just before and shortly after the sack. In a long letter of 409, urging the Roman widow Geruchia not to remarry, Jerome reminded her unhappily of the grim prospects facing any potential husband, now that the return of Brennus, Pyrrhus, or Hannibal seemed imminent. Yet even in the course of his advice to renounce such crumbling realms, he could not help remarking with obvious satisfaction that the provinces of those last two invaders had long since become "tributaries of the Roman *populus*." [26] About 412, in his orotund letter to the patrician Demetrias, he sang in a rather different key the praises of consecrated chastity amid the ruins. Elaborating the account of Demetrias's famous decision not to marry, he imagined her thoughts on the night before the projected nuptials. "Your city, once the world's capital, is now the tomb of the Roman *populus;* and you, an exile on the Libyan coast, will you take for husband yet another exile?" Of course not.

The news of her decision filled the whole Mediterranean world with a joy almost unparalleled.

After Trebia, Trasimene, and Cannae, in which places thousands of the Roman army had been slaughtered, when for the first time Marcellus achieved a victory at Nola, the Roman *populus* did not right itself with such alacrity. With less joy did it learn on an earlier occasion that the ranks of the Gauls had been leveled, the nobility ransomed by gold, and the seedbed of the Roman *genus* preserved within its citadel.[27]

Another venerable, historic society qualifying for the designation *populus* in the writings of Jerome was Israel. He asserted the proud antiquity of the *populus Judaicus* in the course of a reply from Bethlehem to an attack by Magnus, the public orator of the city of Rome, on his mingling pagan and Christian literature.[28] He used the term constantly in discussing the internal affairs, inseparably sacred and secular, of the Chosen People. Speaking of the time when they were least recognizably a polity, Jerome remarked in an early letter that "while Pharaoh lived, the *populus* of Israel did not turn from their work with mud and brick and straws and aspire unto the Lord." [29] Nearly thirty years later, commenting on God's judgment of the Roman Empire, he wrote approvingly of the time when "according to the Law, after the sounding of the trumpet on the tenth day of the seventh month, there was a general fast of the Hebrew *gens,* and the life of him who had preferred satiety to restraint was banished from the *populus.*" [30]

Sometimes Israel is the *populus* par excellence, in the face of whom other peoples are merely "the *gentes.*" This attitude appears clearly in one of Jerome's earliest pieces of scriptural commentary, a treatise on Isaias's vision of the Seraphim (6:1–9), composed at the behest of Pope Damasus around 383.[31] Connected with this point of view is his recurring tendency to speak of two elect *populi,* Israel and its successor. It appears as early as his stay in Chalcis, in a letter "home" to Antonius, a monk of Haemona: "And the Jewish *populus,* because it claimed for itself the chief seats and greetings in the market place, was destroyed and succeeded by the *populus* of the Gentiles, who had previously been accounted as a drop of a bucket." [32] Back in Rome a few years later as Damasus' secretary, Jerome undertook an exegesis of the parable of the Prodigal Son, pointing out that God "disapproves of the pride of the Jews and approves of the repentance of all sinners alike, whether of Gentiles or of Israel. But as to His saying 'two sons,' almost all the Scriptures are full of the calling of two *populi* to the sacraments." [33] The second, he explained further on, is the *"gentilium populus,"* which entered the vineyard at the eleventh hour.[34] Writing some fifteen years later to the priest Evangelus on Melchisedech's priesthood, he discerned therein another type of the predestined relationship between "the former and the latter *populus.*" [35]

Mention of these two singular *populi* occurred again in 404, in Jerome's eulogy for the beloved Paula. There he suggested that the two eyes of the man whose sight was restored by Christ symbolized "the sacraments of both *populi* believing in the Lord." [36] However, we can discern traces of a more generic, neutral use of the word elsewhere in this lengthy work, one of the masterpieces of his mature rhetoric. Inspired by so many memories of their final home together, he addressed Bethlehem: "in you did the source of the Davidic line remain, until at length the virgin gave birth and the Remnant of the *populus,* believing in the Christ, turned to the sons of Israel and freely declared: 'It is to you that the word of God had to speak first; but since you reject it and so judge yourselves unworthy of eternal life, we will turn to the *Gentes.'* " [37] Here is no simplistic opposition of *populus* and *gentes:* the True Remnant is more legitimately the continuator of the old *populus Dei* than are its unfaithful brothers, and as such it turns first to the "sons of Israel" from whom it begins to dissociate itself, and then (in full integrity) to the Gentiles whom it will begin to absorb. In the following chapter it becomes clear that Jerome could consider those Gentiles to consist of many *populi.* Recalling his and Paula's trip to Egypt along the Gaza road, Jerome reports her meditation on the Apostle Philip's encounter there with an Ethiopian eunuch who, "prefiguring the *populi* of the Gentiles, changed his skin, and, while still reading the Old Testament, came upon the spring of the Gospel." [38]

Ecclesiastical bodies, the Roman people, Israel, and other groups which have been objects of God's election—such are *populi,* according to Jerome. What common definition does the least violence to these specific applications of the term? It seems fair and complete to argue that in Jerome's own compositions, *populus* tends most often to stand for a group whose unity is explicitly or implicitly one of law, whose salient attribute is one of some sort of responsibility for policy, whether sacred or civil or both. This is in fact the sense in which he employs the word most widely. Examination of a few further instances should serve to establish how central this usage of *populus* was.

Jerome's first literary effort was an exemplum, telling how Providence finally came to the aid of a woman seven times "executed" for an adultery of which she was innocent. Written slightly after 369, under Evagrius's patronage in the spiritual and material elegance of Maronia's villa near Antioch, it is a good example of the inflated rhetoric so much prized in the student circles from which Jerome had emerged less than five years before. However, the narrative is handled with vigor as well as with careful variation of style and vocabulary. Vercelli in Liguria is the scene of this travesty of earthly justice, in the course of which the blameless victim is denounced by a misled husband, abandoned by the cowardice of her alleged accomplice, and believed by no one. The conviction-hungry prosecutor turns a deaf ear to her torture-defying denials of the charge, and she is brought forth with the wretch of a young man for public execution. "The entire *populus* poured forth to see the sight; in fact, it might have been supposed that the *civitas* was migrating, so dense was the *turba* rushing out through the crowded gates." The sword falls and falls again, but the cruel authorities ignore the increasingly evident miraculous nature of her survival.

At last the *populus* takes up arms to rescue the woman. Every age and sex drive the executioner away. The *coetus* forms a circle about her, and they all can scarcely believe their eyes. The news throws the *urbs* nearby into an uproar, and the entire *caterva* of the constabulary is assembled. From their midst the man charged with the responsibility for condemned persons burst forth, 'staining his snowy locks with dust that he poured upon them,' and exclaimed: 'O *cives*, is it my life you are seeking? Are you making me a substitute for her? You may be compassionate, you may be merciful, you may wish to save the condemned woman, but surely I, who am innocent, ought not to perish.'

The *vulgus* being cut to the heart by this plea, a gloomy sense of frustration descended upon all, and their purpose underwent a remarkable change. Whereas their previous defense of her had seemed the path of duty, it now seemed to be a sort of duty to permit her to be executed.[39]

And they let her face the block again. In these two brief passages, Jerome applies seven names to the group acting with such impulsive sympathy and to the two somewhat external units caught up in their eruption. *Populus* (twice), *civitas/cives* (once each), *coetus, turba,* and *vulgus* all apply to the Vercellians, and *urbs* and *caterva* to the other two elements in this civil disturbance. No very subtle analysis is required to discern the following points. (1) When the group is most confused and thickly packed—most like a mob—it is called *turba* or *coetus*. (2) When seeming to undertake a total migration (striking conceit!), it is called *civitas;* on the other hand, it seems to undergo a certain dissolution when its members are addressed individually as *cives*. (3) It is called *vulgus* when its dissolving emotions bring its new enterprise to naught. (4) *Urbs* simply and neutrally describes the neighboring town, whose population swells the group's ranks for a while. *Caterva* does the same for the small, compact, and practically alien specialty group of provincial police. (5) Jerome's favorite term for the Vercellian group is *populus,* which denotes both its totality (*"totus populus"* in its first appearance; composed of "every age and sex" in its second) and its most vigorous activity (pouring out and arming). It is also the first group-word in each passage, occupying the position of standard-bearer for the variations which follow.

Perhaps five years later, on the blazing frontier of Chalcis, Jerome wrote about quite another kind of judicial process. He was trying to persuade Heliodorus to leave Antioch and join him in the hermit's life. The eschatological advantages of such a choice were perfectly clear to Jerome.

It will come, that day will come, on which this corruptible and mortal will put on incorruption and immortality. Blessed is the servant whom his Lord shall find watching. Then at the sound of the trumpet the earth with its *populi* shall quake with fear; you shall rejoice. The universe will groan mournfully when the Lord is about to judge; *tribus* by *tribus,* men will beat their breasts. Kings once most mighty will tremble with naked flanks. Then Jupiter with his offspring will be displayed truly on fire. Foolish Plato will be brought forward also with his disciples. The reasoning of Aristotle will not avail.

Then you, the illiterate and the poor, shall exult.[40]

However much or little *tribus* may have been equated with *populi* in the normal course of earthly prose, Jerome here presents them united within themselves and with each other before the bar. But once again *populus* is the generic *signifer.*

About twenty years later, solidly established in Bethlehem and in the scriptural studies that would absorb most of the rest of his life, Jerome addressed a letter to the priest Vitalis. It treated the infidelity of Solomon and Achaz in running after the idols of the *gentes,* and then moved on to a strictly political discussion of succession in the southern kingdom: "Ozias, king of Juda, after being struck with leprosy, lived in a house apart and his son Joatham ruled the *imperium* and judged the *populus terrae* up to the day of his father's death and indeed after it." A little further on, a passage from Isaias referring to Ezechias is interpreted to mean that "the son was chosen to succeed to the *imperium* not immediately after the father's death, but after some seditions within the *populus* or periods of interregnum or, certainly, pressing misfortunes of some sort . . ."[41]

That a *populus* can be sacred, secular, and mixed is clear from two chapters of *De Viris Illustribus.* Citing Hegesippus as his source, Jerome reports that the Apostle James, first bishop of Jerusalem, "went into the temple and on bent knees prayed for the *populus.*" And a little further on: "Josephus reports that he was of such sanctity and reputation in the eyes of the *populus,* that

Jerusalem was thought to have been overthrown on account of his execution." [42] In chapter 17, Jerome presents the earthly end of John's disciple Polycarp in a context anything but sacred from the Christian point of view: "While the proconsul was sitting in judgment at Smyrna, and the entire *populus* shouted against him in the amphitheater, he was handed over to the fire." [43] Although all appear in passages relating to the heroic first and second generations of the Church's history, these three *populi* refer to quite different specific communities: one Gentile and unchristian, one Jewish and as yet very little Christian, one a blend of at least those two latter categories. Strikingly similar to Augustine's pattern of usage in both the attributes and the applications which they embody, these three *populi* representing Jerome's central range of usage share a communal consciousness which is either the subject or the object of a moral judgment.

Usage in Scriptural Translations

The preceding conclusions regarding Jerome's use of the word *populus* are strengthened by an examination of the practices which he followed in translating the Hebrew and Greek Scriptures.

It may be argued that the vocabulary of a translation has little bearing on the thought of the translator, since the author is only minimally reflecting his own mind in that process. However, this study is primarily concerned with the vocabulary patterns presented to readers and students of later centuries by Jerome's work —whatever the degree of originality involved therein—and it would be hard to deny that the chief channel of Jerome's influence on medieval culture was the Vulgate. Furthermore, even when this point is granted, there remains the fact that relatively little difference can be discerned between his usage of relevant nouns of association in his "original" compositions and that in the Vulgate. This fact becomes all the more striking after a cursory glance at the texts of the various Old Latin versions of the Bible, from the vocabulary patterns of which Jerome varies a great deal in this regard. In other words, his usage was not simply a reflection of contemporary or recent language; it involved some individual assumptions and interpretations which would play a major part in shaping the Latin of centuries for which the Vulgate became a cornerstone of education.

It should not be surprising to find such indications of personal thought in the text of a translation whose author was constantly defending its fidelity to the original. Jerome was hardly a word-for-word man. Typical of the numerous references to the theory of translation scattered throughout his works is a letter of 394 to the Gothic monks Frithila and Sunnia. In the course of answering their questions about his two versions of the psalms, Jerome attacks the "ill-conceived zeal" of slavish renderings, and asserts the superiority of a method which tends rather more to paraphrase texts and, in summary, "seeks to express itself not by servile literalism, but according to the genius of [one's] own language." [44] Even so, Jerome's notion of word-for-word translation was astonishingly free. Two years before his letter to the two Goths, Jerome accorded Juvencus what is now the earliest surviving literary reference to his work: "Juvencus, a Spaniard of the noblest stock, a priest, translating the four Gospels *paene ad verbum* into hexameter verses . . ." [45] Even if this amazing judgment indicates only that Jerome had not actually seen that translation, it makes quite clear to what extent he felt constrained by details of the written text.

Nor should translations be dismissed or belittled outright as vehicles for discovering what a writer means by a specific word. Probably the most reassuring way to make such a discovery is through the writer's own definition of it—if in fact his usage elsewhere is consistent with that definition, as is the case with *populus* in Augustine's writings. But in the absence of such definition, it may be that the most precise way to determine an author's meaning is to examine his sense of what concepts a particular word can convey from a foreign language to his own. Such an examination can bear sound fruit if his patterns of translation are distinctively different from those of contemporary or recent popularity; if they are internally consistent; and if the contexts of the loci considered can yield an adequate understanding of his interpretation of the parent concepts in the alien tongue. All three conditions can be met by an examination of relevant passages in the Vulgate.

OLD TESTAMENT

It is especially easy to see what Jerome meant by checking his translations of the Old Testament. First of all, the presence of three anterior traditions in three languages—a Hebrew text closely related to the parent of the Masoretic text; the Greek Septuagint; and the varying Old Latin versions, of whose popularity in the Western churches he was painfully aware—puts his final choices into very sharp relief. Secondly, his renderings of the Old Testament, produced in Bethlehem between 389 and 406, represent a far more mature and independent effort than do his versions of the New Testament, written mostly in the 380s and in many places amounting to a cautious revision of the Old Latin rather than a new translation from the Greek.[46]

If we line up the Hebrew, the Septuagint, and the Vulgate versions of some selected texts from the Old Testament, we find a basic pattern of equivalence: עַם (ām)—λαός—populus. Jerome's occasional variations from this pattern emphasize rather than detract from its consistency.

Jerome intended populus to correspond to עַם (ām). This is clear from his steady practice of following the Hebrew rather than the Septuagint when they were at variance; in such cases, the Old Latin versions usually remained strictly faithful to the sacrosanct Septuagint. In Genesis 17:14, "If any male have not the flesh of his foreskin circumcised, that person shall be cut off from his people; he has broken my covenant" (a condition of God's pact with Abraham), the Septuagint and the Italian traditions of the Old Latin had τοῦ γένους and either genere or generatione in the locus underlined; Jerome wrote populo, thus returning to the sense of the original מֵעַמֶּיהָ (meāmeyha). Several African and Gallic versions of the Old Latin preferred populo or plebe, so it may be that Jerome was influenced by them. However, there can be no question of his lonely fidelity to the Hebraica veritas two verses further on: "I will bless her [Sara], and will also give you a son by her; yes, I will bless her, and she shall be the mother of nations; kings of peoples shall descend from her." The Septuagint and all Old Latin versions had ἐθνῶν and gentium in both italicized loci; Jerome followed suit for the first, but for the second he returned with populorum to the original עֲמִים (āmim).[47] It is true that

Isidore of Seville also wrote *populorum* in citing this verse, but his respect for Jerome's version was so major that it would be seriously straining the point not to assume the influence of a Vulgate reading there.[48]

In Genesis 23:11, Abraham is negotiating with the Hethites over the purchase of a tomb for Sara. The Hethite Ephron says to him, "No, my lord! Hear me, I give you the field with the cave that is in it. In the presence of my *people* I give it; bury your dead." Perhaps in the interest of stylistic variety, the Septuagint had τῶν πολιτῶν μου; Jerome, with *filiis populi mei,* returned to בְּנֵי־עַמִּי (*b'nēy-āmi*).[49] In Exodus 20:20, just after God has given the Ten Commandments amid much noise and smoke, the people are afraid. "Moses answered *the people,* 'Do not be afraid, for God has come to you only to test you and put his fear upon you, lest you should sin.'" The Septuagint, perhaps once again seeking to relieve Semitic monotony, put αὐτοῖς for הָעָם (*haam*); Old Latin versions followed with *eis,* but Jerome faithfully wrote *populum.*

Something similar happened with Deuteronomy 7:6, 7, one of the classic constitutional texts of the Old Testament.[50] "For you are a *people* [a] sacred to the Lord, your God; he has chosen you from all the *nations* [b] on the face of the earth to be a *people peculiarly his own.* [c] / It was not because you are the largest of all *nations* [d] that the Lord set his heart on you and chose you, for you are really the smallest of all *nations.* [e]" Schematically, the transferences are as indicated in Table 1.[51]

Table 1

	Hebrew		Septuagint	Vulgate
a.	עַם	(*ām*)	λαός	populus
b.	הָעַמִּים	(*haāmim*)	παρὰ τὰ ἔθνη	de cunctis populis
c.	לְעַם סְגֻלָּה	(*l'ām s'gulah*)	λαὸν	populus
			περιούσιον	peculiaris
d.	הָעַמִּם	(*haāmim*)	τὰ ἔθνη	gentes
e.	הָעַמִּם	(*ḣaāmim*)	τὰ ἔθνη	populis

Why did Jerome follow one Septuagint ἔθνη reading after rejecting two? Perhaps it was for the sake of variety; certainly the use of *gentes* does less violence to the unmistakably political conceptions of this passage in locus *d* than it would anywhere else in these two verses.

An instance somewhat in reverse of the dominant trend is further evidence of Jerome's fastidious use of *populus*. In Exodus 17, the Israelites are at Raphidim, and threaten to stone Moses unless they get some water. In verse 5, "The Lord answered Moses: 'Go over there in front of *the people* [*a*], along with some of the elders *of Israel* [*b*], holding in your hand, as you go, the staff with which you struck the river." *A* is predictably הָעָם (*haām*)—τοῦ λαοῦ *populum* (the Old Latin and Vulgate agree), but for the יִשְׂרָאֵל (yisraēl) of *b*, the Septuagint and Old Latin had τοῦ λαοῦ and *populum*. Jerome put *Israel*. He would not read *populi* into the original text without solid reason.

That Jerome at his strictest considered *populus* the Latin equivalent for עַם (*ām*) (or, more exactly, for what he took עַם to mean), is strongly suggested by his treatment of two appearances of the rather rare Hebrew noun אָם (*am*; plural אֻמִּים, *umim*). It can be considered practically a synonym for עַם (*ām*; plural עַמִּים, *āmim*), and twice Jerome went along with this tendency. In Genesis 25:23, the Lord says to Rebecca: "Two *nations* [*a*] are in your womb; two *peoples* [*b*] shall stem from your body. One *people* [*c*] shall be stronger than the other [*people* (*d*)], and the elder shall serve the younger.'" The translations vary as indicated in Table 2.

Table 2

	Hebrew		Septuagint	Old Latin	Vulgate
a.	גּוֹיִם	(*goyim*)	ἔθνη	gentes *	gentes
				(nationes, populi)	
b.	אֻמִּים	(*umim*)	λαοί	populi	populi
c.	עַם	(*am*)	λαὸς	populus	populus (que)
d.	עַם	(*am*)	λαοῦ	populum	populum

* Minority readings follow in parentheses.

Jerome had followed the same practice earlier, when he translated the Psalter from the Septuagint for Pope Damasus. In Psalm 2:1, "Why do the *nations* rage and the *peoples* utter folly?" Jerome simply followed the Greek and the Old Latin, putting *gentes* and *populi* for ἔθνη and λαοί (in that order). Perhaps at that time he was unaware that λαοί stood for the unusual אֻמִּים (*umim*)—it is hard to tell how much Hebrew he knew during his last stay in Rome.[52] However, when in Bethlehem he translated the Psalter again, this time directly from Hebrew, he judged *tribus* a better equivalent than *populi*.[53] If he had been in the habit of reediting his translations, would he have changed the *populi* of Genesis 25:23 to *tribus* also? This is obviously a futile question, although alluring; however, difficult as it is to demonstrate anything about exact intent from so few passages, it seems fair to argue that אֻמִּים (*umim*) is poorer in truly political connotations in the psalm (being merely a poetic variant for גּוֹיִם) than in the prophecy to Rebecca, where it comes rich with the promise of Israel's ascendancy over Edom. It would seem, in any event, that Jerome was cautious about making *populus* translate any other Hebrew word than עַם (*ām*).

Occasionally he did relax this rigor in favor of words less closely related than עַם (*am*). Genesis 10 gives a genealogy of Noah's descendants to a considerable (and unclear) number of generations. Verse 32 summarizes: "These are the *families* [*a*] of the sons of Noah according to their *descent* [*b*] in their *nations*. [*c*] From these the *nations* [*d*] branched out over the earth after the flood." (See Table 3.)

Table 3

	Hebrew		Septuagint	Old Latin	Vulgate
a.	מִשְׁפְּחֹת	(*mishp'hoth*)	αἱ φύλαι	—	familiae
b.	לְתוֹלְדֹתָם	(*l'tholdotham*)	κατὰ γενέσεις	generationes	populos
c.	בְּגוֹיֵהֶם	(*b'goyehem*)	κατὰ τὰ ἔθνη	—	nationes
d.	הַגּוֹיִם	(*hagoyim*)	τῶν ἐθνῶν	—	gentes

A, c, and *d* are entirely to be expected. What is unusual is Jerome's differing from all three prior traditions in *b* to render תּוֹלְדֹת (*tholdoth*) as *populus*. Elsewhere in Genesis—the genealogies of the posterities of Adam (5:1), Noah previously (6:9), Noah's sons in general (10:1), Sem (11:10), Thare (11:27), Isaac (25:19), and Esau (36:1), for example—he was quite content to translate it as *generatio*, following the normal meaning of the

Hebrew word as well as the Septuagint and the majority of the
Old Latin readings (the variants being *creatura, nativitas, origo,*
and *progenies*). Why this unique departure from the pattern?
Two explanations seem likely.

First of all, 10:32 summarizes rather than introduces a genealogy, and does so much more grandly than any other single verse
in Genesis. It concludes what is called in rabbinical parlance the
Table of Nations, a roll call of all the peoples, languages, and
scripts around the eastern Mediterranean circa 800 B.C. Jerome
may well have decided that he could give greater recognition to
the dignity of the chief groups among Noah's remote, teeming,
and very diversified posterity by listing them according to their
"populos et nationes," than he could by using the more conventional and smaller-scale formula, *"iuxta generationes (cognationes)
et nationes suas."*

Secondly, whether Jerome saw that or not, it seems very likely
that this variation of usage follows a rabbinical interpretation. The
Midrash Haggadol (which is either a thirteenth-century Egyptian
compilation in Arabic by Maimonides' son Abraham, translated
into Hebrew in the fifteenth century by Rabbi David ben-Amram
al-Adeni, or then a Yemenite Hebrew compilation made directly
by al-Adeni) contains an interesting gloss on 10:32. Enumerating
at length the attributes of these "families of the sons of Noah," it
uses the same nouns as the Sacred Text for their "isles," "languages," and "scripts"; but the original תּוֹלְדוֹת (*tholdoth*) is
replaced in the gloss by מְדִינוֹת (*m'dinot*), a word which has always meant "countries" or "states" or at any rate something
much closer to *populi* than to *generationes* or its synonyms. The
most recent editor of the *Midrash Haggadol* for Genesis states that
this "strange" gloss "has no analogues; we have found no precedent for several of the names in it, and its sources are completely
obscure." However, this midrash is an outstanding repository of
unique variants of ancient talmudic statements and of other rabbinical opinions (both halakhic and haggadic, Palestinian as well
as Babylonian) now otherwise extinct—some of them as old as the
first century B.C.[54] Jerome may have made this atypical translation
without benefit of some such midrashic tradition, but it accords
better both with his known habits and with common logic to suppose that he made it under the influence of some authority. In

either case, we have here a striking instance of Jerome's need for a strong reason to translate some other Hebrew word than עַם (ām) as *populus*.

At times Jerome translated עַם (ām) as something other than *populus,* but he tended to do so for some recognizable reason. One revealing example occurs in chapter 25 of 4 Kings, which gives an account of Nabuchodonosor's capture of Jerusalem and subsequent dispersion of the people of Juda. Verse 19 lists, among those who were transported to Babylon:

> Seraias the chief priest, and Sophonias the second priest, and three doorkeepers; and out of the city one eunuch, who was captain of the men of war; and five men of them that had stood before the king, whom he found in the city, and Sopher the captain of the army who exercised the young soldiers of the *people of the land* [*a*]; and threescore men of the *common people* [*b*], who were found in the city.

Both *a* and *b* are עַם־הָאָרֶץ (ām-haarets), and ὁ λαὸς τῆς γῆς. Jerome translated *a* as *populo terrae,* but went behind both the Septuagint and the Hebrew texts to interpret the meaning of *b,* and rendered it as *vulgi. Vulgus* has appeared eight verses earlier in this chapter, translating הָהֲמוֹן (hahēmon)—τὸ στήριγμα—"the remnant of *the common people.*" Why this break in pattern, which on the basis of the text seems rather gratuitous? It seems nearly certain that Jerome was under the influence of a rabbinic interpretation here. As the highly literate elite of priests and scribes rose to social ascendancy in post-exilic Israel, the prestige of the landed gentry, the עַם־הָאָרֶץ (ām-haarets), declined. After Titus's destruction of the Temple and the last vestiges of the Jewish state in A.D. 70, the rabbinic elite, heirs of the priesthood, used that once-proud designation in an ever more pejorative sense, and began to read that interpretation anachronistically into the canonical Scriptures.[55] Jerome's translation has clearly suffered here from his adherence to his masters (in all probability, the Palestinian rabbis to whom he refers so often, if so anonymously): it seems unlikely that the chronicler intended to finish his list of dignitaries taken off to Babylon with sixty peasants or proletarians taken at random; sixty landed magnates suit the context much better. But as least Jerome thought he had a weighty reason for varying the translation.

By far the most common departure that Jerome made from the עַם (*ām*)—λαός—*populus* pattern was in substituting *plebs* for *populus*. His use of this variant may indicate any of three attitudes on his part: an appreciation of the aesthetic value of a vocabulary which could vary itself while still respecting the significant differences of meaning between, for example, *ām* and *goy* (or *populus* and *gens*); respect for Old Latin antecedents, if only in self-defense—his early correspondence with Augustine bears witness to what is the most famous instance of well-meaning and intelligent resistance to the changes with which his translations threatened the familiar liturgies of Latin-speaking congregations; yet a further degree of precision in his understanding of these political terms.

Three Old Testament passages are especially revealing in this regard. Genesis 23 deals with Abraham's purchase of a tomb for Sara from Ephron the Hethite. In verses 7-13, the word עַם (*ām*) appears four times. The first three times, he translated it as *populus,* ignoring in verse 11 (as has already been mentioned) a Septuagint variation. But in verse 13, "And *in their hearing* [Abraham] said to Ephron, 'If you are really willing, hear me. I will give you money for the field; accept it from me that I may bury my dead there,'" the underlined words are rendered as *circumstante plebe.* How can this עַם (*ām*) be considered different from the others? [56] First of all, it is the last of a rather heavy run of them. Secondly, in this verse the general assembly of the Hethites is least prominent. Previously Abraham has "bowed low" before them (verse 7); Ephron has answered from their midst (verse 10) and called upon them to witness his intentions (verse 11); Abraham has "bowed low" again (verse 12), and now practically all attention has been focused on the two men actually negotiating the sale, leaving the עַם (*ām*) of verse 13 in the rather shadowy background. No Old Latin versions of this verse seem to have survived.

In chapters 16-20 of Exodus, which recount the journey of the Israelites from the crossing of the Red Sea to the great theophany and giving of the Commandments on Mount Sinai, the word עַם (*ām*) appears twenty-seven times. Jerome translated it faithfully into *populus* in every instance but one: 19:11. God is speaking: " 'Make them wash their garments and be ready for the third day; for on the third day the Lord will come down on Mount Sinai *before the eyes of all the people'* "—*coram omni plebe.* It could be argued that the people of Israel, just about to receive its constitution, is presented in this verse in an exceptionally humble posture. On the other hand, it would be hard to deny that the Israelites appear quite as lowly in verse 16, where they tremble in the camp, and quite as passive in verse 25, as Moses recites God's message to them.[57] Old Latin readings are at present available for only fifteen of these twenty-seven occurrences of עַם (*ām*), but fourteen of them, including the one in 19:11, translate it (or, to be more exact, λαός) as *populus.* The one exception, 20:20 (αὐτοῖς—*eis*), has already been discussed.[58] So the responsibility for using *plebs* here seems to rest squarely with Jerome.

Psalm 93 (Septuagint reckoning)/94 (Masoretic reckoning) is a sort of national lament, warning the sinners now in power of God's ultimate vengeance. Jerome, following the standard ·contemporary opinion, ascribed it to David. עַם. (*ām*) occurs three times, in verse 5 ("Your *people,* O Lord, they trample down, your inheritance they afflict"), verse 8 ("Understand, you senseless ones among the *people;* and, you fools, when will you be wise?"), and verse 14 ("For the Lord will not cast off his *people,* nor abandon his inheritance"). That "the people" is specifically Israel is made even clearer by a reference to God's universal tutelage of the גּוֹיִם (*goyim*)—ἔθνη—*gentes* in verse 10. Each עַם (*ām*) is given as λαός in the Septuagint, but the Old Latin versions vary widely. All have *populo* in verse 8, almost all have *plebem* in verse 14, and a majority prefer *populum* to *plebem* in verse 5. In his Septuagint-based Psalter (generally called the Gallican Psalter), Jerome followed the Old Latin consensûs, but in his later Psalter *iuxta Hebraeos* he replaced *plebem* by *populum* in verse 14. Considerations of variety obviously. did count in the case of this psalm. Can any significant differences of status or activity be observed among the three appearances of "the people" in this poem? Only with the greatest ingenuity; it seems quite consistently docile in all of them.

Let us summarize the evidence of these three passages, which show us a friendly but still Gentile people, the Israelites triumphantly becoming a fully conscious legal entity, and the plight of their successors in evil days. A check of the surviving Old Latin versions suggests that Jerome ignored those precedents for Exodus. 16-20, followed them at first and then ignored them for Psalm 93/94:14; the Old Latin evidence for the rest of that psalm and for the Hethite incident from Genesis 23 is (as is so often the case) either absent or inconclusive. We can reasonably surmise a concern for variety in the Genesis and Exodus passages, but not in the psalm. It seems reasonable to discern the influence of Jerome's concern for semantic precision in the Genesis passage and the psalm, and possibly even in the section from Exodus.

Perhaps the most striking indication of Jerome's consistency in translating עַם (ām) as populus comes from an examination of his treatment of words with rather similar meanings, such as עֲדַת (ādāt) and קְהָל (qahal), which the Old Testament also uses to designate the group of the Israelites. The section from Exodus just considered provides an excellent example. עֲדַת (ādāt) appears four times between 16:1 and 17:1, the closely related form הָעֵדָה (ha-ēdah) appears in 16:22, and קְהָל (qahal) occurs once, in 16:3. The Septuagint translated all six as συναγωγή (although it usually preferred ἐκκλήσια as an equivalent for קְהָל [qahal]). Jerome turned עֲדַת (ādāt) into multitudo in 16:1 and 17:1, congregatio in 16:2 and 9, and coetus in 16:10. הָעֵדָה (ha-ēdah) (16:22) became multitudo, as did קְהָל (qahal) (16:3). עַם (ām) appears three times among these verses (in 16:4, 27, and 30), and was converted each time into populus. In the rest of the four chapters considered, עַם (ām) (twenty-three times as populus, once as plebs) entirely replaces these other terms as the designation of the group.

It is fairly easy to tell why Jerome varied his Latin equivalents for those three other words. They are a multitudo when engaged in merely herd activity, such as coming to Raphidim in 16:1, being "killed by hunger" in 16:3, or journeying by stages toward Sinai in 17:1. When grumbling against Moses in 16:2 or about to receive his answer through Aaron in 16:9, they become a congregatio. The fact that when they are actually addressed by Aaron in the following verse (16:10) they turn into a coetus could be explained by a desire on Jerome's part to indicate that then they had actually been physically assembled. It could also be accounted for by a desire for variety of wording, as indeed could all the variations in this passage of three dozen verses.

The Old Latin version used by Augustine obediently followed the Septuagint, merely transliterating συναγωγή into *synagoga* in 16:1-3 and putting *populus* for λαός in 16:4. The version used by Ambrose rendered συναγωγή somewhat more freely as *congregatio* in 17:1. Unfortunately, no Old Latin readings seem to be available for the five other loci discussed here, but these are sufficient to indicate the degree of Jerome's originality.

The significant points to be observed here are, first, the utter freedom with which Jerome varied the language of antecedent texts in order to express his interpretation of the narrative,[59] and, second and more important, the contrast between this flexibility and the rigor with which he turned עַם (*ām*) into *populus*.

Granted the frequency of the עַם—λαός—*populus* pattern, it is now necessary to ask what Jerome understood עַם (*ām*)—and hence *populus* (with *plebs* as a minor variant)—to mean. For the Old Testament, the answer is as clear as it is simple: there are two meanings, one vastly more important than the other.

Quite frequently, it can be more or less interchangeable with גּוֹי (*goy*)—ἔθνος—*gens/natio*. Two passages from the Pentateuch are typical. In Exodus 19:5, 6, God gives Moses a message: "'Therefore, if you hearken to my voice and keep my covenant, you shall be my *special possession, dearer to me than all other people* [*a*], though all the earth is mine./ You shall be to me a kingdom of priests, a holy *nation* [*b*]. That is what you must tell the Israelites.'" (See Table 4.) In Jerome's compression of the Septuagint and Old Latin wording of verse 5 it would be unwarranted to see any preference for *populus* over *gens;* he was simply returning once again to the Hebrew, as he did, without need for revision, in the next verse.

Table 4

	Hebrew	Septuagint	Old Latin	Vulgate
a.	סְגֻלָּה מִכָּל־	λαὸς περιούσιος	populus	peculium
	הָעַמִּים	ἀπὸ παντῶν	abundans	de cunctis
	(s'gulah mikal	τῶν ἐθνῶν	prae omnibus	populis
	ha-āmim.)		gentibus	
b.	וְגוֹי (v'goy)	ἔθνος	gens	gens

Deuteronomy 9:1, 2 speak for themselves. " 'Hear, O Israel! You are now about to cross the Jordan to enter in and dispossess *nations* [*a*] greater and stronger than yourselves, having large cities fortified to the sky,/ the Enacim, a *people* [*b*] great and tall. You know of them and have heard it said of them, "Who can stand up against the Enacim?" ' " (See Table 5.)

Table 5

	Hebrew		Septuagint	Old Latin	Vulgate
a.	גּוֹיִם	(*goyim*)	ἔθνη	gentes	nationes
b.	עַם	(*ām*)	λαόν	—	populum

However, Jerome saw that עַם (*ām*) was preeminently the term for the "people of Israel" conceived as a legal-political personality (to use a formulation of Roman inspiration, but quite applicable to the Hebrew notion of Israel [60]). So it appears most frequently in the Old Testament, and Jerome regularly translated it as *populus/plebs*. Several relevant examples from Genesis, Exodus, and 4 Kings have already been considered, but they by no means exhaust the supply, even for those three books. Two other loci in Genesis help define the range of the word's applicability. In 11:6, the Lord comes down to inspect the city (*civitas*) and the tower which the sons of Adam have built at Babel. Observing how much they can achieve, and with what vigor, once they have come to a general agreement, He says, "Truly, they are one *populus* and they all have the same language (*labium*). This is the beginning of what they will do. Hereafter they will not be restrained from anything which they determine to do." [61] On a much smaller scale, the word is used to describe the men of Sodom united by an active consensus (in Genesis 19:4) as they present angry demands to Lot. The word is not conspicuous in those sections detailing God's promises concerning Abraham's posterity: that fundamentally biological group is a גּוֹי (*goy*), a *gens*, rather than an עַם (*ām*)—*populus*. But that latter term crops up with almost oppressive frequency in those sections of Exodus narrating the joint acts and decisions of Israel as it is reconstituted by Moses' mediation of a pact between itself and God. Similarly, when the descendants of those Israelites ignore

God's will as expressed through His prophet's mouth in the tenth
and twelfth chapters of 1 Kings (1 Samuel), and demand a king
instead of the boards of judges instituted by Moses, עַם (ām)—
populus once again fills the text,[62] unaccompanied this time by its
satellite, plebs. Such is the case also in the twenty-fifth chapter of
4 Kings, which narrates the definitive collapse of that experiment
in monarchy before Nabuchodonosor's resettlement policy.[63]

The prophetic books which deal with the validity of Israel's
covenant provide many other examples. The famous marital metaphor of the first and second chapters of Osee uses עַם (ām)—
populus to form the name of the offspring whose legitimacy is in
question (1:9, 2:25, 3:1).[64] The thirty-seventh chapter of Ezechiel
contains two of the most famous allegories in all the literature
of postexilic reassurance, those of the dry bones (verses 1–14) and
of the two sticks (verses 15-28). The latter is particularly instructive about the meaning of עַם—populus. The word appears three
times (verses 18, 23, and 27) in these fourteen verses, along with
four appearances of גּוֹי (goy)—gens/natio. The latter term is applied twice to the surrounding Gentiles (verses 21 and 28) and
twice to Israel in verse 22, where the point at issue is its reunifi-
cation ("I will make them one nation upon the land, in the mountains of Israel, and there shall be one prince for them all. Never
again shall they be two nations, and never again shall they be
divided into two kingdoms"). This reference could hardly be more
political. However, עַם—populus still seems to hold slightly more
title to the central political designation. It is used more frequently
as the noun for the group, and more widely both in meaning and
in distribution throughout the text. In verse 18, the significance
of the miraculous allegory is asked by the "sons of the [prophet's]
populus," and the word recurs in the verses in which God promises
not merely to reunite Israel, but also to purify him and reestab-
lish His pact with him.

NEW TESTAMENT

An examination of Jerome's translation of the New Testament,
undertaken mostly in Rome between 382 and 385,[65] at a time
when he was not yet profoundly under the influence of the Hebraica veritas and probably rather unfamiliar with the specific

Hebrew concepts conveyed by the word עַם, can tell us a great deal about Jerome's understanding of the word *populus*. It also makes very clear the difference between *populus* and *plebs*.

This examination will concentrate on a study of the Vulgate version of the Acts of the Apostles, proceeding thereafter to a consideration of some corroborating evidence from the rest of the New Testament. The Acts of the Apostles is a particularly fruitful book upon which to concentrate. First of all, it is the most intensely political book of the New Testament, or at any rate the book most conscious of group-identification, because it deals with the emergence of the Church in the midst of and then out from Israel, within the context of a Gentile world of Hellenized city-states, subject in varying degrees to the Roman law. Secondly, it is reasonable to suppose that Jerome exercised some care in its revision, since he considered it the composition of Luke, whose style he greatly admired. Thirdly, the relationship of the Vulgate to preceding Old Latin versions is unusually easy to discern in the case of Acts. Jerome rejected the Western Greek tradition. Only three or four Old Latin versions seem to have been current in his generation. The only two which could conceivably be closely related to the text (or texts) on which he worked are based on a European recension of the early or middle fourth century, and are represented today by two almost entirely intact manuscripts, *Gigas* and *Laudianus*.[66] The further fact that Acts was not a favorite or common object of patristic commentary is also helpful to this examination, as it suggests that Jerome may have felt less constrained by solemn precedent or contemporary reputation in matters of usage than he would have felt with, say, the Gospel according to Luke.[67]

A study of the Vulgate Acts, beginning from quantitative data and advancing to critical inspection of significant loci among those data, offers some interesting conclusions strongly in support of previous conclusions about Jerome's use of *populus*. *Populus* appears forty times and *plebs* seventeen, together amounting to an average frequency of twice per chapter. Usually they translate λαός, which never becomes anything else. The four occurrences of δῆμος become *populus*; ὄχλος, a common word usually rendered as *turba,* becomes *populus* three times and *plebs* twice.

That λαός and δῆμος are translated as *populus/plebs* is hardly surprising, but the five instances in which ὄχλος undergoes that transformation are significant. Each one of them involves a vivid crowd reaction to Paul's preaching. The first occurs in 14:13. Paul and Barnabas have been taken for Mercury and Jupiter by the inhabitants of Lystra, "and the priest of the Jupiter that stood at the entrance to the city brought oxen and garlands to the gateways, and *with the people* would have offered sacrifice." Jerome, following the Old Latin, translated σὺν τοῖς ὄχλοις as *cum populis.* Clearly, the projected sacrifice would have been an official public act performed on behalf of a group more coherent than the formless gathering of people which *turba* usually suggested to a Latin audience. However, Jerome's use of the plural form *populi* for a single group could carry implications almost synonymous with those of *turba,* so he did not wander very far from the original in this case. Besides, he was following older Latin precedents.[68]

Two chapters later, he abandoned those precedents. Paul, Silas, Luke, and others have been preaching in Philippi. One day Paul exorcises a girl possessed by a divining spirit, and brings down upon himself and his companions the wrath of her owners, who feel that he has destroyed a valuable source of profit. Dragging Paul and Silas to the agora, they accuse them of disturbing the peace by introducing novel and illegal practices. "And *the people* joined in the attack against them; and the magistrates tore off their clothes and ordered them to be beaten with rods" (16:22). The ὄχλος of this verse, translated as *turba* in the Old Latin version, became *plebs* under Jerome's pen. Here the mob has taken on the character of a plaintiff or a prosecutor, to whose plea the magistrates accede by decreeing punishment.

The same sort of civically conscious interpretation occurs in the case of 17:8. Certain Jews hostile to Paul's message leave the synagogue to rouse the whole Gentile citizenry of Thessalonica against him. When their demand that the ruler, Jason, bring Paul "before the people" (εἰς τὸν δῆμον—*in populum*) fails, they form a mob (ὀχλοποιήσαντες—*et turba facta*) and "stir up the *plebem* and the *principes* of the *civitas* who heard" their charges. Jerome seems to have decided that the *plebs* and the *principes* represented the two chief power elements of that community, and that the former was inadequately represented in that capacity by the word *turba* used in the Old Latin text to translate the original ὄχλος.

In chapter 21 Paul is at Jerusalem, and Jews from Asia Minor arouse against him something rather bigger than a *plebs* (not to mention a *turba*). In verse 27, they incite the whole *populus* (πάντα τὸν ὄχλον) around the Temple by claiming that Paul has profaned it. The results are dramatic in the extreme as well as very decisive: "And the whole *civitas* was thrown into confusion, and the *populus* (λαός) ran together, and seizing Paul, they proceeded to drag him out of the Temple; whereupon the doors were immediately shut" (verse 30). The Roman military tribune quickly finds out that *"tota confunditur Jerusalem."* One charge and another is shouted in the tumultuous crowd (an ὄχλος which Jerome translates as *turba:* verse 34), so that soldiers are needed to escort Paul to the garrison headquarters "owing to the violence of the crowd" (verse 35). This last word is an ὄχλος which Jerome renders as *populus,* despite its association with such disorder. It looks as though he considered *turba* a term too weak, too narrowly associated with random and unrepresentative collections of bodies, to do justice to the fiercely clear and highly significant purpose of this mob. In this judgment he was in accord with his Latin predecessors.[69]

In examining these unusual translations of ὄχλος we have seen that Jerome, in agreement with the Old Latin tradition, used *populus* to designate a group representing what the author considered to be practically the whole Jewish population of Jerusalem, and juridically the wholly responsible city. On the other hand, he used *plebs* (as did none of the Old Latin versions) to denote an important but still partial aspect of the body politic of two Greek cities. This disparity brings us to a consideration of the difference between *plebs* and *populus* in Jerome's Acts.

Sometimes Jerome seems to use *plebs* for the sake of simple variety. This may well have been his motivation in the case of chapter 5, whose seven λαοί became *populus* four times (verse 13, 25, 26, and 37) and *plebs* three times (verses 12, 20, and 34). However, his desire for variety here must be seen as one of independent inspiration: the Old Latin antecedent had turned those seven λαοί into five *plebes* and two *populi;* Jerome followed it in only three instances (verses 20, 26, and 34).

An interesting question is posed by 3:23. Peter, preaching in the Temple after curing a lame beggar, cites Leviticus 23:29: "And it shall be that every soul that will not hearken to that prophet, shall be destroyed from among *the people.*" [70] The Old Latin had *populo* for the λαοῦ of both the Old and the New Testament appearances of that verse. Jerome would follow suit some twenty years later in his translation of the Old Testament source, but in his translation of the quotation in Acts, he turned λαοῦ into *plebe.* This instance provides further evidence of his well-known failure to revise his work, but it is hard to suggest what else it could indicate other than a concern for stylistic variety.

More typical is Jerome's use of *plebs* to make a political distinction, reserving that word for a part of the *populus,* usually the mass of its members considered separately from their leadership. An excellent example of this tendency occurs in the course of chapters 6 and 7, which report the evangelical zeal, the speech before the Sanhedrin, and the martyrdom of the deacon Stephen. In 6:8 it is declared that "Stephen, full of grace and power, was working great wonders and signs among the *people.*" In 7:17 Stephen reminds the Sanhedrin that "when the time of the promise drew near that God had made to Abraham, *the people* increased and multiplied in Egypt." Continuing his summary of Israel's salvation-history, he recounts in verse 34 God's reply to Moses: " 'I have seen all the oppression of my *people* in Egypt, and I have heard their groaning, and I will come to deliver them.' " It is clear that in each of these three verses, reference is being made to an entire community. In each case, Jerome used *populus* for λαός, once (in 7:17) rejecting an Old Latin *plebs.* However, he conformed to the Old Latin use of *plebs* in 6:12: "And they stirred up the *people* and the elders and the Scribes, and, running together, they seized him and brought him to the Sanhedrin." The distinction here between the "people" and the two subsequently named groups of its leaders is obvious, and is emphasized by Jerome's choice of vocabulary.

Occasionally Jerome uses *plebs* to denote the whole community when it is presented in an attitude of subordination, passivity, or general humility. A good example of this third usage is provided by the account of Paul's stay in Pisidian Antioch, contained in verses 14–52 of chapter 13. Λαός appears five times (verses 15, 17 [twice], 24, and 31); the Old Latin Acts turned each appearance into *plebs*. In one instance, verse 24, Jerome wrote *populus* instead. This difference could be explained on the basis of simple variety, but a more substantive explanation seems valid also. To begin with, the synagogue in that city was quite placid, and most untypically receptive to Paul's message. The bulk of its membership is first presented in the most passive of postures: "And entering the synagogue on the Sabbath, they sat down. After the reading of the Law and the Prophets, the rulers (*principes*) of the synagogue sent to them, saying, 'Brethren, if you have any word of exhortation for the *plebs,* speak.'" When Paul addresses them he characterizes Israel as the lowly recipient of divine favor: "'The God of the *plebs* of Israel chose our fathers and exalted the *plebs* when they were sojourners in the land of Egypt, and with uplifted arm led them forth out of it.'" He has at last sent their heirs the promised Savior, and Paul and his companions "'are now witnesses for him to the *plebs.*'" It is only in speaking of their greater precursor and his more total mission that Jerome has Paul vary the pattern: "'John preached before [Jesus'] coming a baptism of repentance to all the *populus* of Israel'" (verse 24).

The high frequency of *plebes* in this incident is not typical of any Latin text of Acts. However, Jerome's changing one of them to *populus* is quite typical of his version of that book. He changed the *populus* of the African tradition into *plebs* four times in the course of his revision of Acts, but changed Old Latin *plebs* into *populus* ten times. No *populus* in the Vulgate Acts replaces any other word in the Old Latin version. Twice, however, an Old Latin *turba* becomes a Vulgate *plebs*. This numerical tally should make it quite clear that *populus* outranked *plebs* in quantitative importance as well as dignity in Jerome's mind. It should also be evident from the preceding discussion of the relationship between these two words that the Old Latin tradition does not show any pattern of usage remotely approaching the consistency of the Vulgate.

A nearly random selection of texts from elsewhere in the New Testament [71] provides much evidence in support of the conclusions derived from Acts about the relationship of *populus* to *plebs*.

An instance of pure vocabulary variation, for example, seems discernible in the Vulgate text of Romans 11:1, 2: "I say then: Has God cast off his *people*? By no means! For I also am an Israelite of the posterity of Abraham, of the tribe of Benjamin./ God has not cast off his *people* whom he foreknew." The Vulgate follows widespread Old Latin traditions exactly in making the λαόν of verse 1 *populum,* and that of verse 2 *plebem.* This may be simply an instance of Jerome's reverence for his predecessors, but it is hard to imagine any reason but variety for this usage. Locating the Old Testament sources of Paul's words does not suggest any more profound explanation, either. Two of the most obvious sources of the reassuring formula "God will not reject His people" are 1 Kings 12:22 and Psalms 93/94:14. For the former locus, Jerome was to use *populum* (Old Latin texts are lacking), and for the latter he used *plebem*—at least he did so in his Roman translation of the Psalter from the Septuagint; in the Psalter according to the Hebrew he was to prefer *populum* for that verse.[72] So even this instance of variety for something like its own sake leads us on to a realization of Jerome's mature preference for the word *populus.*

Even in the early phase of his translator's effort represented by the Vulgate New Testament, Jerome seems to have considered *populus* the standard term for the people of God. This is the case in passages which cite the Old Testament, such as Titus 2:14 (from Exodus 19:5), 1 Peter 2:10 (from Osee 1:9 and 2:24), and 2 Corinthians 6:16 (from Ezechiel 37:27). Jerome's later translations of those sources would simply ratify the usage. This was also his standard practice with passages originating with the New Testament authors, such as Matthew 1:21, which describes the state of Israel's expectancy at the moment of the Savior's conception, or Hebrews 4:9, which discusses Sabbath observances in the infant Church.[73]

Putting aside the question of the relationship between *plebs* and *populus,* we can discern in Jerome's New Testament as well as in his later Old Testament a concern that *populus* be reserved for groups possessing an established communal personality. This is most strikingly demonstrated by Luke 9:13. The Twelve tell Christ that they cannot possibly provide for the five thousand followers He has just told them to feed: "'We have not more than five loaves and two fishes, unless we are to go out and buy food for all this *crowd*.'" The significant word was ὄχλος in the original, and had been rendered as *populus* by most of the Old Latin versions.[74] Jerome, however, judged that the crowd should be called a *turba*. The consciousness of this decision appears incontestable if one considers the rest of the incident in Luke and the account of it in the other three Gospels. In Luke 9:11, 12, 16, and 18, the same group is called an ὄχλος; Jerome and his Old Latin predecessors made it most times a *turba*. In Matthew 14:13–21, the five occurrences of ὄχλος became *turbae* at the hands of all Latin translators; the same thing happened to its single appearance in Mark 6:31–44. In his translation of John 6:1–13, Jerome departed a little from the Old Latin versions by rendering ὄχλος πολὺς once as *multitudo magna* and once as *multitudo maxima,* rather than the more obvious *turba multa*. However, the central point is plain: only once in all these parallel accounts did Jerome really reject his antecedents for the sake of a significant interpretation, and *populus* benefits from the distinction.

So acute is this distinction, in fact, that the Vulgate New Testament seems remarkably free of the rather haphazard juxtaposition of *populi* with *gentes, nationes,* or similar synonymous groups, which occurs so frequently in the Old Testament. Such a usage may at first glance seem to be present in several passages of the Apocalypse,[75] of which 14:6 is typical: "And I saw another angel flying in mid-heaven, having an everlasting gospel to those who dwell upon the earth and to every nation and tribe and tongue and people . . ." (*"et super omnem gentem, et tribum, et linguam, et populum"*). Similar is the formula from Exodus developed in 1 Peter 2:9: "You, however, are a chosen race, a royal priesthood, a holy nation, a purchased people; that you may proclaim the perfections of him who has called you out of darkness into his marvelous light." (*"Vos autem genus electum, regale sacerdotium, gens sancta, populus adquisitionis . . ."*.) However, it should be obvious after a little reflection that these are not instances of conceptual repetition relieved by merely verbal variety. The first passage seeks to exhaust a category, and the second to define one, through the enumeration of successive aspects thereof; neither pas-

sage is simply a stringing together of indifferent synonyms. It may
be that those verses' first transcribers—Galilean fishermen or whatever they were—were ignorant of the difference between these
two reasons for combining words in a series; it is most unlikely
that their supremely Ciceronian translator was.

The central tendencies associated with Jerome's discriminating
use of *populus* in the Vulgate New Testament, and indeed in all
his literary production, are clearly epitomized in his translation of
the Synoptic Gospels' accounts of Jesus' trial before Pilate. The
Gospel according to John is of no relevance to this particular comparison, since its general tendency is to lay responsibility for those
events either—and alternately—on the ruling elite (ἱερεῖς—*pon-
tifices*) or on "the Jews" conceived as a monolithic, unanimous
body. In the narrative of this trial, 18:28–19:16, the Fourth Gospel
uses only one of the words we have been considering—ἔθνος—*gens*,
in 18:35.

The shortest Synoptic account, that of Mark 15:1–15, uses the
word ὄχλος three times (in verses 8, 11, and 15), to refer to the
crowd massed before the praetorium. In verses 8 and 11 Jerome
followed Old Latin antecedents, translating it as *turba;* in verse 15
he again followed tradition, turning it into *populus.* What difference appears from the context? Let us compare them. Verse 8:
"And the *turba* came up, and began to ask that he do for them
as he was wont." Verse 11: "But the chief priests stirred up the
turba to have him release Barabbas to them instead." Verse 15:
"So Pilate, wishing to satisfy the *populus,* released to them Barabbas; but Jesus he scourged and delivered to them to be cruci-
fied." Can one discern in the case of the last verse a Latin sense
that the managed mob had now achieved an act of enduring consequence, and so deserved a somewhat more solemn appellation?
Perhaps; but it is probably more prudent as well as more accurate
to see here simply a respect for either tradition or variety or both.

The slightly fuller narrative contained in Matthew 27:11–25
uses ὄχλος three times (verses 15, 20, and 24), and πᾶς ὁ λαὸς once
(verse 25). All the Old Latin versions translated the three ὄχλοι as
populi, and the majority of them turned the λαός into a *turba!*
Jerome was somewhat more consistent in rendering all four as
some form of *populus.* He may seem a bit out of line with his

usual habits in the case of verse 15: "Now at festival time the procurator used to release to the *populus* a prisoner, whomever they would." But in view of the way he handled ὄχλος in Acts, this translation may not be so inconsistent, after all. In either case, he is quite true to form in verse 20: "But the chief priests and the elders persuaded the *populi* to ask for Barabbas and to destroy Jesus." Here, since a distinction is being made among the elements of the group, we might expect *plebs* to be used; the plural *populi* is very close. When Pilate washes his hands *coram populo* in verse 24, one is disposed to think that Jerome's vocabulary conveys the significance of the moment more acutely than does the original κατέναντι τοῦ ὄχλου; and in the case of verse 25, "And all the *people* answered and said, 'His blood be on us and on our children,' " the only thing surprising is that so many of the Old Latin versions applied the term *turba* to a body so laden with responsibility. For that matter, all the Latin translators' choice of *populus* for ὄχλος in verses 15 and 24 seems much more rationally in line with Roman civic reflexes than does their tame adherence to *turba* in Mark 15:8 and 11.

The language of Luke's account is, as might be expected, much more varied and revealing. A schematic summary of the translation patterns which it evoked may be the most useful way to approach its examination. (See Table 6.)

Table 6

Text	Greek	Old Latin *	Vulgate	Text
22:66	τοῦ λαοῦ	plebis populi	plebis	And as soon as day broke, the elders of the *people* and the chief priests and scribes gathered together; and they led him away into their Sanhedrin, saying, "If thou art the Christ, tell us."
23:1	τὸ πλῆθος	multitudo	multitudo	And the whole *assemblage* rose, and took him before Pilate.

Text	Greek	Old Latin *	Vulgate	Text
23:2	τὸ ἔθνος	gentem	gentem	And they began to accuse him saying, "We have found this man perverting our *nation*,"
4	τοὺς ὄχλους	turbas (turbam) (populum)	turbas	And Pilate said to the chief priests and the *crowds*, "I find no guilt in this man."
5	τὸν λαόν	populum	populum	But they persisted, saying, "He is stirring up the *people*, teaching throughout all Judea, and beginning from Galilee even to this place."
13	τὸν λαὸν	plebis (populi) (omni populo) (plebem)	plebe	And Pilate called together the chief priests and the rulers and the *people*,
14	τὸν λαόν	populum (populos) (plebem)	populum	and said to them, "You have brought before me this man, as one who perverts the *people*. . ."
18	παμπληθεὶ	turba (omnis populus) (multitudo)	turba	But the whole *mob* cried out together, saying, "Away with this man, and release to us Barabbas!"
27	πολὺ πλῆθος τοῦ λαοῦ	multitudo populi (multitudo ingens populi)	multa turba populi	Now there was following him a *great crowd of people*, and of women, who were bewailing and lamenting him.

* Minority readings in parentheses.

The use of *plebs* when the text gives a breakdown of the power structure, as in 22:66 and 23:13, is entirely typical of Jerome. So is the use of *populus* for the generality of the Jews resident in Palestine, or at least for a group of greater compass than the *multa turba* following Jesus to Golgotha (23:27). The fact that that greater group is one essentially composed of citizens comes through, perhaps not quite consciously, in the phrase *et mulierum,* with its implication that women did not really belong. *Gens* makes its appearance early in the hearing (23:2), perhaps entirely synonymous with *populus* (though certainly not with *plebs* or *turba*); however, when Pilate and the spokesmen of the Sanhedrin get down to cases, it abdicates in favor of the more standard term. Nor is the scene devoid of mob tension, for all its precision. *Turba* appears as frequently as *populus,* once in a most revealing conjunction with it (23:27); the freedom with which Jerome uses that word to translate two of the three occurrences of the πλῆθ- stem, as well as the single ὄχλος, while preferring to render the most orderly, least excited πλῆθος of all (that of 23:1) as *multitudo,* could serve as a model of his sense of the proper function of word equivalence in translation.

Finally, even a cursory comparison of the Vulgate text and the Old Latin traditions (so often in disagreement!) shows quickly how crucial Jerome's labors were in bringing to the Latin Church a consensus on the word of Scripture. It should also suggest the relationship in which Jerome's language stood to that of his contemporaries and recent predecessors—fully representative of the general educated usage, but much more careful and consistent than the average.

4 Ideas in Conclusion

What general conclusions can be drawn from the results of this study? A study of this sort finds its proper fulfillment less in some synthetic, self-transcending statement than in offering a coherent body of data and a tested method to students of a wide range of historical problems, but I should like at least to summarize the core of those results and to indicate four kinds of issues to which this inquiry offers useful, perhaps decisive further evidence.

Core Results

It is now possible to describe more fully and at the same time more precisely than before what a *populus* was in the writings—and hence, as far as we can tell, in the minds—of Augustine and Jerome.

A *populus* for them was, first of all, a group of human beings, although each author occasionally allowed himself to conceive of a *populus* of angels—creatures which men have imagined by an analogy with themselves even stricter than that according to which they have pictured their gods. The lower animals could be described by each author as having *genera, familiae,* and even *gentes,* but I have found no reference to a *populus* of subrational creatures.

Rationality is the next characteristic of a *populus* for both authors. Men belong to a *populus* by virtue of their thought, or at least their structured emotions. Only rarely do men belong to a group of that name because of birth, territorial identification, or the simple accident of being together, like strangers in a crowd or the residents of a given cluster of dwellings: the sort of settlement which in some conditions we honor with the name of neighborhood.

What do the men who compose a *populus* think about together? As we see them and their group through the transcribed vision of Augustine and Jerome, we can usually discern their interest in some action or line of action involving common consent; at the very least, we can tell that they are concerned about some event which commands their sentient reaction. Usually these policies, actions, or external events have to do with what we moderns call politics and religion, and with the conflicts, doctrines, or entertainment which tend to inform both of those spheres of mass human commitment.

Most distinctively, a *populus* is a group of sentient human beings involved with a law, or with values subject to juridical review. Sometimes the law in question is a code of ultimate standards, and the judgment divine; sometimes a more secular, man-sized network of regulations and sentences forms the normal milieu of a *populus*.

As it appears in the diversity of literary contexts provided by these two authors, a *populus* can be intensely conscious and active, or comparatively inert, although it is usually active and morally responsible. While we must assume that both authors assumed that the *populi* they mentioned contained a considerable percentage of inactive citizens—not to mention women, children, slaves, and other traditionally voiceless elements of classic Mediterranean society—the silence of those members seems less important than their ultimate participation in the decisions, the tastes, and the behavior subject to judgment which characterize their group, or their participation in its destiny. For both Augustine and Jerome a *populus* tended, in the last analysis, to possess a destiny and a moral character, and by virtue of that near-personality it differed from other kinds of human groups. A *civitas,* for example, might have all those attributes, but it might with equal likelihood appear as simply a city, in the external, descriptive sense of "urban settlement." A *gens* might be as teleological and morally responsible a group as a *populus,* but with at least equal frequency it could be a group unified primarily by genetic origin or language, a society with more beginning and less end.

Finally, a *populus* is usually a comprehensive group for Augustine and Jerome: including the inarticulate women and children of the group as well as its virtual representatives (however anonymous), it normally includes several classes as well. It is usually not what we call "the common people," usually not equivalent to the *plebs,* although that latter group was defined (at least traditionally) by constitutional rather than economic status. At times Augustine in particular contrasts the *populus* as a whole with its leadership, but the latter element appears to be a purely functional elite, and the responsive or compliant mass of the membership certainly includes the rich as well as the poor, the privileged as well as the dependent. The *populus* in such cases enjoys a complementary relationship with its leadership, just like that of the *senatus populusque Romanus* or the *clerus et populus* of the Christian Church.

So far this description covers the range of usage common to Augustine and Jerome. That range corresponds to the widest sector of each author's usage, but in some interesting particulars their patterns of usage are not congruent.

Jerome tends much more than Augustine to apply the word to a group consisting of the lower social classes or the culturally benighted. In this relatively infrequent as well as peripheral usage, he follows the vocabulary patterns of Cicero's speculative dialogues and treatises, whereas Augustine remains faithful to the stricter usage of their common master's orations.

Under the pressure of biblical rather than classical habits of language, Jerome tends to extend the socially comprehensive group-label *populus* to many groups so distant from the reader's center of attention that we find it difficult to discern very much about their distinctive attributes: as far as we can tell, such *populi* might just as well be called *gentes* or *nationes* or even *tribus*. In this not very frequent usage Jerome was influenced by the need to find some Latin phraseology that would reflect a standard Hebrew formula for the diverse Gentiles: thus *gentes et populi* comes to serve as an occasional variant for *gentes et nationes* and the like.

Augustine's total usage differs from Jerome's in a nearly opposite direction. He felt a need at various times in his life to offer fairly elaborate definitions of *populus* and other comparable terms (such as *civitas* and *societas*), and in the process of doing so he lets his readers glimpse a personal insight rich in speculative potential. Even in less self-conscious moods Augustine shows his continuing interest in two attributes of a *populus* which practically become ontological prerequisites: a *populus* must be a *multitudo* of adequate (though unspecified) size, and it must possess a rather special degree of conscious unity. A *gens* may be either family-size or colossal, a *tribus* is typically small and unified by blood and inherited convention, but without respectable size and a certain coherence of mature purpose, a *populus* cannot exist. Neither, presumably, can its normal mode of government, a *res publica*.

The modern reader, reflecting on the historical moment in which Augustine lived and wrote, wonders immediately whether a *populus* (and a *res publica*) can get too big and hence too scattered, losing in the process both function and identity. Conversely, he wonders if a *populus* can consist of other *populi,* either smaller or operating on different planes of interest and communication. Maddeningly enough, Augustine does not seem to have asked himself those obviously important questions.

By rather surprising contrast, a close look at the patterns of word transfer in Jerome's translation of the most constitutional sections of the Old Testament suggests that that isolated and socially maladjusted scholar who never bothered to define a *populus* had a rather definite conception of its content and its proper limits, a conception similar to Augustine's, and yet more strikingly in accord with the traditional language of Roman law.

Rings of Relevant Consequences

Once we have established these descriptive definitions of a *populus* in the writings of Augustine and Jerome, and, perhaps more important, surveyed that central zone in which their usages are congruent, we can hardly help asking what more general conclusions can be derived from that core of data. I think that a great number of conclusions can be drawn from those results, or, to put it rather differently, that they can shed new light on a series of other questions. If the metaphor be permitted, I should like to suggest four rings of issues which this study's information can illuminate.

A look at the first ring of synthesizable results, closest to the core data and most thoroughly shaped by their information, permits us to project a general treatment of the sense of community evident in the written self-revelation of Augustine and Jerome. We can now conclude that these two interestingly comparable contemporaries, influential Fathers of the Church at a crucial period in its history and for quite a few centuries thereafter, expressed a definable sense of identity with, *inter alia,* one kind of human group which they called a *populus.* Several specific *populi* claimed their attention and their allegiance; a few inspired them with sentiments of rejection and even of overt hostility. Five *populi* or aspects thereof seem to have dominated their consciousness.

First of all, both Augustine and Jerome let us know that they belonged to a *populus* called *Christianus.* In its most immediate form, this appears as a local phenomenon, united by a communal liturgy, lively opinions about miracles, doctrine, etc., and no less lively a proclivity for misbehavior. Augustine the discipline-conscious bishop and Jerome the contentious misanthrope expressed their sense of these attributes in different contexts and in rather divergent tones, but their agreement about those attributes themselves is noteworthy. Equally clear is their assumption—indeed, their boast—that these vigorous *populi* to which they belonged belonged equally to young and old (once the waters of baptism had been entered and crossed), to male and female, and to the enslaved, dependent, and privileged members of civil society.

Secondly, and as an extension and elevation of that first identity, Augustine and Jerome belonged to a much vaster *populus* called the Church. It appears in their writings as a federation of orthodox congregations throughout the Roman Empire and occasionally beyond, the lively rancor of whose disputes about dogma, discipline, and precedence attested rather than denied its interior, necessary, and ultimate unity. Sometimes this *populus* appears as a body transcending time and space, struggling under divine tutelage to understand its mysterious identity and purpose. In this guise it often merges with the *populus Dei,* although the historical Israel and even the local churches could share that appellation. What Augustine did with his conception of that transcendent *populus* is well known, or at any rate widely discussed; what Jerome made of it deserves adequate investigation.

Coming back to earth, we can discern a third *populus* to which both authors belonged: the local civil community. Usually urban, neither very intelligent nor politically of much significance, this form of community constantly intrudes on these authors' consciousness, but usually gets rebuffed. Our historical information insists that it must overlap by and large with the local Christian *populus,* but with typical lack of trustworthiness it usually fails to qualify for that identification.

Then there is the *populus Romanus,* a body usually commanding both authors' respectful attention despite the extremely diverse behavior of which it was capable. As Augustine put it so neatly, even its vices were splendid. This community inhabited both the remote historical (and legendary) past and the immediate present; in inverse relationship to the Church, its universal dimensions and its past performance figure more vividly in these authors' works than do its local manifestations or its current concerns. Augustine felt toward this *populus* of his an ambivalence which might, under historical psychoanalysis, turn out to be even more exciting than his problems with his mother, his father, and his mistress. Jerome, despite all his problems with every other form of tie, seems to have been a rather single-minded patriot. (Is that so surprising?)

To present this *populus* as simply the civil counterpart of the religious *populus Christianus* for these two men who were members of both would be to commit a serious anachronism. A purely secular *populus* seems to have been alien to their categories. Even when presented in an anti-Christian context, perhaps especially then, the *populus Romanus* appears in their writings as a body inherently "religious" as well as "political." Shortly before he died, Jean Bayet conveyed to me his growing conviction that the *populus Romanus* came into being as a result of the Roman religious crisis of the second century B.C., a crisis which was resolved by combining plebeian and patrician divinities and rituals into one public pantheon and cult. This durable expedient deserves no little credit for the subsequent expansion of that flexible imperial *res publica,* and only failed when it did because the monotheistic insistence of Christianity responded better to a whole complex of personal spiritual needs which the *religio publica* ignored. Was *populus Christianus* simply another name in the minds of Augustine and Jerome for the religious dimension of the new *populus*

Romanus which had in their century been liturgically revivified, or does the more intense contemporary presence of the former *populus* in their writings unmask a shift of loyalty, yet further evidence of the Church's subversive usurpation? That question really belongs in another ring, farther from the influence of this study's central results and from its most direct extrapolations. Before exploring it further, we should glance at the direct evidence available from a consideration of the fifth *populus* that holds an important place in the writings of these two Roman Christians— the *populus Israel*.

That *populus* was for both of them the historical ancestor and typological alter ego of the Church. Appearing also in the formulaic guise of *populus Israeliticus, Hebraeus, Judaeus, Judaeorum,* etc., it could designate an earlier phase of the continuous *populus Dei* currently manifested in the Church. It was usually distinct from contemporary Jewish communities, to which neither author applied the noun *populus* very often. For Augustine, the *populus Israel* was a historical entity racially and linguistically self-conscious, which had become a special *populus* after being one *gens* among many, and which after rejection of its providential mission seemed not to be much of a *populus* any more. No such evolutionary distinctions appear in the usage patterns of Jerome, who calls the contemporary Jews a *populus* somewhat more frequently than does Augustine.

Augustine occasionally insisted on his (and all his fellow Christians') membership in the *populus Israel,* but that metaphorical insistence is clearly due to the consequences of allegorical rhetoric rather than to any literal, cotidian sense of community. Jerome made the same insistence, perhaps more often: Israel seems to have aroused in him an ambivalence comparable to that which Augustine felt toward Rome. It would be interesting to see whether Jerome in his nonscriptural writings applied the noun *populus* more frequently to Israel (including the Jews after Christ) or to Rome (and civil society in general). Such an inquiry would require a good deal of sheer computing labor (see Appendix B for a model), and frequency alone would not of course prove anything, but the results might be revealing.

The similarities and contrasts between the *populus Romanus* and the *populus Israel* provided Augustine and Jerome with the framework for a number of interesting random observations and speculations, especially fruitful for the former author's theology of history and the ecclesiology of both. All five *populi* are present in their ecclesiology; perhaps in that perspective of their thought all five participate or merge somehow into a single *populus* which absorbed and commanded their integrated allegiance. This is not the place to begin a treatise on the ecclesiological structures of Augustine and Jerome, but it may be an appropriate place to urge this study's results on anyone contemplating such an enterprise.

Neither do I intend at this point to propose a comprehensive description of Augustine's and Jerome's fully developed sense (or senses) of community. That undertaking must await the inductive analysis of other terms than *populus* and the consideration of other data than that available from the analysis of terminology. It should probably include a thorough discussion of the term *sense of community,* which may need to be replaced by a label either more precise or more simply evocative of that profound feeling of belonging which I am trying to isloate and which seems to me so fundamental to many ideas of which we tend to analyze only the surface manifestations. I hope and submit, however, that this study's results provide a firm foundation for that project.

These results also provide solid ground for settling several current issues of scholarly debate which arose originally from the consideration of questions quite different from sense of community. In this second ring of relevant consequences I should like to call attention to two disputes, both treated in appendixes to this study.

The first of these is the fight about Augustine's attitude toward secular society. Did he, in conformity with the Stoic-Ciceronian tradition on natural law, consider human social order a natural good, related to ultimate moral standards and supported by their sanctions? Or did he take a radically spiritual, negative view of earthly institutions, following Tertullian, the Donatist Tychonius, and possibly the postexilic prophets? Put in simpler, modern categories, did Augustine think that the state was capable of attaining and mediating true justice, and therefore able to claim legitimate allegiance?

Faithful and intelligent Augustinians split on this question in the eleventh and twelfth centuries, when it carried more than academic weight; in our own century this problem has once again exercised and irritated the minds of scholars interested in Augustine, and general consensus has by no means been achieved. Appendix A proposes a solution. All the disputants agree that *populus* is a crucial term in the statement of that problem; I hope that the analysis of it made available by this study enables us at last to cross the line between further refinement and satisfactory resolution.

The second dispute, which like all questions concerning Jerome has attracted much less interest, has to do with his authorship of the Vulgate text of the Acts of the Apostles. Most New Testament scholars do not doubt that he produced a Latin manuscript of Acts, but some have suggested that he simply conflated existing Old Latin versions rather than making a coherent, personal effort at translation. Whether or not one credits that suggestion, New Testament scholarship must be interested in the degree of relationship between Jerome's version and the other Old Latin translations current at the time. They are somewhat more diverse and distinctive than is the case with all books of the New Testament, and two of them managed to compete for acceptance with the Vulgate text for centuries to come. Most attempts to treat this set of questions have relied for answers on canons of literary style; this study proposes in Appendix D a very different approach, based on close analysis of comparable patterns of vocabulary usage in the various versions (Greek as well as Latin), and ventures to sketch the outline of a final answer.

This study's results can contribute useful evidence to yet another ring of issues currently in scholarly dispute, but the decisive impact of that information must be indirect in this third ring, since the issues which it touches depend for accurate formulation on evidence or historical argument of a type alien to the proper sphere of verbal content-analysis.

One such issue has already been alluded to: Was Constantine prudent in trying to identify the Christian Church with the Roman Empire for a new reinforcement of loyalty and morale?

The sense of community discernible from this study's data in two highly articulate, fairly well traveled, rather typical middle-class Christian intellectuals one century after Constantine would suggest that his policy had worked. But in order to apply these data to that question, one must make certain that the question has been correctly stated. Is that what Constantine was trying to do? Or should we substitute Theodosius I for Constantine?—and so on. On the other hand, once that question's formulation has been settled, this study's data await a chance to be of use in elaborating the answer.

A second, closely related issue has to do with André Piganiol's ringing declaration that the Roman Empire died from barbarian assassination rather than from natural organic failure.[1] His case contains many elements, but one of them, not the least central, is his argument about morale and public solidarity. As has been suggested, this study's evidence would tend to support strongly the contention that the intellectual community at least felt a keen sense of solidarity with the empire's form of social order in the generation of Augustine and Jerome. On the other hand, this evidence has nothing to say about the factors of demographic and economic decline which may render Piganiol's position purely academic.

A third example from a later period of Western history has to do with the enigmatic Hildebrand's personal view of Christian society. Did he see *sacerdotium* and *regnum* as radically (and properly) opposed, or did he adhere to a simpler, more unitary vision of the right (or actual) order of things? Some have argued for the latter alternative, contrasting Hildebrand's single-mindedness with Augustine's sharper sense of distinctions in an earlier and different environment.[2] The present study suggests that Augustine's language seems to reveal a similarly simplistic set of reflexes, although he lived and functioned in a context of fairly clear division between civil and ecclesiastical spheres of authority. However, this observation is supplementary to the central point, which refers to Hildebrand's rather than to Augustine's thought.

Nevertheless, such observations arising from this study's data might well cast those slightly alien issues in a different light. Do they make Hildebrand appear the authentic Augustinian in the

Investiture Controversy? On the other hand, in view of Augustine's view of the *populus* proposed in Appendix A, does the imperialist position seem more legitimately Augustinian? Or is the startling *populus* of Manegold of Lautenbach, awakening to a dangerous consciousness of its sovereign rights, the true heir returning after centuries of enforced barbarian childhood? To put it both more generally and less captiously, I hope that this study will prove to be useful to continuing discussion of the whole ideological clash brilliantly presented by Henri-Xavier Arquillière in *L'Augustinisme politique,* which is, in fact, the book that first prompted me to think that some of the key terminology appearing in all those contrary positions could stand some exhaustive examination at their common source.

To leave Augustine briefly for the neglected Jerome, I like to entertain the hope that this study may contribute in some small way to a rehabilitation of Jerome as an object of dispassionate study by scholars other than scripture specialists. The continuing but rather desultory debate about Jerome's worth as a translator extends itself easily and validly into a discussion of his abilities as a biblical scholar; unfortunately, that line of discussion bends all too easily to disputes about his competence as a contemporary theologian and a writer—which tend to lack perspective—and finally to recriminations about Jerome as a human being—which lose scholarly justification but still attract small squadrons of licensed intellectuals whose opposing battle-cries have been elaborated by Hans von Campenhausen and Jean Steinmann. I trust that chapter 3 of the present study will suggest a number of ways in which this sort of analysis can affect (dare I say enlighten?) all those levels of discussion.

This study can provide items of useful information for questions yet farther from its central inquiry. One example from this fourth ring of relevance is the theme of progress in Augustine's works.[3] This is just one of numerous intellectual paternities that modern thinkers have alleged of him, and in this case as well as others provable intent is the prime issue. As usual, it is possible to find in his works theoretical statements about human progress which tend to opposite conclusions, and so the debate goes on.

Consequently, demonstrable habit becomes germane: this study contains clear evidence of his assumption that mankind had progressed in military competence (*CD* xviii, 22; cf. p. 44 above) and in general public education (*CD* xxii, 7–8; cf. p. 57 above) since the Flood. Neither of those assumptions is central to this study's concerns, but each seems a reasonable, consistent complement to the patterns of thought and usage with which it is concerned, and since each appears in its own right as a coherent, easily documented attitude of Augustine's, students of his thought on human progress might well find these and similar by-products of this study centrally relevant to their own interests and conclusions.

Comparison with Isidore of Seville

All four of these rings of relevance stand out in sharper relief when we take a bearing on Isidore of Seville's employment of the noun *populus* two hundred years later.

As I have argued elsewhere, Isidore handled that word quite differently than had Augustine and Jerome, both of whom he declared to be his masters. He defined it very strictly, going behind his masters' master to the tradition of pre-Ciceronian grammarians. This fastidious antiquarianism, not too startling on the part of a Hispano-Roman aristocrat in charge of the Visigothic monarchy's attempt to inaugurate a cultural revival, is clearly expressed in the *Differentiae* (1, 445, 450, 472), a vocabulary manual composed around 598, and in his mature monument, the *Etymologiae* (cf. v, 5 and 10; ix, 4, 5–7), completed by 620.

Much of Isidore's usage of the word *populus* is in accordance with this conservative definition, narrower in scope than Augustine's. However, most of his usage refuses to follow suit; in the apparent majority of instances, Isidore's *populus* is a vague, rather characterless group, not unlike the group represented by attribute no. 13 in the tabulation of Appendix B, a peripheral usage somewhat more frequent in Jerome's works than in Augustine's. This *populus*, quite close in its loose polysemy to the modern Spanish *pueblo* or English *people*, seems in Isidore's usage to serve as a frequent synonym to *gens*. The latter noun has become for Isidore a word with much stronger emotional charge in political contexts, and has even taken on a legal, constitutional character. As in the Visigothic law codes, it is the *gens* against which one commits treason. *Gens* enjoys a closer relationship with the *regnum* than does its satellite *populus;* the *populi* with most lively civic consciousness are the local Christian congregations, which one is sometimes tempted to translate as "dioceses."

This grammatical reversal of position reflects a profound change in Isidore's society and in the political realities of the Spanish government. Try as it did to imitate and outdo Byzantine *Romanitas,* the Visigothic kingdom was fundamentally (and, as events were soon to prove, fatally) the *res* of a Germanic *gens.* This shift of usage is all the more revealing for having been, apparently, quite unconscious on Isidore's part.

Basic Contribution

I hope that a glance at such different results (however brief and however distant) will make the various issues situated around the arcs of the four rings of synthetic relevance emanating from the present study appear in sharper perspective and in clearer relationship to this study's core results. I recognize that the orbits farthest from that center of attraction may exercise the greatest attraction for most of this study's potential readers. I accept this disparity with regret but without any sense of cosmic incongruity. Mercury is less interesting to most of us than the moons of Saturn, and for some of us our single moon has none of the allure exercised by the several satellites of that well-ringed, quite inaccessible outer planet. But I think it is now time to abandon this drift of rotational metaphors, including the four intellectual rings from which it got started. None of them should obscure the fact that the basic contribution which this study seeks to make is one of method, designed for use by generations of scholars yet unformed, and for whole families of questions not yet conceived by their perverse professional fertility.

Appendix A
Augustine's Definitions of *Populus* and the Value of Civil Society

Augustine's two definitions of *populus* in books II and XIX of *The City of God* have caused considerable stirring among historians of ideas since the First World War, thanks to an assumption that the difference between them may represent a major split either in Augustine's thought about the state or between his thought and that of his Greco-Roman predecessors.

Several scholars from several national traditions have addressed themselves to that apparent split, and the argument among them has taken on a bewildering variety of issues. I think, however, that two steady questions can be discerned beneath the Protean elusiveness of the debate:

1. Are the two definitions fundamentally opposed?
2. Does Augustine in the final analysis see any moral value in civil society?

The following summary will review several scholarly interpretations according to their stand on the first question; this question has rarely, if ever, been answered without benefit of a decision on the second question. The following lineup of authorities does not pretend to be exhaustive, but I hope that it will indicate the range of opinions and traditions party to the controversy.

Prominent among the scholars who have concluded that the two definitions are significantly opposed are John Neville Figgis, Norman H. Baynes, Sergio Cotta, A. J. Carlyle, and Charles H. McIlwain.

Figgis argued in 1921 that Augustine rejected the stock Ciceronian definition of the state (as most English-speaking authors have translated *res publica*) because he saw that it did not fit the political facts of life, and based his new definition on empirical principles, which he discerned and followed with a ruthless realism that would not be surpassed until Hobbes's time (*The Political Aspects of S. Augustine's "City of God,"* pp. 59–67). Baynes saw individualism rather than empiricism as the signal intellectual virtue in this decision of Augustine's; his departure from Cicero was a consequence of "his individualistic viewpoint" which "declines to regard the State as an entity independent of those who compose it" (*The Political Ideas of St. Augustine's "De Civitate Dei,"* Historical Association Pamphlet, no. 104, pp. 7–8, 11; reprinted in his *Byzantine Studies and Other Essays,* pp. 288–306).

Less interested in those British virtues, Sergio Cotta saw Augustine's originality as a triumph of descriptive over prescriptive reasoning in political philosophy. Writing a quarter-century after Baynes, he saw Augustine's definition-play not as a mere apologetic exercise, but as an integral product of his descriptive insight about society, which naturally rejected "la linea di pensiero giusnaturalistica" of practically all classical authorities, and informed his definitions of *civitas* and *regnum* as well (*La città politica di sant'Agostino,* pp. 24–39, 52–53).

Closer to Figgis and Baynes in time as well as in intellectual categories were the Scotsman Carlyle and the American McIlwain. Both agreed that Augustine had struck off into new territory with the second definition, but they disagreed rather violently about the value of that originality. Carlyle was almost scandalized by the negative character of Augustine's abandonment of the rest of Stoic and patristic tradition in this regard. As he put it in a short essay:

> Whether St. Augustine realised the enormous significance of what he was saying may be doubted; this definition [*CD* XIX, 24] is indeed practically the definition of Cicero, but with the element of law and justice left out, and no more fundamental difference could well be imagined, for Cicero's whole conception of the State turns upon this principle, that it is a means for attaining and preserving justice. ["St. Augustine and the City of God," *The Social and Political Ideas of Some Great Mediaeval Thinkers,* ed. F. J. C. Hearnshaw, p. 50.]

In the monumental *History of Mediaeval Political Theory in the West,* Carlyle had concluded that the second definition was not "a casual or isolated judgment of St. Augustine, corrected perhaps at other times." Referring to other passages in which the political importance of justice is asserted in terms not very alien to those of the older tradition, Carlyle declared that such agreement with Cicero on Augustine's part must be understood in the light of Augustine's "theological conception of justice—a conception which might be regarded as true upon his premises, but which can only be understood as related to those premises (1:164–70, esp. 167–68).

Harvard's McIlwain seemed quite pleased by Augustine's boldness.

He asserted that Augustine's argument in *CD* II, 21 and XIX, 21 "is a *reductio ad absurdum* indeed, but it is the absurdity of heathenism not of Cicero's definition which Augustine means to prove" (*The Growth of Political Thought in the West, from the Greeks to the End of the Middle Ages,* pp. 154–59, esp. p. 157). After close analysis of the terms *civitas* and *regnum* in the famous passage likening empires to large-scale brigandage (*CD* IV, 4) and in *CD* XV, 8, McIlwain concluded that for Augustine, "Justice and justice alone is the only possible bond which can unite men as a true *populus* in a real *res publica.*" Great pagan states had indeed been true *civitates* and *regna,* "but none of them, admirable as some were in other respects, could ever be a true *populus,* its association and its government could never rise to the height of a real *res populi* or *res publica; . . .* No heathen state can ever rise quite to the height of a true commonwealth" (ibid., pp. 158–59). The alternative definition in *CD* XIX, 24 is simply a rhetorical device: notice the clause *"velut si dicatur"* which introduces it. Unfortunately, McIlwain simply dismissed Augustine's outright validation of the *populi* and *res publicae* "of the Athenians, those of any other Greeks, of the Egyptians, of that earlier Babylon of the Assyrians, and of any other *gens* whatsoever" on the grounds that the definition which that validation follows is simply a debating trick. If that is so, how does he account for the phrase *"Secundum probabiliores autem definitiones"* which announces that second definition way back in II, 21? It is almost as though he had not read the few extra lines necessary.

McIlwain's argument probably represents the respectable limit of the opinion that Augustine's two definitions were really at variance. Most of the scholars sharing that view have also concluded that Augustine thereby indicated his low opinion (to put it mildly) of earthly institutions not redeemed by grace. That set of positions has come under strong attack, although most scholars who try to reconcile the two definitions have had to base their cases on distinctions of a fairly ingenious character.

In 1934, Carl-Victor von Horn asserted:

Wichtig ist, ehe man sich an die Betrachtung der Textstelle heranmacht, festzustellen, dass Augustin hier [*CD* XIX, 21] nicht den Staatscharakter eines Staates ohne Gerechtigkeit leugnet, sondern über ihn nur ein abfälliges Werturteil spricht. Aber dies ist in der Literatur zuweilen nicht recht gesehen worden. [*Beiträge zur Staatslehre St. Augustins nach "De civitate Dei,"* pp. 26–32, esp. p. 29.]

Taken at face value, this is rather like saying, "Augustine meant that the unjust state was not just, not that it was not a state." Such a statement may reproduce the final impression of the *Textstelle* in which both definitions appear, but it evades the actual wording of the first definition. Von Horn then went on to argue that Augustine did not so much strike justice out of his new definition of the state as add to it another basis of concord, one which involved a fundamentally similar interest.

The German-trained American Jesuit, Morehouse F. X. Millar, addressed himself to the exact language of the first definition and attacked Carlyle's position on it quite directly, with the aid of a genuine and erudite distinction. In "The Significance of St. Augustine's Criticism of Cicero's Definition of the State," *Philosophia Perennis* 1:99–109, Millar maintained that Augustine's and Cicero's definitions depended on very similar standards of political value. Cicero's Stoic-pantheist conception of justice had just as much "theological bias" as Augustine's Judeo-Christian premises; Augustine's real difference from Cicero lay in his reassertion of a very traditional Roman distinction between the absolute, rational *ius naturale* and purely conventional "temporal" laws. In stressing the relevance to earthly society of the latter type of *ius,* Augustine was indicating that social justice was a matter of multilateral relationships as well as (indeed, rather than) a question of abstract, unilateral, or bilateral intention. On a more general level, the formula proposed in *CD* xix, 24 bears the double principle that "society is natural" but the "concrete state has its basis equally in convention." So Millar recognized some personal empiricism as well as a sophisticated fidelity to Cicero in Augustine's proposing a second definition, and he saw no drastic rejection of civil society among its consequences.

Herbert A. Deane of Columbia University launched quite recently the most comprehensive attack on the tradition running from Figgis to Cotta in the course of his devastating rebuttal of McIlwain's argument in *The Political and Social Ideas of St. Augustine,* pp. 118–29, esp. pp. 120–26. Through careful analysis of *CD* iv, 4 and of several other passages in Augustine's works which McIlwain failed to consider, he shows that McIlwain's position was more artful than sound, and that the definition in xix, 24 is entirely consistent with: (a) Augustine's distinction between *vera iustitia* and the "image of justice found in temporal states"; and (b) his fundamental preoccupation with the unitive power of love, whether divinely inspired or only on the level of selfish interest. I find Deane's argument thoroughly convincing, and only regret that, like almost all commentators on this now-famous pair of definitions, he was not able to look more deeply into the rich im-

plications of Augustine's wider usage of *populus*. Deane does not deny
the gap between the definitions. He minimizes it by saying that it corresponds to a distinction found throughout Augustine's work between
two kinds of justice which, in the last analysis (or in the mind of
God) merge into one; more valuably, in my opinion, he tries to shift
attention away from justice to another moral good (both individual
and social) which he sees as more fundamental to Augustine's total
system of thought.

Several continental scholars had argued along those lines, partly
looking for a prior or higher basis on which to reconcile the definitions,
partly trying to shift the emphasis from justice.

Before the First World War, Ernst Troeltsch firmly maintained that
for all his realism about politics, Augustine never really discarded the
notion that human society was based on some kind of natural law
(*Soziallehren der Christlichen Kirchen und Gruppen*, 1912; see Olive
Wyon's translation, *The Social Teaching of the Christian Churches*,
1:151–52, 155–58, and n. 75). In 1926 Edgar Salin concluded, not unlike
Carlyle and McIlwain, that the second definition was "für den Augen-
blick geformt und Augustinus hat an seinen Wortlaut sich niemals
gebunden," but instead of either dismissing or stressing the novelty of
the definition so conceived, he argued that it represented simply a
Christian variation on the notion of *Gemeinsamkeit* common to Greek
and Roman as well (*Civitas Dei*, pp. 186–87). After the Second World
War, Domenico Pesce discussed the two definitions against the background of classical political thought and concluded that Augustine's departure from Cicero achieved both an interiorization of Cicero's doctrine and a recovery of the level of values which had distinguished
Plato. Pesce admits that Augustine's transformation of Cicero's definition risks becoming "dal punto di visto del valore, neutra," but since
his specific contribution to the older definition was a strong emphasis
on the social role of will, "si passa, nei confronti della concezione
ciceroniana, dell'esterno all'interno, dal piano giuridico a quello etico,
dalle azioni alle intenzione, dalla legge alla determinazione della
volontà o cioè appunto all'amore, ond'è che al concetto di stato (*res
publica*) si sostituisce quello di società (*civitas*)." [*Città terrena e città
celeste nel pensiero antico: Platone, Cicerone, S. Agostino*, pp. 150–60,
esp. p. 153.] Despite the apparent willingness to abandon *populus* and
the wording of the definition itself, Pesce reasserts the unity of both
formulas, which end up in his view returning to the solemn authority
of Plato's hierarchical conception of justice, and hence anything but a
rejection of previous classical tradition. A few years later, Paolo Brezzi

stated this general position in more moderate, accessible terms. Summarizing the views of several other authors, he pointed out that the difference between the two definitions "non esclude ovviamente che la *vera iustitia* (come altrove Agostino chiama quella che si riferisce a Dio —e l'aggettivo è in questo caso davvero qualificativo al massimo) possa completare ed integrare, attraverso l'amore, il precedente tipo di giustizia umana. . ." After all, since Augustine's argument springs from a consideration of human nature, its content and import have to be ethico-rational, and in some way akin to justice of some sort (*Analisi ed interpretazione del "De Civitate Dei" di sant'Agostino*, Quaderni della Cattedra Agostiniana, no. 2, Tolentino, 1960, pp. 47–50). Brezzi's argument reduces to a sort of lowest common denominator the previous attempts to substitute some other social virtue or value for justice in this pair of equations.

Deane's choice of unitive love as the substitute seems most solidly grounded in Augustine's own theory; one can also find areas of congruence for justice and love more easily than for justice and *Gemeinsamkeit*, "the natural-law tradition," or even will (related as it is to love in Augustinian psychology). In this stress on love, Deane joins the tendency of French scholarship, which has not been as impressed by the differences between the two definitions as by the elements underlying both. In his *thèse* of 1927, for example, Gustave Combès saw the two definitions primarily as an opportunity to insist on the eminently spiritual nature of the harmony which Augustine saw unifying all forms of society (*La doctrine politique de Saint Augustin,* pp. 106–07, 109–12).

A quarter-century later, Henri-Xavier Arquillière shifted the center of emphasis to *pax* in his acute analysis of the question of justice in Augustinian social thought, especially as regards these two definitions. He affirms that justice, far from being rejected as a social value, is indeed the central idea of all twenty-two books of *The City of God*. To be sure, Augustine's treatment of it is predominantly in the evangelical terms "dont saint Paul a fait la théologie," but the purpose of his concern with that quality in the two definitions of *populus* is to reassert "la valeur légitime de l'Etat . . . dans toutes les nations antiques" (*L'Augustinisme politique,* 2d ed., Paris, 1955, p. 38). How can a justice so theologically conceived be operative in societies ignorant of and even hostile to God? Because of Providence, all-important to Augustine's view of these matters, and because they managed to achieve a certain degree of internal *pax,* a quality closely related to justice. In any case, Arquillière maintains that Augustine intended no rigorous opposition between the kinds of societies best suited by those two definitions (ibid., pp. 65–71).

In 1952, Gustave Bardy wrote two brief but important notes on the two definitions for the Bibliothèque Augustinienne edition of *The City of God* (*BA* 37:753–55, 759–60). He decided that the second definition represented Augustine's normal and basic thought on the legitimate rights of civil society—the alternative attitude would be obviously absurd in the practical order to which he was seriously committed. What, then, was the point of the first definition? It was an occasion for discussing justice in the abstract; it represents a successful Christianization of the lofty Platonic (as opposed to more pragmatic Roman) conception of justice; and it supported in a memorable formula Augustine's major contention in *The City of God* that states decline when their morals decay. So both definitions are basically about the state (rather than about justice), and the fact that the first explores the higher theoretical reaches of the problem of justice does not deny that quality's normal relationship to normal political life. What Anglo-Saxon scholar has exercised more common sense in coping with this Augustinian conundrum?

In the Cardinal Mercier Lectures at Louvain that same year, Etienne Gilson discussed the pair of definitions, but bypassed the interpretative tangle which I have summarized. Arguing that Augustine rejected both the traditional pagan conception of political society *and* the rigorist consequences of such a rejection, he concentrated his attention on the biblical sources of Augustine's notion *populus* and on the applicability of the model so derived to the Roman experience and to other varieties of secular polity (*Les métamorphoses de la Cité de Dieu*, pp. 38–46). In citing these judicious pages which indicate what I consider the most fruitful direction for further discussions of this sector of Augustine's political thought, I cannot help remembering the very different but in one sense complementary remark made by Troeltsch in 1915, before the dispute about the definitions' relationship got well under way:

Die Augustinische Ethik hat nicht bloss wie alle Väter die durchschnittliche wissenschaftliche Bildung und die politisch-soziale Wirklichkeit aufgenommen, sondern als einer der Führer hat Augustin die christliche und die stoisch-neuplatonische Religiosität verschmolzen und die politisch-soziale Theorie des antiken Naturrechts und der Ciceronianischen Staatsphilosophie in starker christlicher Umfärbung sich angeeignet. Und alles das hat er in einem grossen ethischen System des höchsten Gutes gegliedert um den Gedanken der christlichen Seligkeit und Gottesliebe. Aber das war weder eine neue Kultur . . . [*Augustin, die christliche Antike und das Mittelalter: Im Anschluss an die Schrift "De civitate Dei,"* p. 158; cf. pp. 146–49.]

Unlike Gilson's more extended discussion, this statement is as idealist, abstract, and synthetic as one might expect; yet in its own way it too concentrates on the historical antecedents and consequences of the ideas considered.

One might wish that these two treatments nearly forty years apart would put to rest the definition controversy, but a quick glance at the publication dates of the arguments reviewed above shows that almost the opposite has happened. Perhaps that is justifiable, since the central problem has not really been resolved, even by Deane's well-documented and persuasive distinctions. Since none of the previous attempts to solve that problem have been able to rely on a very wide sample of the crucial terms, I venture now to propose yet another solution, based partly on a new method.

I see no need to recast the problem, although restating it in the hope of refining it somewhat through paraphrase may be of use. I prefer to translate *res publica* as "civil society" rather than as "state," however. As the problem has concerned most of the scholars cited above, it consists of two questions:

1. Are the two definitions ultimately opposed or reconcilable? In other words, does Augustine take one position or two on this issue?

2. Is, therefore, civil society inherently legitimate in Augustine's opinion? Unredeemed by the pervading presence of the City of God, or considered in the abstract, aside from the presence or absence of any such transforming influence—as Bardy points out, Augustine occasionally indulged in such speculation—is civil society morally good (at least potentially), or irretrievably vicious? In other words, does civil society possess any inherent moral validity, and philosophically respectable legitimacy?

How should we tackle such a question? Augustine himself shows us one way, which most of the scholars cited above have for some reason preferred to ignore: that is, through analysis of the logically decisive terms of a speculative definition. I suspect that Augustine would have been rather surprised at all the flurry caused by his dialectical (not rhetorical) device fifteen centuries later, and I think that close atten-

tion to his method of argument and to his general usage of the obviously cardinal term in that argument enables us to recapture his
intent.

To answer the first question, I think that the two definitions are
not only reconcilable, but end up being one, in the sense that the
second absorbs the first. Its terms include the terms of the former definition by an extension of their scope. Stated second, it becomes logically
prior. I have stated this contention in chapter 2 of this study (see pp.
19–20); it may be useful to paraphrase it briefly here in relation to some
of the previous interpretations cited in this appendix. My argument, in
its most narrow statement, is this: If a *populus* of the type outlined in
the second definition agrees to love ethical standards of sufficient lofti-
ness as revealed by the true God, it can hardly help but meet the requirements of the most rigorist interpretation of the first definition.
Such is the achievement of the *populus Dei,* the *res publica Christi.*
Carlyle emphasized the difference between the two definitions because
he thought that Augustine thought that an earthly society could never
match on its own level the definition—synthesizing achievement of
the *populus Dei;* Carlyle's own focus was exclusively on earthly society
(only one aspect, after all, of the "political theory" arising from Augustine's speculation) and on explicit reference to *ius* or *iustitia.* But even
within those limitations of the problem, is it not at least arguable that
the language of the second definition contains the terms of the first, on
the condition that some *consensus iuris* and some agreement about the
nature of *utilitas* are among the *res quas diligit populus?* Carlyle does
not seem to have considered that the question could be posed in this
manner. Neither does McIlwain, who, in his eagerness to defend the
importance of justice to Augustine's conception of *res publica,* simply
dismissed the second definition. Deane's drawing of a distinction between two kinds of justice, a view of Augustine's intention previously
expressed by John O'Meara (*Charter of Christendom: The Significance
of the "City of God,"* pp. 96–101), would lend strong support to my
contention that the two definitions are really two dimensions of one
"definition," although neither of the last two authors puts it that way.

I agree with Bardy (rather than with McIlwain) that the first definition is the clever device, although I think the device of a pair of definitions derives from dialectical rather than from rhetorical method. It
seems to me that Augustine is indulging here in a dialogue between
definitions, making the first statement the contrary, piquant incitement
to discuss, and the second statement the sober reply. The first statement
is set in the heart of a paradox, which Augustine half disowns after

developing its consequences, by promising the reader a *probabilior* treatment of *populus,* the heart of the definition at the heart of the paradox. This dialogue is not a dialectical triad, since it has no third term. The absence of that sort of reassuring capping statement has been perhaps the most disturbing thing about these definitions to our post-Hegelian scholarly world. Why did Augustine leave his dialogue hanging (or is it only we modern interpreters who are caught in that embarrassing position)?

Perhaps because the first definition was designed to fit a paradox so obvious that it did not need to be solemnly described as such. I think that McIlwain is correct in seeing that part of the argument as a *reductio ad absurdum,* and that both he and Bardy are right in referring to Augustine's rhetorical habits in that connection. Marrou has pointed out the unique importance for Augustine of the rhetorical figure of antithesis: "C'est chez lui un mode d'expression si caractéristique qu'on ne peut se contenter de l'inventorier parmi les procédés d'élocution empruntés à l'arsenal de la rhétorique classique: c'est un rythme fondamental qui domine non seulement les mots mais la pensée elle-même; il apparaît lié à la structure même de son esprit" (*Saint Augustin et la fin de la culture classique,* p. 659; cf. pp. 79–80). However, in matching (and topping) the first definition with the second, Augustine moved to the sphere of dialectical discourse, a calmer atmosphere of argument, more conducive to loosely ranging discussion, with a set of conventions quite different from the cut-and-dried rules appropriate to polemic disputation originally developed in the courtroom or the forum rather than in the garden or the banquet chamber. Instead of reducing his opponent to absurdity wtih the intention of leaving him in that state of blatant confusion, Augustine in book xix is in a mood rather like that of his dialogues with his son or his old friends. In that context of "argument" the master's technique is to absorb and advance the statements of his interlocutors rather than to rebut them. Polite recognition of the evident truth by all the civilized participants is the tone properly concluding such a discussion.

If we insist on recasting that late-antique discussion in terms more sympathetic to our modes of argument—and much modern scholarship insists on such recasting—then I propose a loose syllogism oriented to the second basic question elaborated above. It goes like this:

Major proposition: No civil society is valid unless it is a *populus* (i.e., has justice);

Minor proposition: But most (or normal) civil societies are *populi* (because they are unified by love);

Conclusion: Therefore most (or normal) civil societies are valid. The two-term dialectic of definitions operates within or alongside this structure, by changing the scope and hence the name of the essential constituent of a *populus.* Of course Augustine does not state the conclusion to this pseudosyllogism, just as he does not turn his dialogue of definitions into a dialectical triad. But we should be resigned to his maddening habits by now, and might do well to consider William Empson's observation, in *The Structure of Complex Words,* that "Aristotle, for that matter, pointed out that a syllogism might be regarded as a redefinition followed by a tautology" (p. 40). We can be grateful that the presence of a *populus* necessitates the presence of a valid civil society both in this syllogism and in Augustine's own statement of the rigorist paradox in *CD* II, 21. Consequently, if we wish to find out whether Augustine thought civil societies of a valid character were a widespread phenomenon or not (i.e., if we wish to establish the minor proposition), we simply have to see what sorts of society he calls *populi.* This step depends for some of its force on the premise that his usage is generally consistent with the pair of definitions, but I hope chapter 2 has established that consistency adequately.

Selecting as a sample only the work in which these definitions appear, *The City of God,* we can easily see that Augustine is faithful to the remarks about the *populi* and the *res publicae* of the Romans, Greeks, Egyptians, Assyrians, and others with which he concluded XIX, 24. A glance at columns A-H in the tabulations of Appendix B will show that Rome and other Gentile societies qualify normally for the designation *populus,* and that in books I–X such *populi* far outnumber the *populi* of Israel or the Church. Book X is something of a pivot in that regard; although *populus* is a rare word in the four books immediately following, it picks up with book XV as predominantly Israelite or Elect, in which guise it first appears massively in book X. It continues in that guise until book XIX. In the definition-dominated chapters of that book, *populus* is usually either matter-of-factly Roman or abstractly neutral rather than Jewish, Christian, or viciously Gentile. The last three books are a toss-up in regard to that noun's application, although the contemporary Church appears as a *populus* with abnormal frequency in XXII. This very sketchy summary should suffice to indicate how many quite different societies all seemed to be *populi* to Augustine, and hence probably seemed to possess the appropriate quotient of inherent legitimacy.

If further proof-texts are required, I suggest two: the last sentence of XIX, 24 and most of X, 13.

At the very end of developing his second definition, Augustine adds a final sentence insisting on the validity of his critique of pagan society uttered ten years before in II, 21: "In general, however, the *civitas impiorum* does not obey God's command to sacrifice to none beside Himself, and for that reason the mind does not rightly and faithfully command the body in its midst, nor the reason the vices, and so it lacks true justice (*caret iustitiae veritate*)."

If this qualifying remark seems to negate all the foregoing argument about reconciling the two definitions, we should take careful note of two choices of wording:

1. The evil, unjust society here is called a *civitas*, not a *populus*, and is singular and universal. It should be identified with the Other City of the damned, that transcendent society, rather than with any specific historical state. And if Augustine had intended to reconstruct his original paradox, why did he choose *civitas* instead of *populus*, the unmistakably cardinal term in that paradox? It is worth noting that he makes the same shift of terminology in the final sentence of II, 21, just after expressing his concern about current usage of that key term (see chapter 2, p. 21).

2. To say that even such a society lacks *iustitiae veritas* is not quite equivalent to saying that it lacks *iustitia* or even *vera iustitia*. Both Bardy and Deane have remarked the rather elaborate character of this formulation (brief though it is). As in the case of *civitas impiorum*, Augustine's choice of wording seems to be both careful and an indication that he is not just repeating himself again in either thought or vocabulary.

Book x, chapter 13 of *The City of God* seems to me an eloquent piece of evidence that Augustine attributed at least a limited degree of genuine moral probity to historical societies not favored by divine revelation. Book x terminates and culminates the (near-) half of *The City of God* which is dedicated to refuting the values of the pagans. From chapter 8 on, Augustine pays a great deal of attention to the *populus Israel*, which will dominate much of the second (more-than-) half of the work. Five chapters later, Augustine returns to that *populus*, the model of true worship before Christ, the spiritual ancestor of true worshipers since. But even that chosen people, Augustine remarks, needed to have its unique law promulgated in unforgettably dramatic fashion:

Cum igitur oporteret Dei legem in edictis angelorum terribiliter dari, non uni homini paucisve sapientibus, sed universae genti et populo ingenti: coram eodem populo magna facta sunt in monte, ubi lex per unum dabatur, conspiciente multitudine metuenda ac tremenda quae fiebant. Non enim populus Israel sic Moysi credidit, quem ad modum suo Lycurgo Lacedaemonii, quod a Iove seu Apolline leges, quas condidit, accepisset. Cum enim lex dabatur populo, qua coli unus iubebatur Deus, in conspectu ipsius populi, quantum sufficere divina providentia iudicabat, mirabilibus rerum signis ac motibus apparebat ad eandem legem dandam creatori servire creaturam.

Here we see not only a passage heightened by rhyme and rhythm in its prose, but also most of the elements of either definition of *populus* in three sentences containing five appearances of that word. We can tell that a *populus* is (as it should be) a multitude of human beings unified by their concentrated, acutely alert attention to the spectacular effects surrounding the promulgation of their law, which as the reader knows was a law containing "civil" and "religious" regulations as well as an ultimate moral code, and endowing those who were faithful to it with an extraordinary inheritance and destiny. All five appearances of *populus* refer directly to Israel, but in the midst of them appears another group: the Lacedaemonians who surpassed the *populus Israel* in ready responsiveness when they received from Lycurgus a law said to derive from their false gods. Presumably that law was flawed in some ways besides its prescription of idolatry, but if that was the case Augustine surely does not stress it here. If he had applied a common noun to these Lacedaemonians instead of their proper name, what would he have called them?

An answer to that rhetorical question is less important than an appreciation of this group's role in this context. If I may be permitted another quasi-syllogism, I submit that this passage and this virtual *populus* occupy a middle position dialectically as well as spatially between the two definitions of *populus,* of which the former is hostile to pagan society and the latter tolerant. In II, 21 Augustine maintains that only *populi* worshiping the true God could be true *populi;* in x, 13 he remarks that some Gentile societies have in fact been truer to their false gods than Israel was to God Himself; and so we should be prepared to find in XIX, 24 that Augustine has shifted the emphasis of his critique from objective to subjective judgment.

I hope that Augustine would not object too strenuously to this latter-day, synthetic syllogism with *three* terms. I am fairly sure that he would find nothing inappropriate in the empirical character of the historical observation which constitutes the middle term.

Appendix B
Content-Analysis Tables for *Populus* in *The City of God* and for *Gens* in Books xv–xviii

The purpose of the tables which follow is to provide a technique for the statistical analysis of the use of the word *populus* in *The City of God*. The first two columns of the table register the book and chapter of each occurrence of *populus*. The columns numbered 1–13 register the identifiable presence (or absence) in each occurrence of certain attributes, properties, or features associated with that word in Augustine's works. Columns A–H cover the range of specific groups to which that word may be applied in his works. The final column ("Remarks") notes references to the sources of quotations included in the text, as well as occasional observations which may be useful either to clarify a point or to indicate passages of special interest. The appearances of *gens* in books xv–xviii have been similarly recorded in order to provide further comparative basis for part of the analysis attempted in this study.

The text of *The City of God* used is basically that of the Maurist edition reprinted by Gaume Frères—cited in this study as *SAOO*—but compared with (and when necessary corrected by) the text published as vols. 33–37 of *Oeuvres de St. Augustin* (Bibiothèque Augustinienne —cited in this study as *BA*). The latter text reproduces the fourth edition of B. Dombart and A. Kalb (Bibliotheca Teubneriana, Leipzig, 1928–29), but notes the principal variants with the Maurist text as reprinted by Migne and the text appearing as vols. 47 and 48 of *Corpus Christianorum, Series latina*. In view of the variety of authoritative texts available to the reader, I have not included references to pagination.

In general I have followed the frequency table compiled by J. J. R. Rosado in *La Ciudad de Dios* 167 (1954): 420–51. In only a few instances have I been unable to locate occurrences of the word which he reports, or found occurrences which he overlooked. I follow H.-I. Marrou in attributing the wording of chapter titles to Augustine him-

APPENDIX B

self, on the basis both of their antiquity in the manuscript tradition
and of style (see "La division en chapitres des livres de *La Cité de
Dieu*," *Mélanges Joseph de Ghellinck, S. J.*, 1:237–39, 243–45). Marrou
argues that the chapter titles appeared originally as a long index, and
did not interrupt the long flow of chapters within the subtly orches-
trated composition-unit of each book, as they do in most medieval and
modern editions (see also *Saint Augustin et la fin de la culture antique*,
pp. 671–72). By reporting all appearances of *populus* (and *gens*) in
those titles within parentheses, but at the head of each chapter concerned, this tabulation seeks a compromise between Marrou's persuasive
argument and the contrary but quite standard current editorial practice.
Citations from Scripture and from pagan authors have been marked
separately, especially when introduced by an *inquit* or similar formula
(VI, 5), but not when absorbed by a *dixit . . . esse* or comparable construction (the first two *populi* of II, 21).

The attributes (or properties or features) selected for tabulation in
the columns numbered 1–13 will need some explanation. Columns 1–7
refer to attributes which are normally and coherently associated with
the word in Augustine's usage; columns 8–13 refer to features either
unusual in frequency or logically in conflict with any of the first seven.
A solid triangle appears under those headings when I consider that the
attribute in question is explicitly present in that appearance of the
word, a hollow triangle when I feel that it is involved by implication.
Solid and hollow squares register in similar fashion any application of
populus or *gens* to the specific groups or classes of groups designated
by the letters A–H (A–I in the *gens* table). Solid and hollow circles
register both attributes and applications of any appearances of *populus*
and *gens* in source citations. I hope that this variation of geometric
symbols will aid the reader in a visual appreciation of the patterns indicated, without implying an excessive differentiation of intent on
Augustine's part.

A slightly different presentation would be required to prepare the
data recorded in this table for the electronic computer. Although the
present system has been designed for the viewer's convenience, it is
capable of swift translation into a computer program. Only such a
translation would exploit these data fully. Once the cards were
punched, one could quickly get answers to such questions as: Was the
Roman *populus* more concerned with law or with policy than the
Jewish *populus* in Augustine's mind, and did his sense of the historical
disparity of these concerns change over the years in which he composed
The City of God?

Attributes

1. SOCIAL TOTALITY, or multiclass character: The *populus* in question is a group consisting of several social classes or cutting across class lines.
2. ADEQUATE SIZE: The *populus* in question is a *multitudo,* a group of respectable though unspecified numbers.
3. SIMPLE UNITY: This is a special characteristic of the group which to most modern readers may appear a tautologous consideration, since most of these attributes are unifying features anyway. However, Augustine occasionally stresses the importance to a properly constituted *populus* of an ontological unity which will not appear incongruous to readers tolerant of Plotinian categories. "Da unum, et populus est: tolle unum, et turba est." *Sermo* 203; cf. pp. 35–36 of this study.
4. RATIONAL ASSENT, or moral character: The *populus* in question is a group of rational beings who consent to or reject actions of a moral character. (How many human actions lacked that character in Augustine's mind?)
5. POLICY: Some action of political or religious significance—war, migration, worship, etc.—which is often, but not always, the object of the consensus or moral response involved in no. 4. It may seem desirable to classify separately the political and religious aspects of such a group's action, as does R. T. Marshall (cf. p. 14 above, esp. note 6). I began this tabulation recording such a distinction, but soon abandoned the attempt as hopeless. Not just a wasteful duplication, it required too many subjective decisions: How does one assess the "explicitly" or "implicitly" "political" or "religious" character of Israel's conquest of Canaan, or the Roman practice of *evocatio* (by which an army commander wooed away the gods of a hostile city or army)? It became very clear to me that Augustine's mind rarely separated church and state, at least not on the level of vocabulary deployment.
6. LAW: This can be political or religious, as above; also doctrine or ideology related to the fundamental laws of the group. Once again, how does one neatly separate the juridical and doctrinal aspects of the Mosaic Law (unless discussed in close detail, as Augustine rarely does), or of Roman legislation concerning the cult of the emperor's *genius* (cf. J. Bayet, *Histoire politique et psychologique de la religion romaine,* pp. 277–79)?

7. DESTINY: This applies especially in the sense of divine promise or prophetic consciousness thereof.

8. GENETIC ASSOCIATION: The group in question is unified by the fact or myth of common physical descent.

9. LINGUISTIC ASSOCIATION: The group in question is characterized by a common language, which may or may not be its exclusive property.

10. TERRITORIAL ASSOCIATION: This is sometimes very important to a group's cohesion, sometimes not too relevant. Canaan and Attica were in certain periods essential to the self-definition of Jews and of Athenians, but at other times became only sentimentally important.

11. LOWER-CLASS STATUS: The *populus* in question is one of the less-favored classes of a larger society, like the "common people" in English—a minor but steady usage in the works of Cicero. This feature conflicts directly with no. 1; in a very few instances I have placed a hollow circle in both columns, because the case seemed unclear. In several instances I have done so to indicate that the *populus* in question consists of several classes but is distinct from a small elite group in regard to some common policy (e.g., those *populi* of book VI who are the vast majority of Roman citizens left in enthusiastic superstitious ignorance by a tiny group of sophisticated priests or philosophers; similarly, the audience in theaters).

12. OTHER ATTRIBUTES: This did not turn out to be a useful heading, but I have left it in the table for possible future use and because that uselessness is eloquent testimony to the neatness of Augustine's use of vocabulary.

13. ACCIDENTAL CONTIGUITY: The group in question happens to live together or to find itself together at one place or moment, but little else can be said about either the reasons for its gathering or its behavior once gathered. Cf. the *locus commanentium* of XXII, 8 (p. 58 of this study). Augustine rarely uses *populus* for such a featureless group; Isidore of Seville frequently does.

Applications

A. Israel, or the Chosen People under some other title, before Christ.

B. The Jews during or after the rejection of Christ.

C. The Christian Church on earth.

D. The Christian Church in heaven, or the angels.

E. The *populus Dei* without historical differentiation; this application can easily overlap, explicitly or implicitly, with A, C, or D.

F. Rome: the kingdom, republic, or empire, or other forms or manifestations (often local) of Roman secular society.

G. Other historical, secular societies, either specific (the *populus Assyriorum*) or general ("no *populus* can expect to possess its territory in perpetual peace").

H. The transcendent antagonist of E: *populus terrenus, impius,* etc., without historical differentiation.

The same sets of attributes and applications can be applied to Augustine's use of *gens* simply by substituting one noun for the other in the preceding descriptions. I have not yet encountered a *gens Dei* or *gens sancta* parallel to the *populus Dei* of E; by contrast, almost any *gens* imaginable is a group including several classes, high and low (no. 1). However, it seemed pointlessly confusing to change the sequence of sets by suppressing those two columns for the tabulation of *gens*. I have added one column to the set of applications:

I. The Gentiles, in opposition to A or B: basically a Hebraism, but one popular with Christian writers. This usage can overlap all too easily with G, depending on our understanding of the author's intent.

The applications which I have selected for tabulation practically chose themselves after my first reading of *The City of God* years ago; formulating the attributes was more difficult, and more dependent on subjective decisions. I realize fully that there is a certain amount of circular logic in arranging argument-supporting data according to categories derived from the completed argument, a circularity not entirely in accord with the spirit of induction to which this study has declared allegiance. Since this tabulation was begun after most of my conclusions had been drawn, I could hardly pretend to forget them. Even had the timing of this study been different, the alternative would have been to select some set of a priori features straight out of modern political or social theory, and try to fit Augustine's usage into that pattern. Both Marshall and del Estal have done so.

In trying to label the properties of Augustine's *populus,* I have, by contrast, stayed as close as seemed reasonable to the terms of Augustine's own definition. Heading no. 1, for example, tries to pin down the breadth of association connecting this group which is something *sociatus:* Augustine could have used many other participles to characterize the manner of its gathering, and I hesitated to ignore that choice. (If modern justification seems called for, see William Empson's discussion of "appreciative" and "depreciative pregnancy" as elements in the proper definition of words rich in implications, in *The Structure of*

Complex Words, pages 16–17.) Heading 2 pays homage to his frequent insistence that it must be a *multitudo;* no. 3 recognizes his infrequent but striking assertion of its high degree of categorical unity, reflected in the term *communio* and in some of the implications of the adjective *concors*, which relates more directly to the cluster of features gathered under heading 4. That heading associates several of the words in his definitions: *consensus, rationalis,* and *concors,* not to mention the *dilectio* and *amor* which play such central roles in all his thought. Heading 5 refers to the objects of all those states of rational assent, the *utilitas* or interests on which they agree (or should agree), the *res quas diligit populus.* No. 6 deals with the sacrosanct *jus* and *justitia* which in his most elevated moods Augustine saw as climaxing and validating this kind of group's association, as well as with the more cotidian *leges* and *doctrina* which they entailed. The destiny of no. 7 and territory of no. 10 come from usages not covered by his definitions, but not excluded by them, either; so does the genetic and linguistic unity of headings 8 and 9, which also figures in his definitions (or near-definitions) of *gens.* Headings 11 and 13 are designed for features proper to other words, appearing only abnormally in association with Augustine's *populus.*

There is of course a good deal of deductive subjectivity in the compromise between fourth-century Latin and twentieth-century English which these formulations represent. I wonder, however, if historical reasoning can ever escape circular logic of the sort involved here, and I suspect that the historian of ideas should be especially wary of renouncing all subjectivity in the illusion of a pure fidelity to the inductive spirit.

Despite some lubricity of method, tabulation of the sort undertaken here has something to offer traditional humanistic criticism: another basis, in some cases a more solid basis, for selecting texts to be analyzed in depth. Classical criticism has long recognized the value—indeed, the necessity—of choosing such passages after having isolated certain units natural to the work in question. For example, to a student of *The City of God* interested in any of the issues connected with the meaning of the word *populus,* it is obvious that books ɪɪ and xɪx constitute thematic units to which he should pay special attention. They deal with the same basic question (What sort of human community is truly valid?). Within each of these books one can isolate topical units of smaller scale. The author himself states that ɪɪ, 19–22 and xɪx, 21, 23–24 discuss the same issue (the relationship of justice to a true commonwealth), and it is entirely fitting that they should contain the classic pair of definitions to which so much attention has properly been paid. Finally, the sensitive analyst who respects the lessons of form-criticism as well as exact chronology must worry about the relation of the thematic and topical units which he has discerned to the author's and his audience's actual units of composition and attention.

Statistical tables can add a new dimension and a check to the critic's concern about these three types of units by showing if any of them corresponds to a unit of frequency—in the present one, the frequency of a word's (or a neat idea's) appearance. It should be heartening to see that xix, 21, 23–24 has the highest frequency of *populus* occurrences of any three-chapter set in *The City of God,* and that the statistically comparable four-chapter set of ii, 19–22 has the second highest frequency. The evidence of those frequency units confirms what seemed obvious about the relationship as well as the importance of these two units of composition, each of which would have been digestible at one sitting to ancient or medieval audiences with serious inclinations.

Frequency units can do more than that, however. When one looks for another area of *The City of God* to investigate as a control to the conclusions reached after analyzing the classic definitions in ii, 19–22, and xix, 21, 23–24, what should one pick? Usually passages that have struck the imagination of the modern reader, like the pirate's "excellent and elegant" reply to Alexander the Great in iv, 4, get chosen. It is dangerous to reach general conclusions (as does McIlwain) after concentrating on such a passage in the work of a rhetorician as skilled in special effects as Augustine was, but in all practicality what else is there to do? A much safer choice is suggested by the frequency chart, which shows that the highest frequencies per book of *populus* (the key word in the classic definitions) occur respectively in xvii, xviii, and xvi, the salvation-history which makes long and dismal reading for most modern historians. When one notices that xvii is a neat thematic unit clearly labeled by the author, with topical units flowing into one another so smoothly, and with so little digression as to make it one of *The City of God*'s most unified (and atypical) books, and in that respect quite unlike its two neighbors, one should conclude that the whole trio deserves closer attention.

So far I have discussed only the "vertical" frequency evidence available in the following chart. When one considers also the "horizontal" density of content and reference data which it presents, a great deal more of the chart's utility becomes evident. A quick look at the spread of the usage patterns of *populus* in those three books indicates that *populus* is used much more neatly and steadily (one might say "consistently") in xvii than in xvi or xviii—in other words, that the usage-density unit may bear some correlation to the character of the thematic and topical units. In chapter 2 of this study (pp. 49–51) I have tried to show how this correlation helps to describe the overall literary and intellectual character of those books, as well as the employment of *populus* therein. The probability that a fair lapse of time occurred between Augustine's completing xvii and beginning xviii makes all the more interesting the similarities between xvi and xviii: as in the case of ii and xix, the observable correlations become strongly suggestive evidence of Augustine's fundamental consistency of literary habit, especially when he was dealing with consistent themes and subject matter.

Checking the density as well as the frequency units for ii and xix should further reassure the traditional critic about the exceptional weight of *populus* in the passages he has analyzed. Should he feel the need of further controls, or find the usage pattern of xvi–xviii not especially instructive, then he should notice chapters 8 and 13 of book x, two chapters coterminous on this chart, which together contain no less than thirteen appearances of *populus*. The eight appearances in chapter 8 have little to offer, but the five appearances in chapter 13 exhibit a spread of attributes quite similar to that of the definition passages (though not so thickly clumped), as well as applying to Israel and, at least by strong implication, to a Gentile group which turns out to be the Spartans receiving their fundamental law from Lycurgus—an application far richer in historical content than any of the comparable loci of ii, 19–22 or xix, 21, 23–24. Rereading that chapter, I was struck by several features that had somehow not stuck in my memory before: a fine specimen of *Reimprosa,* in which *gens* renders good stylistic service to five *populi;* a *populus* which is big, conscious, attentive—indeed, wide awake with awe—and which in the massive unity of its concentration on the spectacle supplied by its Lawgiver to ratify the authority of His mediators (the angels as well as Moses) invites comparison with the Spartan fidelity of a comparable group less favored by a judgment-making Providence. In other words, this chapter contains most (if not all) of the elements of the two great definitions, enriched and extended by important literary and historical dimensions which they lack. It is perhaps not so incidental that this chapter occupies spatially as well as dialectically a middle position between the two abstract definitions: only *populi* worshiping the true God are true *populi* (ii, 21); but we observe that some Gentile communities were truer to their false gods than Israel was to God Himself; (x, 13); consequently, the emphasis changes from objective to subjective judgment (xix, 24).

At the end of Appendix A I have indicated how decisive I consider this usually neglected chapter in settling the question of Augustine's respect for the value of secular society. One final example: The two highest chapter frequency-units are xvi, 43 (which seemed reasonable to me) and xxii, 8 (which didn't). The attribute spread of the latter chapter is not particularly remarkable, although it is neater than normal; but nowhere else in *The City of God* is *populus* applied in such long, unbroken sequence to the Christian Church. Such an exception deserves attention. On rereading, one notices that this rather lengthy chapter forms a tight unit of composition and attention, building to a superb rhetorical climax, constituting a beautifully rounded topic (with clear subtopics) in the typically Augustinian thematic unit of chapters 4–10 (which echo x, 8, incidentally); that it is intensely personal, beginning with a forty-year-old reminiscence and culminating in a recent series of events in Augustine's own cathedral church which are also treated in four of his most clearly linked and obviously tachygraphed sermons (what an ideal overlap for generic and stylistic comparison!). One must conclude that this a passage worthy of close analysis. In fact, one discovers that Augustine there uses *populus* for Christian congregations in a usage less widely spread than the definitions but more vivid; one feels close to the reason why shortly after Augustine's time the *populi Christiani* were the most vigorous *populi* in the once-Roman world.

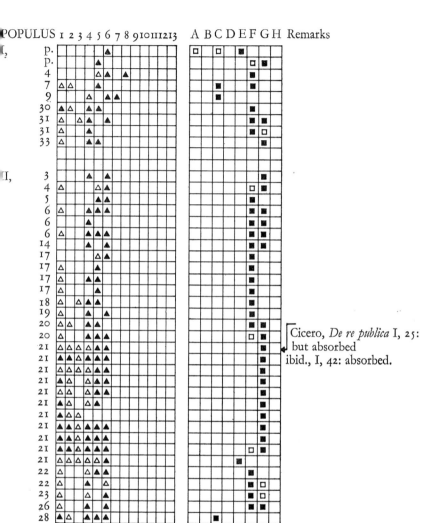

Cicero, *De re publica* I, 25: but absorbed
ibid., I, 42: absorbed.

POPULUS III,	1	2	3	4	5	6	7	8	9	10	11	12	13	A	B	C	D	E	F	G	H	Remarks
1	△				▲		▲												■	■		
1	△		△		▲	▲								■								
1	△				▲	▲								■								
2			△			△	▲												■			
2	△			▲	▲	▲													■			
10						●															●	Sallust, *Catiline* VI
13	△				△	▲													■			
14	△				▲				▲		△								■	■		
14	▲		△	▲															■			
14	△		△		▲														■	■		
14	△		△	▲	▲															■		
14	△		▲		▲														■	■		
15	△				△	▲	▲												■			
15					▲						▲								■			
15	△				▲														■			
15	△				▲														■			
15	△				△	▲													■			
15	△				▲	▲	▲												■			
16	△				▲	▲	△												■			
17	△				▲	▲													■			
17	△				▲	▲													■			
18	△	△			△	▲													■			
18	▲	▲				▲													□			
19	▲	△			△	▲		△											■			
20	△	△			▲	▲													■			
20	△	△			▲	▲													■			
20	▲	△			▲	▲													■			
20	▲	▲			▲	▲	▲	△								□				■		
24	△	△			▲					△									■			
26	▲				▲														■			
31	△				▲					△									■			

POPULUS 1 2 3 4 5 6 7 8 9 10 11 12 13   A B C D E F G H   Remarks

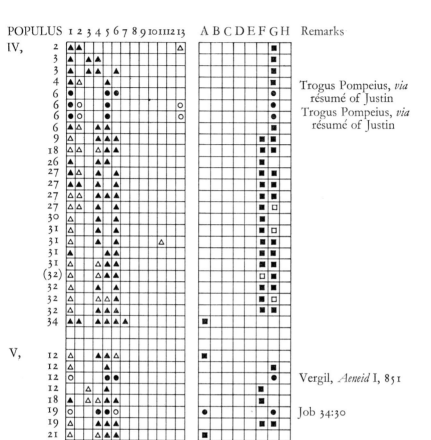

IV,
2
3
3
4
6   Trogus Pompeius, *via* résumé of Justin
6
6   Trogus Pompeius, *via* résumé of Justin
6
9
18
26
27
27
27
27
30
31
31
31
31
(32)
32
32
32
34

V,
12
12
12   Vergil, *Aeneid* I, 851
12
18
19   Job 34:30
19
21
26

POPULUS 1 2 3 4 5 6 7 8 9 10 11 12 13 A B C D E F G H Remarks

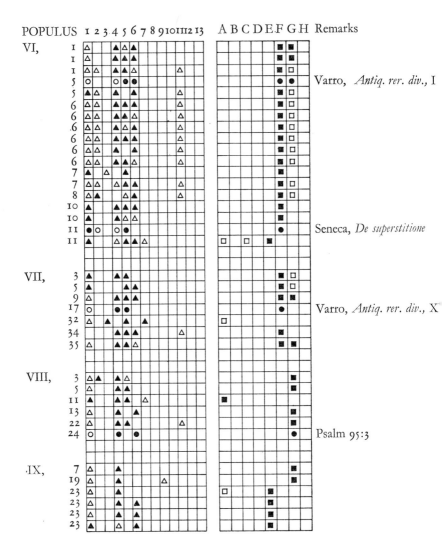

Varro, *Antiq. rer. div.*, I

Seneca, *De superstitione*

Varro, *Antiq. rer. div.*, X

Psalm 95:3

POPULUS 1 2 3 4 5 6 7 8 9 10 11 12 13   A B C D E F G H   Remarks

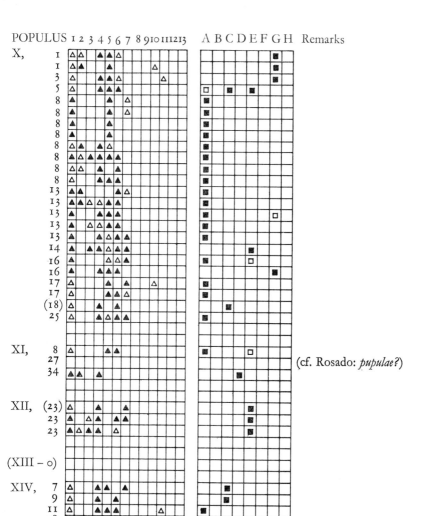

(cf. Rosado: *pupulae?*)

POPULUS 1 2 3 4 5 6 7 8 9 10 11 12 13   A B C D E F G H   Remarks

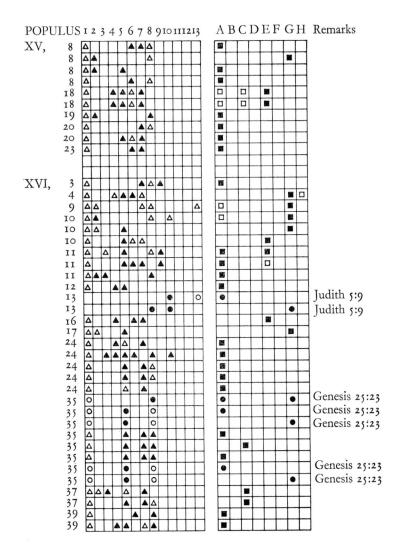

		A B C D E F G H	Remarks
XV,	8		
	8		
	8		
	8		
	18		
	18		
	19		
	20		
	20		
	23		
XVI,	3		
	4		
	9		
	10		
	10		
	10		
	11		
	11		
	11		
	12		
	13		Judith 5:9
	13		Judith 5:9
	16		
	17		
	24		
	24		
	24		
	24		
	24		
	35		Genesis 25:23
	35		Genesis 25:23
	35		Genesis 25:23
	35		
	35		
	35		
	35		Genesis 25:23
	35		Genesis 25:23
	37		
	37		
	39		
	39		

POPULUS 1 2 3 4 5 6 7 8 9 10 11 12 13   A B C D E F G H   Remarks

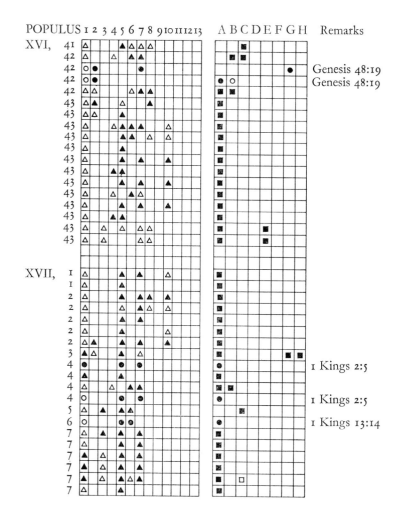

XVI, 41
42
42   Genesis 48:19
42   Genesis 48:19
42
43
43
43
43
43
43
43
43
43
43
43
43
43

XVII, 1
1
2
2
2
2
2
3
4   1 Kings 2:5
4
4
4   1 Kings 2:5
5
6   1 Kings 13:14
7
7
7
7
7
7

151

POPULUS 1 2 3 4 5 6 7 8 9 10 11 12 13   A B C D E F G H   Remarks

XVII,

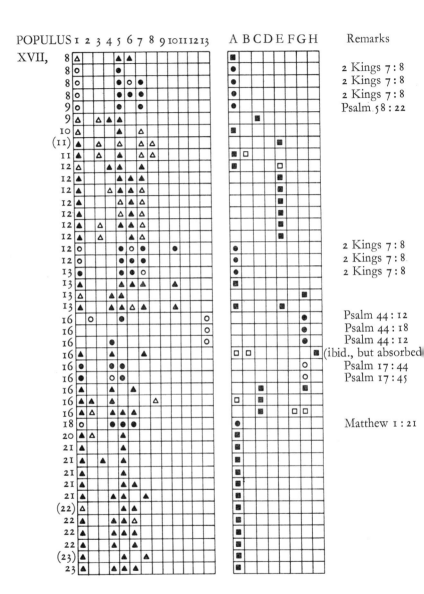

	Remarks
8	
8	2 Kings 7 : 8
8	2 Kings 7 : 8
8	2 Kings 7 : 8
9	Psalm 58 : 22
9	
10	
(11)	
11	
12	
12	
12	
12	
12	
12	
12	
12	2 Kings 7 : 8
12	2 Kings 7 : 8
13	2 Kings 7 : 8
13	
13	
13	
16	Psalm 44 : 12
16	Psalm 44 : 18
16	Psalm 44 : 12
16	(ibid., but absorbed)
16	Psalm 17 : 44
16	Psalm 17 : 45
16	
16	
16	
18	Matthew 1 : 21
20	
21	
21	
21	
21	
21	
(22)	
22	
22	
22	
(23)	
23	

POPULUS	1	2	3	4	5	6	7	8	9	10	11	12	13	A	B	C	D	E	F	G	H	Remarks
XVIII, 2	▲			▲																■		
2	▲	△		▲				△													■	
2	○			○		○														●		Varro, *De gente p. Rom.*
7	▲	▲		▲										■								
8	△			▲	▲		△							■								
8	△			▲										■								
(11)	△			▲										■								
11	△			▲										■								
11	△			▲	▲	▲								■								
11	△			▲		△		△						■								
11	△	△		▲		▲		▲						■								
11	△			▲										■								
12	△			▲	△	▲		▲						■								
12	△	△		▲	△	△							△					□				
13	▲			▲	▲	△								■								
13	○				●		○													●		Varro, ibid.
20	△	△	△	▲										■								
22	▲	△		▲	▲															■		
22	▲			▲		▲		▲						■								
22	▲			▲										■								
24	▲	△	△	▲				△						■								
25	▲			▲	▲	▲		△						■								
25	△			▲				△						■								
25	△				▲	▲								■								
27	△			▲	▲	▲								■								
28	○				●	●	○		○					●								Osee 1:10
28	△				▲	▲											■		■	■		
28	△		△		▲		△										■		■	■		
29	△			▲	▲	▲	▲							■								
29	○			●	●									●								Isaias 53:8

153

POPULUS	1	2	3	4	5	6	7	8	9	10	11	12	13	A	B	C	D	E	F	G	H	Remarks
XVIII, 32	△		▲	▲																	■	
32	△			△		△	▲								■							
32	○		●																		●	Habaccuc 3:10
32	○			●										●								
32	△		▲	▲																	■	
32	△		▲	▲												■					■	
32	○			●										○				○				Habaccuc 3:16
32	△		▲				▲														■	Sophonias 3:9
33	○							●	●	●										●		Sophonias 3:9
33	○		●			●	●							●								Daniel 6:14
34	●			●																	●	Ezechiel 37:24
34	●	○	●			●	●							●								
36	△			▲				△						■								
38	△		△		▲									■	■	■						
39	△			▲	▲			▲						■								
41	▲	▲		▲		▲										■						
41	▲			▲	▲	▲													□	□	■	
41	▲		△	▲		▲								■								
41	▲			▲		▲										■						
43	▲			▲		▲		▲								■						
45	△			▲		▲								■								
45	△			▲																■		
46	△		△		▲	△								■	■							
47	△		▲		▲									■								
47	△				▲									■								
47	△				▲													■				
47	△				▲		△							■								
50	▲	△		▲	▲													■		■		
52	△			▲		△								■					□			
52	▲				▲	△								■					□			

154

Complex distribution chart with row labels "POPULUS XIX" and verse/line numbers, a 13-column grid (filled ▲ and open △ triangles), an A–H grid (filled ■ and open □ squares, ● ○ circles), and a Remarks column.

POPULUS XIX	1 2 3 4 5 6 7 8 9 10 11 12 13	A B C D E F G H	Remarks
15	▲ · ▲ ▲	■	
(19)	▲ · ▲ ▲	· ■	
21	△ · · ▲ △	□ ■	Cicero, *De re pub.* I,
21	△ · · ▲ △	■ ■	25: absorbed
21	▲ ▲ ▲ ▲ ▲ ▲	□ ■	ibid, I, 42: absorbed
21	▲ · △ ▲ · ▲	□ ■	
21	△ △ △ △ △ △	■	
21	△ △ △ △ ▲ △	■	
21	△ ▲	■	
21	△ △ △ △ △	■	
21	△ · △ ▲ · ▲	■	
21	▲ ▲ · ▲ · ▲	■	
21	▲ △ ▲ · ▲ △	■	
21	△ · · △ ▲	■	
23	△ · △ · ▲	■	
23	▲ · ▲ · ▲	· ■	
23	▲ △ ▲ ▲ ▲ ▲	■	
23	▲ △ ▲ ▲ ▲ ▲	■	
23	▲ △ ▲ ▲ ▲ ▲	■	
23	▲ △ ▲ ▲ ▲ ▲	■	
23	▲ △ ▲ ▲ ▲ ▲	■	
(24)	△ △ △ △ △	■ ■	
24	△ · △ △ △	■	
24	▲ ▲ ▲ ▲	■	
24	△ · ▲ △	■	
24	▲ ▲ ▲ △	■	
24	▲ ▲ ▲ △	■	
24	▲ ▲ ▲ △	■ ■	
24	▲ △ △ ▲ ▲	■	
24	△ · ▲ ▲ ▲	■	
24	▲ ▲ ▲ ▲ △	■ ■	
24	△ △ ▲ ▲ △	■ ■	
(26)	△ · ▲ · ▲ · · ▲	■	
(26)	△ · ▲ · ▲ · · △	■	
26	○ · · ● · ●	● ○	Psalm 143:15
26	△ △ ▲ ▲ ▲	■ ■	
26	△ · △ ▲ · ▲	■	
26	▲ · △ ▲ ▲ · ▲	■	

POPULUS 1 2 3 4 5 6 7 8 9 10 11 12 13   A B C D E F G H   Remarks

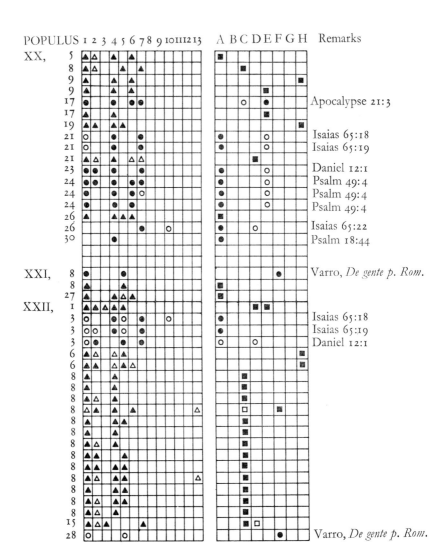

POPULUS	Remarks
XX, 5	
8	
9	
9	
17	Apocalypse 21:3
17	
19	
21	Isaias 65:18
21	Isaias 65:19
21	
23	Daniel 12:1
24	Psalm 49:4
24	Psalm 49:4
24	Psalm 49:4
26	
26	Isaias 65:22
30	Psalm 18:44
XXI, 8	Varro, *De gente p. Rom.*
8	
27	
XXII, 1	
3	Isaias 65:18
3	Isaias 65:19
3	Daniel 12:1
6	
6	
8	
8	
8	
8	
8	
8	
8	
8	
8	
8	
8	
8	
15	
28	Varro, *De gente p. Rom.*

GENS 1 2 3 4 5 6 7 8 9 10 11 12 13   A B C D E F G H I   Remarks

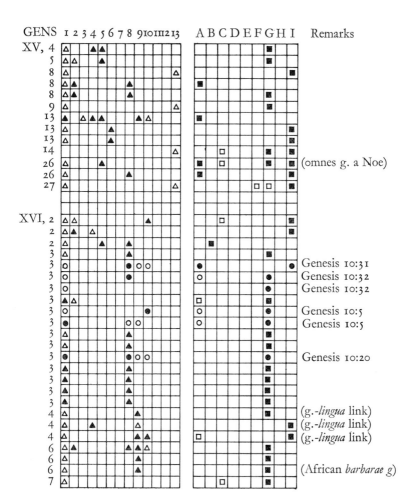

GENS		Remarks
XV, 4		
5		
8		
8		
8		
9		
13		
13		
13		
14		
26		(omnes g. a Noe)
26		
27		
XVI, 2		
2		
2		
3		
3		Genesis 10:31
3		Genesis 10:32
3		Genesis 10:32
3		
3		Genesis 10:5
3		Genesis 10:5
3		
3		
3		Genesis 10:20
3		
3		
3		
3		
4		(g.-lingua link)
4		(g.-lingua link)
4		(g.-lingua link)
6		
6		
6		(African barbarae g)
7		

GENS	1	2	3	4	5	6	7	8	9	10	11	12	13	A	B	C	D	E	F	G	H	I	Remarks
XVI, 8	△		△																			■	
8	△					▲														■			
8	△					▲														■			
8	△					▲														■			
8	△					▲														■			
8	△					▲														■			
8	△				▲	▲														■			
8	▲	△																		■			
8	△					▲														■			
8	△		△			△														■			
9	△					△	△							□						■			
10	△		△			▲								■						■			
11	△		▲				▲													■		□	
11	△					▲	△							■									
11						▲	▲															■	
11	△					▲	▲							■									
11	△				▲		▲							■									
11	△			▲			▲															■	
11	△		△			▲	▲							□						■			
11	△	▲				▲	△							■									
11	△		△			▲								□						■			
11	▲					△	▲													■			
11	△					▲								□						■			
11	△		▲			▲	▲							□						□			
11	△						▲							■									
11	△					▲														■			
11	△	▲				▲								□						■			
11	△					▲		△						□						■			
11	△					▲														■			
11	△					▲								■						■			
11	△					▲								□						■			
13	△					△		△												■			
13	△			▲		▲								■									
15	△					△	▲													■			
15	△					▲	▲							□						■			
16	●	●				●	●		●					●									Genesis 12:2
16	○	●				●	●		●					●									Genesis 12:2
16	▲		▲				▲							■									
16	△	△			▲	▲								□		□			□	■			
(17)	▲	▲		▲																■		■	
17	▲	▲		△																■		■	
18	▲	△				▲								□		□			□	■			
18	△	▲					▲	△						■									

158

GENS	1 2 3 4 5 6 7 8 9 10 11 12 13	A B C D E F G H I	Remarks
XVI, 21			
21			
21			
21			
21			
23			
24			(regnum g. Israelit.)
24			
24			
(26)			
26			Genesis 17:4
26			Genesis 17:5
26			Genesis 17:6
26			Genesis 17:16
26			Genesis 17:20
26			Genesis 17:20
26			
26			
28			Genesis 17:5
28			Genesis 17:16
28			Genesis 17:16
28			Genesis 17:5
29			Genesis 18:18
29			Genesis 18:18
29			
29			
32			Genesis 21:13
32			Genesis 22:18
32			
34			
35			Genesis 25:23
35			
36			Genesis 26:4
36			Genesis 26:4
37			Genesis 27:29
37			
37			
38			Genesis 28:3
38			Genesis 28:3
41			Genesis 49:10
41			Genesis 49:10
42			(Christianae gentes)
42			Genesis 48:19
42			Genesis 48:19

GENS	1	2	3	4	5	6	7	8	9	10	11	12	13	A	B	C	D	E	F	G	H	I	Remarks
XVI,43	▲	▲					▲							■									
43	▲	▲		▲		▲	▲							■									
43	▲																					■	
43	▲		▲			▲	▲	▲						■									
43	▲		▲			▲		▲						□		□			□	■			
43	△					△	▲							■		□			■				
XVII,1	△					△	▲							■									
1	△				▲	△										□				□	□	■	
2	○	●						●						●									Genesis 12:1
2	△					▲								■									
2	△			▲	▲											□			□	□		□	
2	△			▲	▲		▲															■	
2	△			△	▲	▲	▲							■									
2	△	▲																	□	■		□	
3	△				▲	▲								■									
3	△			▲	▲											□			□	■			
4	△			▲												□						■	
4	△				▲														□	■			
5	△	△												■	□								
7	△	△	△	▲			▲							■									
7	△	▲		▲		▲									■								
11	△	▲		△										■									
12	○	○		●																		●	Psalm 88:51
12	△	△	▲																	□	■		
12	△	▲	▲															□				■	
12	△	△	▲	▲														□		□	■		
12	△		▲	△														□				■	
12	○	○		●																		●	Psalm 88:51
12	△	▲	▲																			■	
13	△		▲											■									(synonym for *populus*)
16	△		△															□		□	■	■	
16	△		△																			■	
16	○		●																			●	Psalm 17:44
16	△																		□			■	(populus gentium)
17	○		●																			●	Psalm 21:28
17	○		●																			●	Psalm 21:29
20	△	▲																				■	Eccli. 36:2
20	○	●																				●	Eccli. 36:3
20	○	●	●																			●	
22	▲	△		▲	▲									■									(synonym for *populus*?)
23	▲	△	△	▲			▲							■									
23	△		▲																	■	■	■	

GENS 1 2 3 4 5 6 7 8 9 10 11 12 13 A B C D E F G H I Remarks

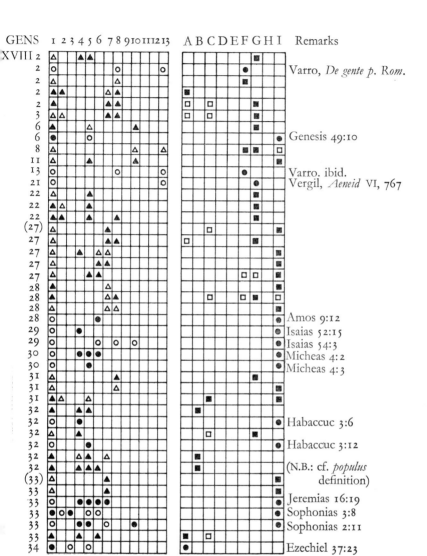

GENS	Remarks
XVIII 2	
2	Varro, *De gente p. Rom.*
2	
2	
2	
3	
6	
6	Genesis 49:10
8	
11	
13	Varro. ibid.
21	Vergil, *Aeneid* VI, 767
22	
22	
22	
(27)	
27	
27	
27	
27	
28	
28	
28	
28	Amos 9:12
29	Isaias 52:15
29	Isaias 54:3
30	Micheas 4:2
30	Micheas 4:3
31	
31	
31	
32	
32	Habaccuc 3:6
32	
32	Habaccuc 3:12
32	
32	(N.B.: cf. *populus*
(33)	definition)
33	
33	Jeremias 16:19
33	Sophonias 3:8
33	Sophonias 2:11
33	
34	Ezechiel 37:23

161

GENS 1 2 3 4 5 6 7 8 9 10 11 12 13   A B C D E F G H I   Remarks

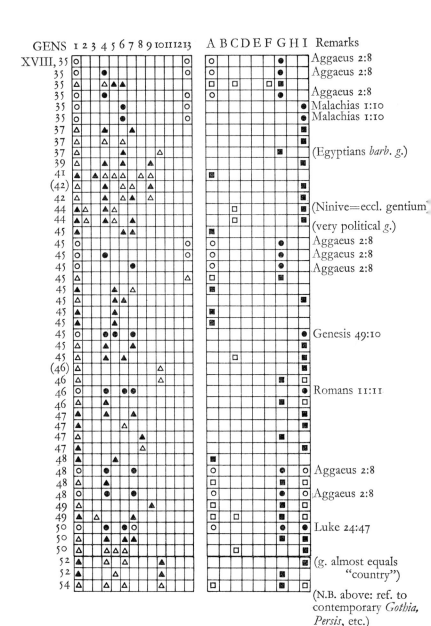

GENS	Remarks
XVIII, 35	Aggaeus 2:8
35	Aggaeus 2:8
35	
35	Aggaeus 2:8
35	Malachias 1:10
35	Malachias 1:10
37	
37	
37	(Egyptians *barb. g.*)
39	
41	
(42)	
42	
44	(Ninive=eccl. gentium
44	(very political *g.*)
45	
45	Aggaeus 2:8
45	Aggaeus 2:8
45	Aggaeus 2:8
45	
45	
45	
45	
45	
45	Genesis 49:10
45	
45	
(46)	
46	
46	Romans 11:11
46	
47	
47	
47	
47	
48	
48	Aggaeus 2:8
48	
48	Aggaeus 2:8
49	
49	
50	Luke 24:47
50	
50	
52	(g. almost equals
52	"country")
54	

(N.B. above: ref. to contemporary *Gothia, Persis,* etc.)

Appendix C
Sources Used in the Study of Scriptural Passages

Research on Jerome's translation of the Old Testament began with a search through standard dictionaries and concordances. Three proved to be especially useful: *Wilhelm Gesenius' Hebräisches und Aramäisches Handwörterbuch über das Alte Testament,* rev. F. Buhl, 17th ed. (Leipzig, 1915); the treatment of עַם on pp. 596–97 is very useful, for example. The *Konkordanz zum Hebräischen Alten Testament,* by G. Lisowsky, contains a thorough compilation of that word's appearances on pp. 1073–86. The *Theologisches Wörterbuch zum Neuen Testament,* ed. Gerhard Kittel, contains much useful material on Old Testament antecedents; the lengthy study on λαός in 4:29–57 is an impressive example. The passages actually cited in the text of this study have been chosen finally on the basis of their political relevance to this inquiry and of the degree to which they are typical of usage patterns. The following editions of Scripture have been used: *Biblia Hebraica,* ed. R. Kittel; the Rahlfs edition of the Septuagint; the Grammatica edition of the Clementine Vulgate; *Biblia Sacra iuxta latinam vulgatam versionem ad codicum fidem,* genl. ed. A. Gasquet: vol. 1, *Genesis,* ed. H. Quentin; vol. 2, *Exodus & Leviticus,* ed. H. Quentin; vol. 3, *Numeri & Deuteronomium,* ed. H. Quentin and others. These last two editions varied in no way relevant to this research. *S. Hieronymi Psalterium iuxta Hebraeos,* ed. Henri de Ste.-Marie. *Le Psautier Romain et les autres anciens psautiers latins,* ed. Robert Weber.

Bibliorum sacrorum latinae versiones antiquae, seu Vetus Italica, ed. Pierre Sabatier, remains indispensable despite its frustrating incompleteness; fortunately for this study, it is now beginning to be supplemented by *Vetus Latina: Die Reste der altlateinischen Bibel nach Petrus Sabatier neu gesammelt und herausgegeben von der Erzabtei Beuron.* Vol. 2, *Genesis,* ed. B. Fischer, is the only volume of those so far extant in this excellent series that was of significant assistance to this research. For English translations this chapter uses the Confraternity versions of

163

the *Old Testament* (intr. and comm. J. Grispino) and the *New Testament*. These versions' only real merits are their neutral simplicity of language and their conscious adherence to the Vulgate, but those virtues become paramount in a study of the Vulgate. The abbreviations used in citing individual books of the Bible are those employed by the Clementine and San Girolamo editions of the Vulgate. The transliteration of Hebrew words, however, follows a pattern improvised for the occasion (though combining features of two or three more standard patterns).

The Greek Old Testaments of Aquila, Symmachus, and Theodotion have not been cited in the text, because in few cases cited do their readings vary significantly enough from those of the Septuagint. In any case Jerome's important departure from contemporary practice was in preferring Hebrew witness to the Septuagint, and his preference for any of these three versions was based on their generally greater fidelity to the Hebrew.

The question of Jerome's Hebrew texts is a vexed one, but there seems to be general agreement that it is safe to use the present Masoretic *textus receptus* as the closest possible approximation to his models (of which there were evidently many, of varying quality as well). On this question, cf. E. F. Sutcliffe, "St. Jerome's Hebrew Manuscripts," *Biblica* 29 (1948): 112–25, and Benjamin Kedar-Kopfstein, "Divergent Hebrew Readings in Jerome's Isaiah," *Textus* 4 (1964): 176–210; the latter article discusses the question in regard to the entire Hebrew Bible despite its title. In cases of major dispute, this study has tended to follow the final judgments of Jean Steinmann, in view of his own special expertise as a translator of Hebrew. Cf. also, for dating, L. H. Cottineau, "Chronologie des versions bibliques de St. Jérôme," *Miscellanea Geronimiana,* pp. 43–68.

Genesis is a particularly rewarding book for a study of this kind, because of the unusually complete support available from the San Girolamo Vulgate and the Benediktbeuron Vetus Latina. There is also a thesis by Felix Reuschenbach, "Hieronymus als Übersetzer der Genesis," of which even the available first two chapters are of use, while several chapters of vol. 2 appear from the table of contents to be of great potential help to this research. Jerome himself seems to have been unusually preoccupied with this book. The Vulgate Pentateuch, the last of his efforts at translating Hebrew, appeared in 406, and so presumably represents the culmination of his technique in that project; on the other hand, his interest in the first of those five books spans the whole period of his Old Testament translating, as is shown by his

Quaestiones Hebraicae in Genesim, composed at the beginning of his stay in Bethlehem, that is, between 389 and 392. As F. Cavallera points out, this is a unique work for Jerome, being the only instance of his approaching the sacred text by means of the very prestigious Alexandrian genre of the *quaestio* (a problematic, selective approach quite different from the verse-by-verse Hebrew *commentarium.*—"Les 'Quaestiones Hebraicae in Genesim' de Saint Jérôme et les 'Quaestiones in Genesim' de Saint Augustin," *Miscellanea Agostiniana,* 2 [1931]: 360–62). Study of New Testament data began with a search through the Kittel *Theologisches Wörterbuch zum Neuen Testament* and the *Concordantiae Novi Testament Graeci,* ed. Alfred Schmoller, published with Eberhard Nestle's edition of the New Testament (*Novum Testamentum Graece*). The biblical texts used have been the latter and *Nouum Testamentum Domini Nostri Iesu Christi Latine, secundum editionem Sancti Hieronymi,* ed. J. Wordsworth and H. J. White: vol. 1, *The Gospels,* and vol. 3, fasc. 1, *the Acts of the Apostles,* were published in 1889–98 and 1905, respectively. Two general introductions to the area of New Testament study have been especially useful. Alfred Wikenhauser, *New Testament Introduction,* trans. Joseph Cunningham; and Marie-Joseph Lagrange, *Introduction à l'étude du Nouveau Testament:* pt. 2, *Critique textuelle;* vol. 2, *La critique rationelle.* Lagrange is exhaustively authoritative, but Wikenhauser is both more up to date and occasionally more acute in his bibliographical selections. Adolf Jülicher, *Einleitung in das Neue Testament,* while less specifically relevant than the previous two works, was nonetheless useful in a general way (esp. pp. 391–415). For introduction to the apparatus of textual criticism, this study has relied heavily on Heinrich Vogels, *Handbuch der Textkritik des Neuen Testaments.* Vastly more complete, but outdated on some important points and occasionally reflecting special premises of the author, is Hermann von Soden's *Die Schriften des Neuen Testaments:* vol. 1, *Untersuchungen;* pts. 2 and 3, "Die Textformen." Not to be entirely discounted because of its age is Frederick Scrivener, *A Plain Introduction to the Criticism of the New Testament,* ed. Edward Miller, vol. 2. It is not without value to observe, by a comparison of these three works, the progress of New Testament "historiography" over the last three scholarly generations.

In an attempt to establish the general features of the Old Latin versions of the New Testament (outside of Acts), nine published manuscripts have been examined besides the indispensable work of Sabatier:

a Codex Vercellensis, late fourth-century, quite possibly transcribed by Eusebius, bishop of Vercelli (died 371), and so perhaps the oldest surviving MS of the Latin Gospels. Edited (after the edition of I. A. Irico, Milan, 1748) by Johannes Belsheim (*Codex Vercellensis*). Now in the episcopal treasury of Vercelli.

b Codex Veronensis, a sumptuous transcription of the Gospels in silver ink on purple parchment, probably executed in northern Italy in the fifth century. Edited by Belsheim (*Codex Veronensis*) it was re-edited much more carefully by E. S. Buchanan (*The Four Gospels from the Codex Veronensis* [b], Old Latin Biblical Texts 6). Belsheim points out its affinities with *a*, but Buchanan stresses instead its relationship to Corbeiensis (*ff*^{2}: see below) and to the Old Syriac tradition. The ratio of textual variations per leaf of *b*, and *ff*^{2} in the Four Gospels (Matt.:Mark:Luke:John) is 4:8:5:6; or, "when both *mss*. were whole, they must have exhibited 11,500 variants one from the other" (Buchanan, p. xiv). Buchanan ends his examination by suggesting that these two closely related MSS represent the texts of the Gospels accepted in the churches of northern Italy and Gaul, respectively, before the Vulgate. Now in the library of the cathedral chapter at Verona.

c Codex Colbertinus, a Gospel MS of the twelfth century; the only complete Old Latin MS of the Gospels, it is not entirely free of the Vulgate text (as is hardly surprising, considering its date). Related in certain sections to *ff*^{2} and Palatinus (*e:* see below), the greater part of its text seems to represent a stubborn Gallic tradition (perhaps with a few Irish or Spanish elements, too). Published first by Sabatier, it has been reedited by Belsheim (*Codex Colbertinus Parisiensis*) and by Heinrich Vogels (*Evangelium Colbertinum*, Bonner Biblische Beiträge, no. 4).

d The Latin half of Codex Bezae Cantabrigiensis, a bilingual MS containing the Gospels, Acts, and fragments of 3 John. Probably composed in the fifth or early sixth century in a region where Latin was the prevalent vernacular tongue, but Greek was still in use for the liturgy—perhaps Sicily or even Sardinia—it may have been brought thence to Lyons by Florus, bishop of that city (died 860). Used at Trent by the bishop of Clermont in 1546, it was bought in 1562 by Theodore de Bèze, after having been looted from the monastery of St. Irenaeus in Lyons by Huguenot troops; in 1581 de Bèze gave it to the University of Cambridge, where it is at present. The Latin text is not simply a translation of the Greek, but represents in some places an African tradition with few surviving relatives. Used by Sabatier, Codex Bezae was published in toto by F. H. Scrivener (*Bezae Codex Cantabrigiensis*), and its text of Acts has been superbly studied by J. H. Ropes (cf. Appendix D, p. 171).

e Codex Palatinus, a very defective but splendid (silver ink on purple parchment) Gospel MS of disputed provenance, but clearly representing an early African tradition closely related to that of Cyprian (died 256) and of the even earlier Bobbio Fragments (*k:* see below). Written in the fifth century, it was brought from Trent in the early nineteenth century to the Hofbibliothek in Vienna, where it is now (with the exception of a few leaves in Dublin and Rome). Edited by Belsheim (*Evangelium Palatinum*), Heinrich Vogels has made it the object of a thorough study, *Evangelium Palatinum: Studien zur ältesten Geschichte der lateinischen Evangelienübersetzung.*

f Codex Brixianus, a sixth-century Gospel MS in silver ink on purple parchment, probably composed in northern Italy under Ostrogothic patronage. Published by Wordsworth and White along with the Vulgate in vol. 1 of their New Testament, since they were convinced that it was the text on which Jerome worked. It has since been demoted to the status of a descendant of an earlier Latin-Gothic bilingual Bible, greatly altered to conform to the increasingly popular Vulgate. Now in Brescia, property of the cathedral chapter.

*ff*² Codex Corbeiensis II, Gospel MS probably composed in southern Gaul or Italy. Edited by Belsheim (*Codex f² Corbeiensis*), and by E. S. Buchanan (*The Four Gospels from the Codex Corbeiensis . . . together with fragments of the Catholic Epistles, of the Acts and of the Apocalypse from the Fleury Palimpsest,* Old Latin Biblical Texts 5). Buchanan points out its agreements with the Old Syriac, Irenaeus, and Origen in some ancient readings now otherwise lost, and dates it 375–425. Belsheim notes its agreements with Lugdunensis, and dates it more conservatively (for once); Vogels suggests the fifth century, and points to its agreements with *a, b, e,* and the Vulgate. Brought from Corbie to Paris in 1638, it is now in the Bibliothèque Nationale.

i Codex Vindobonensis, fragments of the Gospels of Luke and Mark in silver on purple. Written in the seventh or early eighth century, it displays affinities for *b* and *e*. Edited by Belsheim (*Codex Vindobonensis*). Brought from an Augustinian monastery in Naples to Vienna in 1717, it was in the Hofbibliothek.

k Codex Bobbiensis, a fragmentary MS of the Gospels of Mark and Matthew composed somewhere in North Africa (perhaps as far east as Egypt) in the fifth century. It is the oldest witness of any size to the African version used by Cyprian, and is closely related to *e*, although clearly older, less free in wording, and much more carelessly transcribed. Even though St. Columban was not especially partial to the African version in his writings, it is now generally agreed that this may be the Bible which he brought with him to Bobbio in 613. Edited by John Wordsworth, W. Sanday, and H. J. White (*Portions of the Gospels according to St. Mark and St. Matthew from the Bobbio Ms.,* etc., Old Latin Biblical Texts 2). It is now in the Biblioteca Nazionale, Turin.

Two modern composite texts of the Old Latin have been of considerable interest, though not always of major usefulness: Hans, Freiherr von Soden, ed., *Das lateinische Neue Testament in Afrika zur Zeit Cyprians,* Texte und Untersuchungen zur geschichte der altchristlichen Literatur, vol. 33; and Heinrich Vogels, ed., *Vulgatastudien, die Evangelien der Vulgata untersucht auf ihre lateinische und griechische Vorlage.* Von Soden's work strives to reconstruct the New Testament from *k, e,* the Fleury Palimpsest (*h*) (see Appendix D, p. 172), and patristic citations from Tertullian, Cyprian, and others; disagreements are harmonized cautiously and conservatively. Vogels' text is really a composite text, rather daringly compounded from several "European" MSS, especially *b* and *ff*².

The question of Jerome's model remains a vexed one as far as the Latin traditions are concerned (all agree that he rejected the "Western" Greek text, preferring a text or texts much closer to Codices Vaticanus and Sinaiticus). There is general agreement that Jerome intended to produce a version faithful both to his notion of the Greek original and to the at least minimally literate vernacular of the Latin Church (presumably, to be more specific, of the city of Rome or at least of northern and central urban Italy). It is clear that so distinguished and congregation-conscious an African as Augustine felt great respect for versions of the Bible then current in Italy. Nearly universal agreement has been accorded the statement of Hermann Rönsch that "Die Sprache der Itala und sporadisch auch die der Vulgata ist der Hauptsache nach unverkennbar mit der römischen *Volkssprache* (lingua *vulgata rustica,* sermo *cottidianus, plebeius, rusticus,* etc.) identisch . . . Sie wurde in Afrika zuerst Schrift- und Büchersprache und errang sich dort bald eine Literatur, während sie anderwörts, in der Stadt Rom, in Italien und den übrigen Provinzen des römischen Staates, zwar auch im Gebrauch war, . . . Sie kann deshalb auch *afrikanische* Latinität genannt werden" (*Itala und Vulgata, das Sprachidiom der urchrist-lichen Itala und der katholischen Vulgata: unter Berücksichtigung der römischen Volkssprache*, p. 12). L. Ziegler soon pointed out the defects in Rönsch's conception of an "ideale Itala," and established a more flexible and securely documented description of Christian Bible Latin before Jerome (*Die lateinischen Bibelübersetzungen vor Hieronymus und die Itala des Augustins*, pp. 53–60 and passim). Jerome's commitment to this variety of speech obviously rules out any attempt to select one existing MS tradition as his model simply on the basis of stylistic preferences which it would be easy to establish from his letters and treatises (or even his scriptural commentaries). However, it would be at least equally irresponsible to suggest that he had samples of all the existing Old Latin traditions before him as he worked on his version (although nothing rules out the possibility that he may have compared MSS of several rather diverse traditions).

It is certain that there were several such traditions current in the West in the 380s. First of all, there was the crude but venerable African tradition, represented by the sources combined in von Soden's text, and in a way underlying all later efforts. Secondly, there were a number of European versions that had sprung up in the fourth century (and perhaps earlier); some had interacted with African versions to produce such recensions as *e* and one of the probable ancestors of *c*. This process is described with great subtlety and precision in Paul Capelle, *Le Texte du psautier latin en Afrique*, Collectanea Biblica Latina, vol. 4 (Rome, 1913). These European versions form a group different *en bloc* from the African versions, but within that *bloc* it is possible to discern three or even four families: an Italian family whose purest scion is *b;* another (North) Italian or Gallic one now represented by *ff*² and the non-Vulgate, non-Gothic elements of *f;* the rather solitary but surely Italian *a;* and perhaps another family around Lyons, no exemplar of which contains texts useful to this study of the New Testament (Lagrange, *Introduction à l'étude du Nouveau Testament*, pt. 2, vol. 2, pp. 254–58).

In presenting "Old-Latin readings" for comparison with Vulgate readings, this study seeks to avoid the excessive haste of Wordsworth's and White's enthusiasm for *f* (probably the only noteworthy defect in that splendid undertaking), Sabatier's equivocal practice of presenting a "Versio Antiqua" with variant readings in the apparatus, and Vogel's much more sophisticated harmonization in the *Vulgatastudien*. Where there is no disagreement among representatives of the African and the three European families *à la Lagrange* which are relevant—whether from unanimity or from the absence of readings from some representatives—one "Old-Latin reading" appears in the text. Where there is disagreement, the four families are counted equally, and minority readings appear in parentheses. Giving all four equal weight seems justifiable for two reasons: (1) While it is true that Jerome's education and papal secretaryship at Rome (359–67, 382–85) and his happy sojourn in the bosom of the church of Aquileia (ca. 370–74), not to mention his birth and childhood somewhere near the latter city, would argue strongly for his attachment to versions current in Italy, one cannot ignore his considerable knowledge of Tertullian and the enduring prestige of African traditions, or his respect for Hilary and other Gallic Fathers (cf. *De Viris Illustribus,* chaps. 53 and 100). His trip to Trier had a decisive influence on his religious vocation, and the first scriptural works mentioned in his life are those he copied in Gaul (where he may have stayed for as long as three years). (2) It is not impossible that Veronensis (*b*), so close to the Vulgate in phrasing as well as in the individual words considered in this study, may turn out to be another Brixianus (*f*).

Appendix D
The Sources of Acts and Their Relationship

This appendix has a triple purpose. First of all, it discusses the texts and secondary authorities employed in this study's examination of the Acts of the Apostles—as in Appendix C, only much more thoroughly. Secondly, it treats an objection which has been raised to Jerome's integral authorship of the Vulgate version of Acts. Finally, and partly as an extension of that treatment, it attempts to clarify the relationship of the Vulgate text and the other Latin versions. This section ends with a tabulation of all the appearances of *populus* and *plebs* in those translations, and a brief summary of that table's potential relevance to some debates still current in biblical scholarship.

The most complete and profound study so far of the text of the Acts of the Apostles is James Hardy Ropes, *The Text of Acts* (vol. 3 of pt. 1 (*The Acts of the Apostles*) of *The Beginnings of Christianity*, ed. F. J. Foakes Jackson and Kirsopp Lake). The core of this volume is a comparison of the "Western" text *D* (the Greek side of Codex Bezae Cantabrigiensis) and several Old Latin translations (*d, h,* and citations from Irenaeus, Tertullian, Cyprian, Augustine, and other sources) with the authoritative "Alexandrian" (or "Old Uncial") text of *B* (Codex Vaticanus, a fourth-century Egyptian MS). This latter text disagrees with the Greek *textus receptus* as published by Nestle in no way relevant to the present study. The Vulgate text used is that of Wordsworth and White, vol. 3, fasc. 1; the apparatus to this thorough edition contains a great number of Old Latin variants as well as the variants in Vulgate MSS.

Six Old Latin texts have been consulted directly:

> *d* The Latin side of Codex Bezae, edited by Ropes (see Appendix C above). Its base seems to have been a text kin to Gigas (see below), but farther from African versions like *h* than either Gigas, Laudianus (see below), or the Vulgate. Its

value as an independent Old Latin text has been much debated since the late seventeenth century (Ropes, pp. lxxvi-lxxx).

h Codex Floriacensis or the Fleury Palimpsest, written in Africa in the sixth century. A free rendering of the purest form of "Western" Greek text known to us in continuous sections, it is almost entirely like the text of Cyprian, and so must represent an African tradition current in the early third century. Augustine cited it in 404 against Felix the Manichee. Published by Ropes, it has been edited carefully by Buchanan in 1907 (see Appendix C above), after the edition of Berger (1889). Scraped with pumice in the late seventh or early eighth century to receive part of Isidore of Seville's *De Mundo,* it belonged in the eleventh century to the abbey of Fleury, and is now in the Bibliothèque Nationale.

Cy Peter Corssen, ed. *Der Cyprianische Text der Acta apostolorum.* Very fragmentary, hardly ever relevant to this study.

Luc Cal A. M. Coleman, ed. *The Biblical Text of Lucifer of Cagliari (Acts).* Based on the Hartel edition of Lucifer (Vienna, 1886). Less fragmentary than *Cy,* more often relevant to this study, but practically identical with Gigas. Lucifer wrote between 355 and 362, while exiled from his see; he brought his Bible with him from the West.

gig Codex Gigas Holmiensis, a huge Bible composed shortly after 1239, probably in Bohemia. Its text of Acts and of the Apocalypse are Old Latin, in the case of Acts representing with exceptional purity a version widely current in the mid-fourth century, probably of Gallic or Italian (though not Roman) origin. Its excellent, lively Latin remained very popular for centuries, blending with the Vulgate to produce many other MSS. Taken from Bohemia as war booty in 1648, it soon entered the Royal Library of Stockholm, where the Acts text was first recognized as Old Latin and published by Johannes Belsheim (*Die Apostelgeschichte und die Offenbarung Johannis*).

e Codex Laudianus, the Latin side of a bilingual text of Acts. The Greek side, *E,* is the oldest complete "Antiochian" version (a recension of the "Western" and "Alexandrian" versions, closer to the latter). The Latin text is partly based on a "Westernized" Greek text, and hence not entirely adjusted to its parallel Greek column; it preserves its native idiom better than does *d*, and remarkably few distinctively African renderings survive into it. Quite close to both *gig* and the Vulgate, its relationship to them has been much disputed; Ropes suggests a common European ancestor for all three (p. cxi). *Ee* must have been written before 536, the date of an inscription on its last page bearing the name of Flavius Pancratius, δουξ of Sardinia (among others). The scribe seems to have known Greek better than Latin, although the Latin column is dominant. Probably written in Sardinia as a copy of an older bilingual, it probably traveled to Rome or southern Italy, and may well have come to England ca. 650 with Benedict Biscop and Ceolfrid. Bede used it as the text for his *Expositio Actuum Apostolorum* and *Retractatio* (ca. 710 and between 725 and 731, respectively); the scribe of Codex Amiatinus (ca. 716) used some of it. Then it came to Würzburg, perhaps with Burchard, who was consecrated Bishop of that see by Boniface in 741. After the sack of the monastery there by Swedish soldiers in 1631, *Ee* was bought by the agents of Archbishop Laud, who gave it in 1636 to the Bodleian Library at Oxford, where it is now. Edited by Belsheim (*Acta Apostolorum ante Hieronymum latine translata ex codice latino-graeco Laudiano Oxoniensi,* Forhandlinger i Videnskals-Selskabet i Christiania), it had previously been used by Sabatier and others.

Hans Von Soden's *Lateinische Neue Testament in Afrika zur Zeit Cyprians* is very useful for criticism and text history as well as for text. Among the numerous analyses of the contents and themes of Acts (see Wikenhauser, *New Testament Introduction,* pp. 320–45, for up-to-date summaries), Adolf Harnack's *The Acts of the Apostles,* New Testament Studies, vol. 3, trans. J. R. Wilkinson, is especially useful for its treatment of "Lands, Nations, Cities, and Houses" (chap. 2, pp. 49–116), which includes a consideration of λαός and ἔθνος as general terms.

What were the antecedents of the Vulgate Acts? There is general agreement that Jerome rejected the "Western" Greek text in favor of a text closer to *B* than to *E* (e.g., Wordsworth and White, Acts, pp. x-xiii; Hermann von Soden, *Die Schriften des Neuen Testaments,* vol. 1, pt. 3, pp. 1798–1802). However, as regards his Old Latin "model" there is little consensus. Most authorities agree that there was an African text of Acts (as of the whole Bible) current ca. 250, surviving in *Cy* and *h*.

Then came a new recension of European inspiration ca. 350, represented (probably quite freshly) by *gig.* To this recension *e* is somehow related, as is the Vulgate; *d* is distantly if at all related. In an article of 1914 ("Kritische Analyse der Lateinischen Übersetzungen der Apostelgeschichte," *Zeitschrift für die neutestamentliche Wissenschaft* 3:163–88, esp. 182–88), Jülicher suggested *e* as a representative of the version upon which Jerome worked. This suggestion was vigorously attacked by Albert C. Clark in *The Acts of the Apostles, a Critical Edition, with Introduction and Notes,* pp. 234–46. Lagrange (*Introduction à l'étude de Nouveau Testament,* pt. 2, vol. 2, pp. 433–35, 438–39) followed and strengthened Clark's argument based essentially on *e*'s numerous Hellenisms, and asserted that *e*'s similarities to the Vulgate are due to Vulgate influence; the opposite hypothesis "n'est pas vraisemblable, car Jérôme n'eût pas pris comme base un aussi mauvais latin." Wikenhauser accepts this judgment without discussion (p. 103).

The present study, tracing vocabulary patterns in search of a central concept or set of notions rather than along syntactical or stylistic lines, may suggest the feasibility of proposing *e* once again, as either the Vulgate model or a recension (in the light of the Greek text) much closer to that model than *gig.* The results of this study's collation indicate, briefly, that *e* is much closer to the Vulgate than *gig* in the usage of *populus, plebs,* and selected instances of *turba,* but that the Vulgate differs from *e* precisely because it has a consistent pattern of usage in regard to those words and *e* does not (or at any rate has none of equally clear consistency). For more detailed results, see the tabulation and argument summary which terminate this Appendix. One immediate consequence has been the acceptance of *e*'s readings as "Old Latin readings"; substituting *gig* readings for them would simply make Jerome's usage appear even more individual and internally consistent than it does by comparison with *e.*

Much of the above is based, of course, on the premise that Jerome really revised or retranslated Acts. F. Cavallera has maintained ("Saint Jérôme et la Vulgate des Actes, des Epitres et de l'Apocalypse," *Bulletin de litterature écclesiastique,* 1920, pp. 269–92) that he simply incorporated preexisting Latin versions of those books into his New Testament. The reason given is that his citations of those books in later letters is often inconsistent with their Vulgate form. This argument has been largely rejected, mostly on the basis of Jerome's own testimony. *De Viris Illustribus,* chap. 135: "Novum Testamentum Graece fidei reddidi; Vetus iuxta Hebraicam transtuli" (Altchristlichen Literatur, 14: 56). *Ep.* 71:5, written in 398 to Lucinius: "Nouum Testamentum

Graecae reddidi auctoritati. ut enim ueterum librorum fides de Hebraeis uoluminibus examinanda est; ita nouorum Graeci sermonis normam desiderat." *Ep.* 112:20, written 404 to St. Augustine: ". . . si me, ut dicis, in noui Testamenti emendatione suscipis, exponisque causam cur suscipias; quia plurimi linguae Graecae habentes scientiam, de meo possint opere iudicare: eandem integritatem debueras etiam in ueteri credere Testamento, quod non nostra confinximus, sed ut apud Hebraeos inuenimus, diuina transtulimus" (*CSEL* 55:6, 391). The alternative to taking these statements at face value is deciding that Jerome was an outright falsifier, which requires better proof than instances which could easily be laid to his notorious failure to be consistent about his editions. Furthermore, within the limits of their competence, the results of the present study strongly suggest that Jerome either revised Acts himself or took over a version extremely consistent with his usage of *populus* and *plebs,* far closer than any Old Latin version now in existence. The latter alternative postulates too much to be accepted without further evidence.

A tabulation of the loci relevant to *populus/plebs* usage in the Acts of the Apostles follows on pages 176–78.

Tabulation of loci relevant to populus/plebs usage in the Acts of the Apostles

Key to symbols

Cy Cyprian
D   Codex Bezae, Greek (where varying from TR)
d   Codex Bezae, Latin
e   Laudianus; Latin
gig Gigas
h   Fleury Palimpsest
l   Latin translation of Irenaeus' commentary

LC Lucifer of Cagliari
TR Greek *textus receptus* (very close to Vaticanus)
Vg Vulgate
vS von Soden's composite African text (where it supplements either Cy or h)
(—) word not used

Verse	TR	d (& D)	Cy (& vS)	h	gig	e	Vg
2:47	λαόν	mundum / D-κόσμον				populum	plebem
3: 9	λαὸς	populus	populus	populus	populus; LC	populus	populus
11	λαὸς	(—); D	populus	populus	populus	populus	populus
12	λαόν	eos; αὐτούς	populum	populum	illos	populum	populum
23	λαοῦ	populo	populo; I	populo	plebe	populo	plebe
4: 1	λαόν	populum		populum	populum; LC	populum	populum
2	λαόν	populum		populum	plebem; LC	populum	populum
8	λαοῦ	populi	populi; I	populi	populi	populi	populi
10	λαῷ	populo	populo; I	populo	plebi	populo	plebe
17	λαόν	populum		populum	populum; LC	plebem	populum

Ref	Greek						
21	λαόν	populum			populum; LC	populum	populum
25	λαοὶ	populi	populi-l	populi	populi; LC	populi	populi
27	λαοῖς	populis	populis-l	populis	populis; LC	populo	populis
5:12	λαῷ	populo			plebe; LC	populo	plebe
13	λαός	populos			plebs; LC	plebs	populus
20	λαῷ	populo			populum; LC	plebi	plebi
25	λαόν	populum		populum	populum; LC	plebem	populum
26	λαόν	populum		populo	populum; LC	populum	populum
34	λαῷ	populum		plebi	populo	plebi	plebi
37	λαόν	populum		plebem	populum	plebem	populum
6:8	λαῷ	populo	plebe-vS	plebem	populo	populo	populo
12	λαόν	populum			populum	plebem	plebem
7:17	λαός	populus			populus	plebs	populus
34	λαοῦ	populi		. . . m	populi	populi	populi
10:2	λαῷ		populo-l	plebem	plebe	plebi	plebi
41	λαῷ	populo	populo-l		populo	populo	populo
42	λαῷ	populo	populo-l		populo	populo	populo
12:4	λαῷ	populo			plebi; LC	plebi	populo
11	λαοῦ	populi			plebis; LC	plebis	plebis
22	δῆμος	populus			populus; LC	populus	populus
13:15	λαόν	populum			plebem	plebem	plebem
17	λαοῦ	populi			populi	plebis	plebis
	λαὸν	populum			populum	plebem	plebem
24	λαῷ	populo			populo	plebi	populo
31	λαόν	populum			plebem	plebem	plebem

Tabulation of loci relevant to populus/plebs usage in the Acts of the Apostles (cont.)

Verse	TR	d (& D)	Cy (& vS)	h	gig	e	Vg
14:13	ὄχλοις	turba	(turba-IΓ)	plebe	turbis	populis	populis
15:14	λαὸν	populum	populum-IνS		plebem	populum	populum
16:22	ὄχλος	turba			turba; LC	turba	populus
17: 5	δῆμον	populum			populum	populum	populum
8	ὄχλον	turbam			turbas	civitatem	plebem
18:10	λαός	populus		plebs	populus	po(r)pulus	populus
19: 4	λαῷ	populo			plebi	plebi	populus
30	δῆμον	turbam			turbam	populum	populum
33	δήμῳ	populo			populum	populum	populum
21:27	ὄχλον	turbam			turbam	populum	populum
28	λαοῦ	populum			(—)	plebem	populum
30	λαοῦ	populi			populi	populi	populi
35	ὄχλου	populi; λαοῦ			populi	populi	populi
36	πλῆθος	multitudo (—);			multitudo	multitudo	multitudo
	τοῦ λαοῦ	πλῆθος (—)			(—)	populi	populi
39	λαόν	populum			populum	populum	populum
40	λαῷ	eos; αὐτούς			populum	plebem	plebem
23: 5	λαοῦ		plebis-vS		populi	populi	populi
26:17	λαοῦ				plebe	populo	populo
23	λαῷ		plebi-vS		plebi	populo	populo
28:17	λαῷ				plebem	plebem	plebem
26	λαὸν				plebem	populum	populum
27	λαοῦ				plebis	populi	populi

A summary of the data relevant to the question of whether *gig* or *e* is closer to *Vg*:

A. Of the 58 loci cited above,

Vg, *gig* and *e* agree	23 times
Vg agrees with *e* but not with *gig*	16 times
Vg agrees with *gig* but not with *e*	10 times
Vg differs from both *e* and *gig*	6 times

   (*e* = *gig* 4 of those times)

B. Four of the above loci seem specially revealing:

   16:22, in which *Vg* departs from all Latin antecedents and from the obvious translation of Greek *TR* and *D;*

   14:13, in which *Vg* and *e* disagree on the one hand with *gig* and both Greek traditions, and on the other hand with the African Latin tradition;

   21:36, in which *Vg* and *e* disagree with *gig*, which seems closer to the Western (*D*) than to the Alexandrian (*TR*) Greek tradition;

   3:12, in which case *Vg* and *e* adhere to the Alexandrian Greek tradition (*TR*), but differ from *gig*, which adheres to the Western Greek tradition (*D*) even more clearly than in the previous instance.

C. It may be argued that the above data show that *e* is derived from *Vg*, but then how does one account for the numerous and sometimes substantial differences between the two—either by alleging a rather haphazard conflation of *Vg*, *gig* (and something else?) on the part of the scribe of *e*, or by positing a fourth, lost version. Both alternatives demand more of common logic than the simpler argument that Jerome made more use of *e* than of *gig*.

Appendix E
Populus and *Plebs* in the Vulgate and the Old Latin Gospels

The following tabulation is designed as a supplementary aid in assessing the degree of Jerome's originality in translating the Gospels, especially the Synoptic accounts of Jesus' encounter with Roman justice.

As in the tabulation in Appendix D, only *populus* and *plebs* are registered in completeness; however, the great majority of the occurrences of *turba* and *multitudo* in the relevant verses are recorded as well.

It should not be surprising to note that Jerome's employment of those words in these instances is much less free, much more faithful to antecedent versions, than in his translation of Acts. The chief events recounted—one of Jesus' most reassuring social miracles and the rejection of his universal redemptive mission by cowardly Gentile authority as well as by the bloodthirsty spokesmen of perversely stubborn Israel— were familiar both to the liturgy and to the private meditation of Latin Christians. Jerome was much less free to tamper with phrases dear to lay sensibilities and to clerical authority in the case of these emotionally charged passages than in his later, more mature translation of the much less popular (indeed, relatively neglected) Acts of the Apostles.

For a discussion of synthetic conclusions based on this tabulation, see chap. 3, pp. 102–08.

Tabulation of *loci relevant to* populus/plebs *usage in the Gospels*

Key to symbols

- *a* Codex Vercellensis
- *b* Codex Veronensis
- *c* Codex Colbertinus
- *d* Latin side of Codex Bezae Cantabrigiensis
- *e* Codex Palatinus
- *f* Codex Brixianus (where varying from *Vg*)
- *ff²* Codex Corbeiensis
- *H* Hilary of Poitiers' commentary
- *i* Codex Vindobonensis
- *k* Codex Bobbiensis
- *TR* Greek *textus receptus* (close to Codices Vaticanus and Sinaiticus)
- *Vg* Vulgate
- *VL* Old Latin version(s)
- *vS* von Soden's composite text (also including *k* and *e*)
- (—) word not used

Verse	TR	African VL (*vS, k, e*)	"European" VL (*ff², f, c; H*)	Italian (1) VL (*a*) (& *d*)*	Italian (2) VL (*b, i*)	*Vg*
Matt. 1:21	λαὸν	populum-*vSk*	populum-*cff²*	p . . . -*a*	populum-*b*	populum
Matt. 14:13	ὄχλοι	turbae-*vSk*	turbae-*cff²*	turbae-*ad*	turbae-*b*	turbae
14	ὄχλον	turbam-*vSk*	turbam-*cff²*	turbam-*ad*	turbam-*b*	turbam
15	ὄχλους	turbas-*vSk*	turbas-*cff²*	turbam-*a*; as-*d*	turbas-*b*	turbas
19	ὄχλους	turbas-*vS*	turbam-*cff²* H	turbam-*d*	turbam-*b*	turbam
	ὄχλους	turbis-*vS*	turbis-*cff²* H	turbis-*ad*	turbis-*b*	turbis
Mark 6:34	ὄχλον	turbam-*e*	turbam-*c*; / turbas-*ff²*	turbam-*ad*	turbam-*b*	turbam

Tabulation of loci relevant to populus/plebs usage in the Gospels (cont.)

Verse	TR	African VL (vS, k, e)	"European" VL (ff², f, c; H)	Italian (1) VL (a) (&d)*	Italian (2) VL (b, i)	Vg
Luke 9:11	ὄχλοι	turbae-vSe	turbae-cff²	turbae-ad	turbae-b	turbae
12	ὄχλον	turbam-vSe	turbas-cff²	turbam-a; as-d	turbam-b	turbas
13	λαὸν	populum-vSe	populum-cff²	populum-ad	turbam-b	turbam
16	ὄχλῳ	populo-vSe	turbis-c; turbam-ff²	turbis-ad	turbas-b	turbas
18	ὄχλοι	homines-vSe	**turbae-cff²**	**turbae-ad**	**turbae-b**	**turbae**
John 6:2	ὄχλος	turba	multitudo magna-cff²; turbae multae-f	turba	turba	multitudo magna
5	πολύς	magna-vSe	multitudo maxima-cff²; turba multa-f	multa-ad	multa-b	multitudo
	πολὺς	multa		multae-ad	multae-b	maxima
Mark 15:8	ὄχλος	turba-vSe; turba-vSk	turba-cff²	turba-ad		turba
11	ὄχλον	**populo**-vS; **turba**-k;	turbis-c; turbae-ff²	tur . . . -a; turbas-d		turbam
15	ὄχλῳ	illis-vS; **populo**-k	populo-c; illis-ff²	(—)-d		populo
Matt. 27:1	λαοῦ		plebis-cff²	plebis-a	plebis-b	populi
15	ὄχλῳ		populo-c; populum-ff²	populo-ad	populo-b	populo
20	ὄχλους		populo-c; populis-ff²	populo-a; turbis-d	populo-b	populis
24	ὄχλον		populo-cff²	populo-ad	populo-b	populo
25	λαὸς		turba-cff²	turba-a; populus-d	turba-b	populus
Luke 22:66	λαοῦ	plebis-vSe	populi-c; plebis-ff²	populi-ad	plebis-bi	plebis

Luke 23:		multitudo-vSe	multitudo-cff^2	multitudo-ad	multitudo-bi	multitudo
1	πλῆθος	multitudo-vSe	multitudo-cff^2	multitudo-ad	multitudo-bi	multitudo
2	ἔθνος	gentem-vSe	gentem-cff^2	gentem-ad	gentem-bi	gentem
4	ὄχλους	turbas-vSe	populum-c; turbas-ff^2	turbam-a	turbas-bi	turbas
5	**λαόν**	**populum-vSe**	**populum-cff^2**	populum-ad	populum-bi	populum
13	**λαὸν**	**plebis-vSe**	**populo-c; populi-f; plebis-ff^2**	populi-a; plebem-d	plebis-b	plebe
14	λαόν	populum-vSe	populos-c; populum-ff^2	populum-a; plebem-d	populum-b	populum
18	παμπληθεὶ	turba-vSe	populus-c; turba-ff^2; multitudo-f	populus-ad	turba-b	turba
27	πολὺ πλῆθος τοῦ λαοῦ	multitudo populi-vSe	multitudo populi-cff^2 f	multitudo ingens populi-a	multitudo populi-b	multa turba populi

* This juxtaposition is for convenience only, and in no way suggests kinship between these two versions; d's readings for these words are exactly like a 14 times, but exactly like b 15 times. All that this fact might serve to suggest is the Italian origin of d, which is not too far from the current theory.

Abbreviations Used in the Notes

AM	*Augustinus Magister.*
BA	Bibliothèque Augustinienne. *Oeuvres de Saint Augustin.*
CCSL	*Corpus Christianorum, Series latina.*
CD	Augustine, *De Civitate Dei.*
CSEL	*Corpus Scriptorum Ecclesiasticorum Latinorum.*
Dods *CG*	*The City of God,* trans. Marcus Dods.
DVI	Jerome, *De Viris Illustribus.*
Ep.	*Epistula* (any author).
Loeb *CG*	Loeb Classical Library edition of Augustine's *City of God,* trans. G. E. McCracken.
MA 1	*Miscellanea Agostiniana,* vol. 1 (*S. Augustini Sermones post Maurinos reperti;* ed. G. Morin).
MA 2	*Miscellanea Agostiniana,* vol. 2 (*Studi Agostiniani*).
Migne	*Patrologiae Cursus Completus* or *Patrologia Latina,* genl. ed. J. P. Migne.
SAOO	*Sancti Augustini opera omnia,* 11 vols. (the Maurist edition).
SI	*S. Augustini Tractatus sive Sermones inediti,* ed. G. Morin.

Notes

1 For my conclusions concerning Isidore of Seville, see my Ph.D. dissertation, "Sense of Community in the Early Middle Ages: 'Populus' and other Sociopolitical Terms in the Works of Jerome, Augustine, and Isidore of Seville" (Harvard, 1966), chap. 4. That chapter's basic contentions appeared in condensed and differently oriented form in "The Political Grammar of Isidore of Seville," *Actes du quatrième Congrès International de la Philosophie Médiévale* [Montréal, Aug.–Sept. 1967]: *Arts libéraux et philosophie au moyen âge* (Montreal–Paris, 1969), pp. 763–75.

2 This description is based on a variety of sources and impressions; I have not been able to find a satisfactory general treatment of this word's meaning in the classical vocabulary. See A. Ernout-A. Meillet, *Dictionnaire étymologique de la langue latine*, p. 522; unfortunately, the *Thesaurus Linguae Latinae* has not yet reached the letter *P*. For a discussion of the meanings of *populus* in the legal literature, see n. 29 to chap. 2, below; for its use by one influential and comprehensive author, see H. Merguet, *Lexikon zu den Reden des Cicero*, 3:645–65; and *Lexikon zu den philosophischen Schriften Cicero's*, 3:104–09. For authoritative confirmation of the description which I offer here, I rely finally on a conversation (1 Dec. 1969) with Jean Bayet, who suggested furthermore that *populus* became a prominent word (and notion) as a result of the Roman solution of the religious crisis of the second century B.C., that is, the fusion into a comprehensive public cult of the plebeian and patrician gods and rituals. Cf. his allusions to that merger in *Histoire politique et psychologique de la religion romaine*, chaps. 7–8, esp. pp. 106 ff., 144 ff. This view of the evolution of the *populus* is cast into deeper and complementary perspective by the article of Jean Gagé, "La *plebs* et le *populus* et leurs encadrements respectifs dans la Rome de la première moitié du Ve siècle avant J.-C.," *Revue historique* 493 (Jan.–Mar. 1970): 5–30. Gagé argues that the *populus* of the primitive Roman republic (derived etymologically from *pubes*) was a

manpower pool of youths ready for quick mobilization and generally quartered outside the walls of the city (so that entry into the society of the Quirites, the mature citizens, was literally an "opening of doors").

After steady territorial expansion and military specialization had consigned to oblivion this original *"populus* spécifique," its name drifted upward to become the standard classical designation of the "société légale" consisting of "l'ensemble des *cives Romani"* (p. 10). What a striking parallel this earliest discernible usage offers to the *populus Francorum* or *populus gentis Gothorum* of a millennium later! No less striking, of course, are the fundamental differences between such sporadically political warrior-bands, normally obedient rather than commanding or sovereign, and the *populi* of classical and patristic Christian literature on which this study concentrates.

3 In a provocative book often more subtle than finally persuasive, David Hackett Fischer insists that historical reasoning is neither deductive (in the manner of Aristotle and Ramus) nor inductive (cf. Mill, Keynes, or Carnap); properly understood, it should be described as "adductive" (Fischer's own term). Without challenging those definitions, I find it instructive to consider Fischer's observation that Charles Sanders Peirce defined induction "rather specially" as "the experimental testing of a theory," which "does nothing but determine a value" (*Historians' Fallacies: Toward a Logic of Historical Thought,* pp. xv–xvi), and I find encouragement and consolation in his related exhortation: "If historical research were as empirical as it can be, then we might hope to see very large heuristic hypotheses put to very small controlled tests" (p. 25). This study of the exact value of an important word hopes to make just that sort of contribution to several of the grand heuristic hypotheses of intellectual history, and two of its appendixes were designed as specific examples of such testing.

4 For a strong assertion of Augustine's value as a representative of the culture of his age, see Henri-Irénée Marrou, *Saint Augustin et la fin de la culture antique,* pp. x–xii, 662. Jerome he sees (or saw in 1938) as quite the contrary in general significance, because of the private nature of his personal concerns and the idiosyncracy of his literary erudition. According to such a view, Jerome's case has at least the value of a good control.

5 The semantic problem at issue here might well be reconsidered without recourse to the terminology of consistency. That model for judging range of meaning and usage can raise as many questions as it answers, at least partly because of its peculiar susceptibility to relative or subjective application. For instance: "inconsistency," the definitional contrary of "consistency," may be synonymous with "contradiction," or may describe a usage "less than consistent" with the usage serving as the base for comparison, but not in polar opposition to it. Consider the horrid tangle we uncover when we begin to ponder the strict consequences of asking whether Author X (or his usage x of meaning

x) is "more consistent"—or "less inconsistent" (and what's the difference there?)—than Y or y or *y*. And so on.

William Empson (I am grateful to Prof. R. W. B. Lewis of Yale for
introducing me to his work) has developed several "identity equations"
which might do a less tendentious job of assessing the proper range of
words like *populus:* see *The Structure of Complex Words,* chap. 2
("Statements in Words"), esp. pp. 39–44, 47–55, and 75–80. He proposes five neatly charted identity equations for dealing with words rich
in philosophical, scientific, or complex ideological value, like *God,
electron, law,* and *nature.* His discussion concentrates on the problem of
establishing a viable hierarchy among various senses of such words, dis-
tinguishing, for example, what he calls the "chief," "head," "dominant,"
"central," "root," and "primary" meanings; he also stresses the importance of sensitivity to any shift within that structure of meanings. To
such a discussion the categories of consistency appear wholly irrelevant,
and I for one am sorely tempted to abandon them. Unfortunately, I
fear that analyses like Empson's are too unfamiliar to current historical
discourse in English, and so feel compelled here to continue tackling
the consistency model on its own slippery ground.

6 Marshall goes so far as to assert that *civitas* is usually a socioreligious
rather than a political term in *The City of God,* and that this sort of
distinction was a product of Augustine's own mind: "St. Augustine
does not want to confuse what is political with what is socioreligious"
(p. 35; cf. also p. 43). See p. 45 for his dismissal of *populus Romanus;*
some of his most forthright assertions of the primacy of *civitas* in his
concern occur on pp. iv, 3, 8, and 26.

7 At first glance rather similar, but actually more useful in arrangement,
is H. Hohensee's *The Augustinian Concept of Authority.* It is almost
entirely an anthology of passages in which the word *auctoritas* occurs,
with only two pages of what the author modestly calls "summary
exegesis." However, it is also equipped with an analytical index to the
passages compiled, guiding the reader to which of those passages refer
to the nature, the active or passive aspects, the persons or things subject
to *auctoritas,* certain virtues or vices closely related thereto, etc. The
Rosado tabulation is accompanied by no such breakdown.

8 *Populus, plebs,* and their plural forms in reference to the Church for
Ratzinger (pp. 159–69); *plebs, plebeius,* etc. (even including *populus*)
as terms for the dependent classes in Seyfarth (pp. 104–27). Cf. nn.
53, 39, and 48 to chap. 2, below.

9 See n. 53 to chap. 2, below.

Chapter 2

1 The basic text of Augustine's works used in this study is *SAOO. The
City of God* occupies vol. 7. One of the chief attractions of this hand-
some edition is the very full and sensitive analytical index which occu-

pies vol. 11, pt. 2; it seems to be largely the work of Coustant, Guesnié, and Martène. Since this attractive edition is not generally available, this study cites also the corresponding references in the complete works of Augustine which appeared in vols. 32–47 of Migne. This edition simply reprinted the Maurist text. For *The City of God* this study also cites the text appearing in vols. 47 and 48 of *CCSL*—which is based on the edition of Bernard Dombart and Alfons Kalb (4th ed., Leipzig, 1928–29), but takes cognizance of the Maurist text. I have also consulted Loeb *CG*. Another English translation used in this chapter is that of Dods *CG*. Several volumes of *BA* have also been consulted. *The City of God*, ed. F.-J. Thonnard and M. A. Devynck, intro. and notes by G. Bardy and others, trans. G. Combès and others, appears in vols. 33–37: the Latin text of this excellent and extremely useful bilingual edition is based on that of *CCSL*, vols. 47–48 with further attention to the Maurist tradition. For general bibliographical guidance I have followed Martin Schanz, Carl Hosius, and Gustav Krüger, *Geschichte der römischen Litteratur*, vol. 4, *Die römische Litteratur von Constantin bis zum Gesetzgebungswerk Justinians*, pt. 2, pp. 398–472 (esp. pp. 402–04, 415–19, 454–61); the more condensed but often more judicious and more up-to-date *Patrology* of Berthold Altaner, trans. Hilda Graef, pp. 487–534, and the spare but nearly exhaustive *Bibliographia Augustiniana*, ed. Carl Andresen. Unless otherwise attributed, translations are mine.

For general assessment and interpretation of Augustine, I have tended to follow the judgments of Henri-Irénée Marrou in *Saint Augustin et la fin de la culture antique* (1958) (a "4th ed." including his 1938 Paris thesis and his 1949 *Retractatio*), and of F. Van der Meer, *Augustine the Bishop*, trans. Brian Battershaw and G. R. Lamb. Far less definitive in intent, but still of great utility, is Gustave Bardy's summary of much of his work in the field, *Saint Augustin, l'homme et l'oeuvre* (1948). The dissertation on which this study is based was completed before the publication of Peter Brown's magisterial *Augustine of Hippo: a Biography* (1967): a definitive biography indeed, and a storehouse of erudite and sensitive judgments on many doctrinal, historical, and social issues besides. The last stages of this study's revision owe much to Brown's masterpiece in matters of detail as well as general interpretation.

2 M. Tullius Cicero, *De Re Publica*, ed. K. Ziegler. The argument which Augustine recapitulates begins in book II, chap. 42 (p. 78), and continues through most of the now very fragmentary book III. However, the definition under discussion appears intact earlier in the dialogue, in book I, chap. 25 (pp. 24–25). The *Laelius* mentions the occasion and main *personae* of this dialogue in book IV, chap. 14.

3 "Populum autem non omnem coetum multitudinis, sed coetum iuris consensu et utilitatis communione sociatum esse determinat. Docet deinde quanta sit in disputando definitionis utilitas: atque ex illis suis

definitionibus colligit tunc esse rem publicam, id est rem populi, cum bene ac iuste geritur, sive ab uno rege, sive a paucis optimatibus, sive ab universo populo. Cum vero iniustus est rex, quem tyrannum, more graeco, appellavit; aut iniusti optimates, quorum consensum dixit esse factionem; aut iniustus ipse populus, cui nomen usitatum non reperit, nisi ut etiam ipsum tyrannum vocaret: non iam vitiosam, sicut pridie fuerat disputatum, sed, sicut ratio ex illis definitionibus connexa docuisset, omnino nullam esse rem publicam: quoniam non esset res populi, cum tyrannus eam factiove capesseret; nec ipse populus iam populus esset, si esset iniustus, quoniam non esset multitudo iuris consensu et utilitatis communione sociata, sicut populus fuerat definitus" (*SAOO* 7, col. 75; Migne 41, col. 67; *CCSL* 47:53–54; Loeb *CG* 1:220–21 [with some revision]).

4 "Enitar enim suo loco, ut ostendam secundum definitiones ipsius Ciceronis, quibus quid sit res publica, et quid sit populus, loquente Scipione, breviter posuit . . . nunquam illam fuisse rem publicam, quia nunquam in ea fuit vera iustitia. Secundum probabiliores autem definitiones, pro suo modo quodam res publica fuit: et melius ab antiquioribus Romanis, quam a posterioribus, administrata est" (*SAOO* 7, col. 77; Migne 41, col. 68; *CCSL* 47:55).

5 It is clear from a letter of Augustine's to Evodius, bishop of Uzalis (*Ep.* 169, 1), that books i–v had been finished sometime during 415. A reference to an imperial decree on pagan worship in book xviii, chap. 54, dates the completion of that book at 424 or 425. Dates of individual works of Augustine appear in most convenient order and in accordance with the latest research in two otherwise cursory introductions to the subject: Henri-Irénée Marrou, *Saint Augustin et l'augustinisme*, pp. 182–86; and Hugh Pope, *St. Augustine of Hippo*, pp. 328–60. For the sermons, see A. Kunzelmann, "Die Chronologie der Sermones des hl. Augustinus," *MA* 2:417–520. Dates of letters are derived from a variety of sources, such as the Maurist editors and secondary treatments.

6 The first words of book xix, chap. 21 announce the resumption of the topic: "Quapropter nunc est locus ut quam potero breviter ac dilucide expediam, quod in secundo huius operis libro me demonstraturum esse promisi . . ." (*SAOO* 7, col. 906; Migne 41, col. 648; *CCSL* 48:687). The consequent argument occupies the rest of this lengthy chapter. For one discussion of Augustine's attitude in *The City of God* and elsewhere toward the pagan fascination with superhuman achievement as a civic boast and a personal consolation, see Charles Norris Cochrane, *Christianity and Classical Culture*, esp. pp. 109–13, 486–500, 513–15.

7 See John J. O'Meara, *Porphyry's Philosophy from Oracles in Augustine*, (*Etudes Augustiniennes*), esp. pt. 2, pp. 49–64. Cf. Pierre Courcelle, *Les lettres grecques en Occident, de Macrobe à Cassiodore*, Bibliothèque des Ecoles Françaises d'Athènes et de Rome, fasc. 159, p. 168.

8 "Si autem populus non isto, sed alio definiatur modo, velut si dicatur,

populus est coetus multitudinis rationalis, rerum quas diligit concordi communione sociatus: profecto ut videatur qualis quisque populus sit, illa sunt intuenda quae diligit. . . . Secundum istam definitionem nostram populus Romanus populus est; et res eius sine dubitatione res publica. Quid autem primis temporibus suis, quidve sequentibus populus ille dilexerit, et quibus moribus ad cruentissimas seditiones, atque inde ad socialia atque civilia bella perveniens, ipsam concordiam quae salus quodammodo est populi, ruperit atque corruperit, testatur historia: de qua in praecedentibus libris multa posuimus. Nec ideo tamen vel ipsum non esse populum, nec eius dixerim rem non esse rem publicam, quamdiu manet qualiscumque rationalis multitudinis coetus, rerum quas diligit concordi communione sociatus. Quod autem de isto populo et de ista re publica dixi, hoc de Atheniensium vel quorumcumque Graecorum, hoc de Aegyptiorum, hoc de illa priore Babylone Assyriorum, quando in rebus suis publicis imperia vel parva vel magna tenuerunt, et de alia quacumque aliarum gentium intelligar dixisse atque sensisse" (*SAOO* 7, col. 917; Migne 41, cols. 655–56; *CCSL* 48:695–96; Loeb *CG* 6:230–33 [with some revision]).
For a discussion of how much further Augustine went in this second definition, and in what direction, see Appendix A.

9 See Appendix A for a fuller discussion of this question, with current bibliographical background.

10 ". . . vera autem iustitia non est nisi in ea re publica, cuius conditor rectorque Christus est, si et ipsam rem publicam placet dicere, quoniam eam rem populi esse negare non possumus. Si autem hoc nomen, quod alibi aliterque vulgatum est, ab usu nostrae locutionis est forte remotius, in ea certe civitate est vera iustitia, de qua scriptura sancta dicit: 'Gloriosa dicta sunt de te, civitas Dei' " (*SAOO* 7, col. 77; Migne 41, cols. 68–69; *CCSL* 47:55; Loeb *CG* 1:224–27). The scriptural reference, which Augustine uses over and over again in *The City of God,* is to Ps. 86:3. Cf. remarks on "true justice" in Appendix A.

11 Representative of this awareness and of Augustine's normal attitude toward semantic cleverness is his admonition, in a letter of 418 to his fellow bishop Asellicus, against confusing the ordinary people by out-of-the-way usages: ". . . non tamen debemus consuetudinem sermonis humani inepta loquacitate confundere, et in rebus discernendis frequentata vocabula perturbata significatione miscere . . ." (*Epistola* 196: *SAOO* 2, col. 1103; Migne 33, col. 897). Rudolph Berlinger discusses the more aesthetic and philosophical side of Augustine's semantic practice in *Augustins dialogische Metaphysik,* pp. 19–28 (esp. p. 21), 31, 216–21. Augustine's attitude toward the social function of language, especially of particular items of vocabulary, is examined in relation to his pedagogic theories as expressed in *De Magistro* (389) and in the second book of *De Doctrina Christiana* (ca. 397), in Ulrich Duchrow's *Sprachverständnis und biblisches Hören bei Augustin,* pp. 118–22. Part

of Duchrow's argument maintains that the theory expressed in those early works and adhered to in his general practice is quite consistent with the elevated word-theory developed in *De Trinitate* (ca. 400–416), esp. in book x, chap. 2. Neither of these rather abstract studies would seem to disagree with Joseph Finaert's conclusion that Augustine strove throughout his literarily productive life for consistency of vocabulary usage, and that he showed a very conservative attitude toward neologisms (*L'Evolution littéraire de Saint Augustin*, Collection d'Etudes Latines, 17:19–27). For a similar judgment, arising from a different approach, see Giuseppina Bellissima, "Sant'Agostino grammatico," *AM*, pp. 35–42.

12 For a thorough and definitive treatment of Augustine's relationship with the work of Cicero, see Maurice Testard, *Saint Augustin et Cicéron*. In vol. 1, *Cicéron dans la formation et dans l'oeuvre de Saint Augustin*, see chap. 4, "Cicéron et la vie morale de St. Augustin," pp. 131–54; chap. 7, "La répartition des citations," pp. 185–204; chap. 9, "Jugements de St. Augustin sur Cicéron," pp. 231–54; and chap. 10, "Traitement du texte cicéronien des citations," pp. 255–92. Pp. 39–42 of vol. 2, *Répertoire des textes*, treat the passages cited in nn. 3 and 6 of this chapter, using them to reconstruct part of book III of the *De Re Publica*. The bibliography is extremely full.

13 Karl Hermann Schelkle has treated Augustine's use of Vergil's works with judicious thoroughness in *Virgil in der Deutung Augustins*, Tübinger Beiträge zur Altertumswissenschaft, no. 32. Pp. 8–175 list and comment on all the *loci citati* so far identified. Felipe Martínez Morán discusses the psychological and ideological points of connection between the two men, especially as discernible in *The City of God*, in the course of a rather diffuse and lyrical article, "El espíritu virgiliano en la Ciudad de Dios," *Estudios sobre la "Ciudad de Dios,"* 1:433–58. John O'Meara's article, "Augustine the Artist and the *Aeneid*," in *Mélanges offerts à Mademoiselle Christine Mohrmann*, pp. 252–61, is a close study of Augustine's exploitation of parts of the *Aeneid* for his own *Confessions;* the conclusions derived are of considerable relevance for the general question of Augustine's dependence on Vergil. All three authors pay some attention to the evident fact that Vergil outshone all other Latin poets in Augustine's eyes; S. Angus points out that Augustine cites Vergil about seventy times in *The City of God*—"more than the total of his quotations from all the other poets" (*The Sources of the First Ten Books of Augustine's "De Civitate Dei,"* pp. 12–13).

14 The question of Neoplatonic influence on Augustine has not proved to be of much direct illumination to my research. John O'Meara's *Charter of Christendom* gives on pp. 62–68 a convenient summary of the controversy about the extent of Augustine's Neoplatonism, which began in 1888 with Boissier's and Harnack's independent conclusions that Augustine was more Neoplatonist than Christian at the time of his

conversion in Milan (386–87), and only gradually turned into a sincerely orthodox Catholic. The extreme statement of this position probably occurred in Prosper Alfaric's thesis, *L'Evolution intellectuelle de Saint Augustin: Du Manichéisme au Néoplatonisme* (1918), which went so far as to assert that Augustine's intellectual position at that time was dominated "avant tout de Plotin. Elle modifie assez sensiblement la doctrine du Maître pour l'adapter aux enseignements de la foi catholique. Mais elle transforme encore davantage le Catholicisme pour le mettre d'accord avec la philosophie plotinienne et elle ne le considère que comme une forme inférieure de la sagesse, bonne seulement pour les intelligences faibles ou encore novices" (p. 515; see pp. 361–527 for his full argument). An attack on this sort of position led by C. Boyer resulted after a quarter-century in its almost total discrediting. See Pierre Courcelle, *Les lettres grecques en Occident, de Macrobe à Cassiodore*, pp. 156–76, and H.-I. Marrou's impatient remark in *Saint Augustin et la fin de la culture antique*, pp. 628–31, that Alfaric seems to have confused Augustine with Synesius of Cyrene. Most current scholarship seems to operate on the conviction that Neoplatonic influence on the intellectually mature Augustine was not really decisive, and that strictly Platonic influence on him was extremely indirect, despite the respect for that distant figure so eloquently expressed in *CD* VIII, 1, 4–7, and in *De Vera Religione* (composed in Tagaste, 389–90), VII. Typical of this current of thought is M. F. Sciacca's *Saint Augustin et le Néoplatonisme* (1956), the central interest of which is the question, "Quel enseignement véritablement nouveau Augustin peut-il tirer des platoniciens?" (p. 5; cf. pp. 11, 14, 17–19 for his general conclusions; for his more summary account of Augustine's encounter with the *Platonici*, see his *S. Agostino* (1949), 1:44–54.

A further question not yet settled is that of the relative influence on Augustine of particular Neoplatonist authors. Paul Henry argued vigorously for the dominance of Plotinus in *Plotin et l'Occident: Firmicus Maternus, Marius Victorinus, Saint Augustin et Macrobe*, Spicilegium sacrum Lovaniense, fasc. 15, (1934); see esp. pp. 213–40. John O'Meara has seconded Theiller's nomination of Porphyry, in *The Young Augustine* (1954), pp. 131–55. The major issues and positions of this continuing argument have been summarized by Pierre Courcelle in "Litiges sur la lecture des 'Libri Platonicorum' par saint Augustin," *Augustiniana* (1954), pp. 9–23.

Scholarship on this question seems to be very cautious about suggesting Platonism or Neoplatonism as significant sources of political or social models in Augustine's thought. An example of the most extreme position in that direction is Edgar Salin's suggestion that Augustine decided to write twenty-two books on the City of God because Plato's *Republic* had ten books according to the old reckoning, and Plato's *Laws* had twelve. "Indem er beide Zahlen vereint, sagt Augustinus, welchem grossen Gegner er sich gewachsen, sich überlegen fühlt, und zugleich sagt er, indem er gerade die Staatswerke Platons nacheifernd aufeinandertürmen will, unwiderleglich die letzte Absicht seines eigenen Werkes: theologische Politik, nicht politische Theologie,—Staatsgründung, nicht Geschichtsbetrachtung" (*Civitas Dei*, p. 174). The more modest view of Viktor Stegemann, that certain partly Platonic ideas of Philo's and Origen's about an οὐράνιος πόλις reached Augustine through Ambrose, has gained wider present acceptance. See his *Augustins Gottesstaat*, Heidelberger Abhandlungen zur Philosophie und ihrer Geschichte, no. 15, (1928), pp. 26–35. A very compact summary of the debate on this and related issues is given in J. Ratzinger's "Herkunft und Sinn der *Civitas*-Lehre Augustins," *AM*, pp. 965–80, esp. pp. 969–71, 979.

15 The question of Augustine's familiarity with Greek has influenced the direction of my research only in a negative sense. Augustine's schoolboy resistance to Greek, largely due to his teachers' methods and in spite of the allure of the subject matter, is recalled in *Confessions* I, 14: "Cur ergo graecam etiam grammaticam oderam talia cantantem? Nam et Homerus peritus texere tales fabellas, et dulcissime vanus est, et mihi tamen amarus erat puero . . . Videlicet difficultas, difficultas omnino ediscendae peregrinae linguae, quasi felle aspergebat omnes suavitates graecas fabularum narrationum" (*SAOO* 1, col. 146; Migne 32, col. 671). It is generally agreed that Augustine never overcame that *difficultas*, despite later efforts to do so; however, opinions have varied on the extent of his discomfort with Greek, especially after 400. Seventy years ago, L. Grandgeorge expressed the dominant current opinion when he stated simply that "Saint Augustine ignorait la langue grecque" (*Saint Augustin et le néo-platonisme*, Bibliothèque de l'Ecole des Hautes Etudes, Sciences Religieuses 8 (1896): 50). Hans Becker disagreed strongly in *Augustin: Studien zu seiner geistigen Entwicklung* (1908), in which, after a lengthy mustering of texts (pp. 120–38), he claimed that by 400 "Augustin das Griechische derart beherrscht hat, dass er ohne Schwierigkeiten lesen und verstehen könnte . . . er ganze griechische Aussprüche im Kopfe gehabt hat; . . . Augustin das Griechische nicht nur oberflächlich, sondern ziemlich genau gekannt hat" (pp. 131, 137; see pp. 138–47 on his knowledge of Hebrew—none, really—and of Punic—some colloquial command). Two years before, S. Angus had formulated a much less enthusiastic interpretation: "On the testimony of Augustine's works he had a limited working knowledge of biblical Greek, a very slight working knowledge of patristic Greek and apparently no working knowledge of classical Greek" (p. 276; see pp. 236–73 for his treatment of Augustinian texts and his understanding of a "working knowledge"). Marrou accepted Angus's formulation in *Saint Augustin et la fin de la culture antique*, pp. 28–37 ("Il sait un peu; il n'en sait pas beaucoup") and 631–37, despite the attempt of Courcelle to demonstrate that Augustine's control of biblical Greek was

quite good after 410 or so, and that he read the *Enneads* in Greek
around 415 (*Les lettres grecques en Occident,* pp. 137–53, 183–94).
Most recently, Gerald Bonner argues for the acceptance of Angus's thesis
without modifications (*St. Augustine of Hippo: Life and Controversies*
[1963], pp. 394–95). *In medio stat* the opinion of Irénée Chevalier, who
asserts, on the basis of very thorough comparison of Augustine's theological semantics with the usages of several Greek Fathers, that "il nous
apparaît clairement que l'évêque d'Hippone pouvait controller sur
l'original grec les traductions existantes, voire même les refaire. Il se
livra à cet examen critique, chaque fois qu'il en vit l'utilité, soit pour
ses commentaires exégétiques, soit pour les témoignages des Pères dans
ses controverses et ses exposés doctrinaux. Mais la langue grecque lui
offrit toujours quelque difficulté et il ne sut jamais l'écrire" (*S. Augustin
et la pensée grecque,* Collectanea Friburgensia, fasc. 33, [1940], pp.
100–02).

Once again, as in the case of the Platonic/Neoplatonic influences
discussed in the previous note, this interesting question fails to penetrate
the periphery of my research. Even if it is true that Augustine reread
the *Enneads* in entirety and in Greek, around 415, the numerous
passages in *The City of God* which give rise to this supposition (best
treated in Henry, pp. 121–30) are completely irrelevant to the kind of
social and political questions with which I am concerned. Consequently,
the field is left (at least for the present) to the influence of biblical and
Roman models.

16   In his article "Platonisches und biblisches Denken bei Augustinus," *AM,*
pp. 285–92, Ephraem Hendrikx argues that in his preference for the
concrete and historical mode of thought over the abstract speculation
characteristic of the Greek Fathers, Augustine represents a return to
the biblical conceptual framework of the earlier Church. The central
thesis of Heinrich Scholz's commentary on *The City of God—Glaube
und Unglaube in der Weltgeschichte* (1911)—is that its central theme
is the unending conflict between those who know God and those who
do not: a conception much more Jewish and primitive Christian than
Greek (see pp. 20–69, 165–74, and passim). The brief credit given
Plato, Plotinus, and the Stoics on pp. 71–76 does not alter his basic
argument. A more general but also more comprehensive and more
judicious presentation of the theory that the Two Cities idea developed
from Jewish sources under the influence of early Christian experience
is given by Etienne Gilson in *Les métamorphoses de la Cité de Dieu*
(1952), pp. 11–24, 45–54. Viktor Stegemann suggests several Old Testament themes which seem to have had special influence on *The City of
God* (pp. 44–49, 51). Eduard Stakemeier stresses the importance of the
Apocalypse (especially its "lineare Geschichtsdenken") to Augustine's
magnum opus (*Civitas Dei; Die Geschichtstheologie des heiligen Augustinus als Apologie der Kirche* [1955], pp. 21–29). Gerhart B. Ladner,
besides giving a closely documented summary of current opinions on the

history of the Two Cities idea, points out the importance to Augustine's thought of the Pauline doctrine of the old and the new man (*The Idea of Reform, Its Impact on Christian Thought and Action in the Age of the Fathers*, [1959], pp. 242–49, 263–66).

17 Cf. Cicero's *Laelius de Amicitia* iv, 14: "Quod idem Scipioni videbatur, qui quidem, quasi praesagiret, perpaucis ante mortem diebus cum et Philus et Manilius adesset et alii plures, tuque etiam, Scaevola, mecum venisses, triduum disseruit de re publica, cuius disputationis fuit extremum fere de immortalitate animorum, quae se in quiete per visum ex Africano audisse dicebat." Viktor Poschl, in "Augustinus und die römische Geschichtsauffassung," *AM*, pp. 957–63, argues that although Augustine is the great debunker of the Roman historical tradition, the method and assumptions of his attack are entirely consistent with that tradition, and in fact derive from it. Poschl names Cato, Cicero (through his *De Re Publica*), Sallust, Livy, Lucan and Tacitus as the classic repositories of this tradition, which he says is characterized first of all by moral determinism: "Einmal dadurch, dass hier politische Grösse und politischer Verfall auf moralische Ursachen zurückgeführt werden. Mit diesem Moralismus der römischen Geschichtsbetrachtung hängt aufs engste zusammen das Schuldgefühl, das mehr oder weniger alle Römer erfüllt, die sich mit der Geschichte ihres Volkes befassen, und der erstaunliche Pessimismus, der aus ihrem Äusserungen spricht" (p. 957). For an assessment of Augustine's use of Roman historians in the first 10 books of *The City of God*, see Angus, pp. 26–35 (Livy), 38–41 (Sallust, Varro), 42–49 (the epitomizers Florus and Eutropius), 49–50 (Livy and the two epitomizers).

18 Carlyle maintains that Augustine's departure from Cicero on this question cost him following in later centuries, which simply ignored his original contribution to this matter of definition. See esp. "St. Augustine and the *City of God*," *The Social and Political Ideas of Some Great Mediaeval Thinkers*, ed. F. J. C. Hearnshaw, esp. pp. 51–52. Gilson disagrees with this opinion, although he agrees that Augustine is seriously straining Cicero's terminology in *CD* ii, 21 and xix, 21 (esp. pp. 38, 42). The whole point of Arquillière's *L'Augustinisme politique* is that the assessment of the state which Augustine intended was severely distorted in subsequent centuries by theocratic theorists, but Arquillière's analysis of these two definitions in no way agrees with Carlyle's: he sees them as aspects of the same conception and goes so far as to say that with *CD* xix, 24, "l'auteur du *De civitate Dei* rejoint Saint Paul et toute la tradition patristique antérieure" ("L'essence de l'augustinisme politique," *AM*, p. 993). (This article [pp. 991–1002 of *AM*] is a convenient summary of his thesis, enhanced by discussion of some of the opinions generated by his book on the subject; pp. 995–1001 suggest some broad outlines for a study of *augustinisme politique* up to the present.)

19 There is no shortage of studies of Augustine's style according to purist

standards of Ciceronic-humanist latinity; they proliferated in the nineteenth century and until quite recently continued to dominate significant areas of scholarship: most of the studies of Augustine's language
in the Patristic Studies series of the Catholic University of America,
for example, pay at least token reverence to such stylistic norms. Only
one representative of that tradition, the work of Regnier (see below) has
been of some general illumination to my research. A new approach, in-
corporating the previous erudition and superseding the judgments resulting from it, examines the literary production of early Christian
figures in the light of internal consistency with their own aesthetic
standards, social purpose, etc.; I have found its results very illuminating.
The general approach and many of the specific criteria are most con-
veniently condensed in Josef Schrijnen's *Charakteristik des altchristlichen
Latein*, Latinitas Christianorum primaeva, fasc. 1 (1932), and in Christine Mohrmann's "Altchristliches Latein. Entstehung und Entwicklung
der Theorie der altchristlichen Sondersprache," *Etudes sur le latin des
chrétiens* (cited hereafter as Mohrmann, *Etudes*) (1958) 1:3–19. For
overall aspects of Augustine's style, see Mohrmann's articles, "Saint
Augustine and the 'Eloquentia'," "Comment saint Augustin s'est
familiarisé avec le latin des chrétiens," *Etudes*, 1:351–70, 383–89; "Saint
Augustin écrivain," *Etudes*, (1961), 2:247–75; Joseph Finaert, *L'Evolution littéraire de Saint Augustin*, passim and pp. 39–56, 71–82. For the
Epistolae, see also M. Pellegrino, "Osservazioni sullo stile delle Lettere
di S. Agostino," *Mélanges offerts à Mademoiselle Christine Mohrmann*,
pp. 240–51.

20 For a classicist's approach, see A. Regnier, *De la latinité des sermons de
Saint Augustin* (1886). For a more useful approach, see Joseph Finaert,
Saint Augustin rhéteur (1939) which discusses *The City of God* and also
the *Confessions* as well as the sermons. Some further insights along the
same lines are offered in Mohrmann's "Saint Augustin prédicateur,"
Etudes, 1:391–402. For Augustine's relationship to the history of the
sermo humilis, see Erich Auerbach, *Literary Language and Its Public
in Late Latin Antiquity and in the Middle Ages*, trans. Ralph Manheim,
Bollingen Series, no. 74, pp. 27–58.

21 For a classicist, grammatical approach, see Sr. M. Columkille Colbert,
The Syntax of the De Civitate Dei of St. Augustine, Patristic Studies,
vol. 4 (1923). For a typical treatment, pp. 95–101. Erich Auerbach
suggests some critical principles for another approach (pp. 42, 43, 68).
I have been unable to lay hands upon the work of C.-I. Balmus, *Etude
sur le style de Saint Augustin* (Paris, 1930). Joseph Finaert offers some
brief observations on the style of *The City of God* in *Saint Augustin
rhéteur*, pp. 37–39, 79–81. Aside from the above, there seems to be
little work on the style of Augustine's magnum opus.

22 The *Confessions* have been very thoroughly studied indeed. Christine
Mohrmann sees them as the parent of a whole new theory of literary

style formulated by Augustine ("Saint Augustine and the 'Eloquentia,'" *Etudes*, 1:369). See also her "Considerazioni sulle *Confessioni* di sant' Agostino," *Etudes*, 2:277–323 (esp. 308–23). The most fresh and thorough study of the *Confessions* from a purely literary point of view is Melchior Verheijen's *Eloquentia pedisequa: Observations sur le style des Confessions de saint Augustin*, Latinitas Christianorum primaeva, 10. Pp. 95–104 offer some interesting comparisons with *The City of God* and the sermons. For a more organic consideration of some of these points of style, see M. Pellegrino, *Le Confessioni di s. Agostino* (1956), pp. 178–203.

23   In fact, Augustine uses *populus* more narrowly than Cicero does in his philosophical works, according to the copious examples proposed in H. Merguet's exhaustive treatment of that word in his *Lexikon zu den philosophischen Schriften Cicero's*, 3 (1894): 104–09. Surprisingly, his twenty pages on that word in *Lexikon zu den Reden des Cicero*, 3 (1882): 645–65, report a usage quite strictly in accordance with Augustine's as well as with Cicero's own definition, and so in accordance with Augustine's usage. So it seems that, despite Augustine's independence in reshaping Cicero's formal definition, his divergence from Cicero in actual usage was in the direction of even greater fidelity than Cicero himself was capable of in speculative works. The variation in Cicero's own usage may indicate that the narrower usage of *populus* was more in accordance with the standard forum and courtroom language of the late republic, and that possibility should suggest in turn both how conservative and how eminently rhetorical Augustine's exploitation of his Ciceronian legacy was. In discussing the relationship of Augustine's rhetoric to Cicero's, Marrou maintains that, with the partial exception of his most popular sermons, Augustine indulged in syntactical novelty far less than most authors since the Silver Age. Furthermore (and more significantly), Augustine considered literary purity above all a matter of vocabulary (rather than of morphology or syntax), and in this sense of priority was very close to "la conception étroite du *latine dicere*" of his great republican model, whose own stylistic precepts "portent principalement sur le choix des mots, *elegantia*, qu'on doit sélectionner avec soin en n'employant que ceux qui ont pour eux le bon usage, en évitant les néologismes, les archaïsmes, les termes techniques ou familiers" (*Saint Augustin et la fin de la culture antique*, pp. 77–79).

24   This research into Augustine's usage of *populus* began with an examination of all the examples cited in the analytical *Index Generalis* which fills *SAOO*, vol. 11, pt. 2. This was followed by a skimming of *The City of God* and a more random sampling of other works, particularly the collected sermons and letters. Passages cited in secondary works provided some further examples. Less than 20 percent of all the loci examined are in any way cited in this chapter, the goal of which has

been a representative selection from a variety of genres and contexts, rather than exhaustive treatment. After my research had been completed, I became aware of two studies rather similar to mine: R. T. Marshall's *Studies in the Political and Socio-Religious Terminology of the "De Civitate Dei,"* Patristic Studies, vol. 86, and Gabriel del Estal and Juan José R. Rosado's "Equivalencia de 'civitas' en el *De Civitate Dei,"* *Estudios sobre la "Ciudad de Dios"* 2:367–454. For a discussion of the differences between my research and theirs, see the discussion of method in chap. 1, pp. 13–15, above.

Even though most commentators agree that the word *populus* is of considerable importance to the formulation of Augustine's political and social thought, very few have paid much attention to its actual semantic value in his writings. This is true even of Gilson, despite his pointing out the significance of the term in chap. 1 of *Métamorphoses* (published the same year as Marshall's study). Two years later (the same date as del Estal's study) appeared Josef Ratzinger's *Volk und Haus Gottes in Augustins Lehre von der Kirche,* Münchener Theologische Studien, 2, vol. 7, (1954), which pays considerable attention on pp. 159–68, 255–62, and 293–95 to the problem of establishing the meaning of the terms *civitas* and *populus* through sampling actual usage. However, in the last two sections the usage established is that of Augustine's classical models rather than that of Augustine himself, and the first section, which studies Augustine's own works, is concerned exclusively with establishing the difference between *populus* and *populi* as terms for Church groups. Even there, the number of *loci citati* is neither large nor very varied. Six years later, Sergio Cotta treated the "concept" of *populus* on pp. 23–44 of his *Città politica di sant'Agostino* (of which I was also unaware until lately), but his discussion is an extreme example of the definition-bound, deductive method which characterizes the studies of Marshall and del Estal (which Cotta cites). Most of the pages cited deal with the two formal definitions and their natural-law background; the sort of thing Cotta is after is typified by his conclusion about Augustine's definitions (and hence "concepts") of *civitas, populus,* and *regnum:* ". . . manifestamente si equivalgono, facendo tutte perno su tre elementi: 1) la pluralità dei componenti; 2) il vincolo di una regola commune; 3) l' accettazione generale di questa regola. Nel caso del popolo è messo in evidenza anche un quarto elemento: il *fine,* cui la sociologia moderna attribuisce così grande importanza quale strumento di coagulazione di ogni associazione" (p. 52). So despite Gilson's implicit suggestion, *populus* continues to run a poor second to *civitas* in current literature. In the case of the one prima facie exception, Ratzinger's research is really directed toward his notion of *Volk* rather than toward the word *populus* which was its normal (but not exclusive) vehicle of expression in the works of Augustine and his spiritual ancestors.

25 "Quid enim est res publica, nisi res populi? Res ergo communis, res utique civitatis. Quid est autem civitas, nisi multitudo hominum in quoddam vinculum redacta concordiae? Apud eos enim ita legitur: 'Brevi multitudo dispersa atque vaga, concordia civitas facta erat.' Quae porro praecepta concordiae in suis templis unquam illi legenda censuerunt? Quandoquidem miseri quaerere cogebantur, quonam modo sine offensione cuiusquam eorum discordes inter se deos suos colere possent: quos si imitari discordando vellent, rupto concordiae vinculo civitas laberetur" (*Ep.* 138: *SAOO* 2, col. 617; Migne 33, col. 529). Augustine used a very close variation of this definition two years later in a letter written to his friend Macedonius, then Vicar of Africa: " 'Qui gloriatur, in Domino glorietur.' Hoc nobis velimus, hoc civitati cuius cives sumus: non enim aliunde beata civitas, aliunde homo; cum aliud civitas non sit, quam concors hominum multitudo" (*Ep.* 155: *SAOO* 2, col. 805; Migne 33, col. 670). In *CD* xv, 8, composed perhaps six to ten years later, Augustine varied the formula once more. He explains how Cain could be said to have built a *civitas* in the name of his son Enoch: ". . . quia nec constitui tunc ab uno poterat civitas, quae nihil aliud est quam hominum multitudo aliquo societatis vinculo colligata: sed cum illius hominis familia tanta numerositate cresceret, ut haberet iam populi quantitatem, tunc potuit utique fieri, ut et constitueret et nomen primogeniti sui constitutae imponeret civitati" (*SAOO* 7, col. 618; Migne 41, col. 447; *CCSL* 48:464). If it is not equally clear from the third passage as it is from the first that *populus* equals *civitas,* it is nonetheless clear that enough population to make a *populus* is a necessary factor in the creation of a *civitas:* both are first of all a *multitudo.* For Augustine's relationships with Marcellinus and Macedonius, see Marie A. McNamara, *Friendship in St. Augustine,* Studia Friburgensia, n.s., 20: 132–36. For Marcellinus, cf. also Angus, pp. 68–69. On this last citation and conclusion, cf. p. 45, above, and n. 80, below.

26 For a recent restatement and summary of that apologetic situation, see E. Stakemeier, pp. 9–20. The first clear emergence of the idea of the two opposed but connected societies in Augustine's work occurs in *De Vera Religione,* written at Tagaste in 389 and 390, chaps. 26–28: "Hic dicitur vetus homo, et exterior, et terrenus, etiamsi obtineat eam, quam vulgus vocat felicitatem, in bene constituta terrena civitate, sive sub regibus, sive sub principibus, sive sub legibus, sive sub his omnibus: aliter enim bene constitui populus non potest, etiam qui terrena sectatur: habet quippe et ipse modum quemdam pulchritudinis suae. . . . Sic proportione universum genus humanum, . . . ut in duo genera distributum appareat. Quorum in uno est turba impiorum terreni hominis imaginem ab initio usque ad finem gerentium. In altero series populi uni Deo dediti, sed ab Adam usque ad Iohannem Baptistam terreni hominis vitam gerentis servili quadam iustitia: cuius historia vetus Testamentum vocatur, quasi terrenum pollicens regnum, quae tota

nihil aliud est quam imago novi populi, et novi Testamenti pollicentis regnum coelorum. Cuius populi vita interim temporalis incipit a Domini adventu in humilitate, usque ad diem iudicii, quando in claritate venturus est. . . . Resurget ergo pius populus, ut veteris hominis sui reliquias transformet in novum. Resurget autem impius populus, qui ab initio usque ad finem veterem hominem gessit, ut in secundam mortem praecipitetur. . . . Quisquis autem populi terreni temporibus usque ad illuminationem interioris hominis meruit pervenire, genus humanum adiuvit, . . ." (*SAOO* 1, cols. 1232–33; Migne 34, cols. 143–44). In these passages it is clear that the two *populi* (the *terrenus* member of the pair being once called a *turba*) live in and are destined for *civitates* and *regna,* within which they may possibly be entirely contained, but with which they are evidently not equated. Notice also the presence of "a certain mode of beauty," closely related to harmony and order, even in earthly *civitates.*

27 *Ep.* 91: *SAOO* 2, cols. 334–35; Migne 33, cols. 314–17. The pagans of Calama, a very Punic city about thirty-five miles inland from Hippo, and only since A.D. 283 a Roman *colonia,* had rioted against an imperial edict of June 407 forbidding public pagan worship. Nectarius, whom Augustine addresses as "Domino eximio meritoque honorabili fratri," argued their case. Augustine's intimate friend Possidius was then bishop of Calama. Writing at least partly on Possidius's behalf, Augustine replied (among other things) that such worship was not conducive to the frugality, continence, marital fidelity, probity, and other virtues which such authors as Cicero and Sallust knew and taught to be essential to the well-being of a *civitas.* On Calama and this incident, see Van der Meer, pp. 39–42, Pope, pp. 28, 120, and Brown, p. 287 (which relates this letter to Augustine's correspondence with Paulinus of Nola about the religious integrity of entities like the Roman people and the Heavenly Jerusalem). On Possidius, see McNamara, pp. 121–24, and pp. 12–19 of the introduction to Possidius's *Sancti Augustini Vita,* ed. and trans. Herbert T. Weiskotten.

28 "An putatis civitatem in parietibus deputandam? Civitas in civibus est, non in parietibus. . . . Nonne Deus pepercerat civitati, quia civitas migraverat, et perniciem illius ignis evaserat?" (*De Urbis Excidio sermo: SAOO* 6, cols. 1052 and, for the latter reference, 1053; Migne 40, cols. 721–23; *De Excidio Urbis Romae,* ed. and trans. Marie Vianney O'Reilly, Patristic Studies, 89: 66–70; *CCSL* 46: 258–60). On this sermon, see n. 32 below; but cf. the "civitas universa" in *SAOO* 6, col. 1048, showing another and wider usage of which *populus* seems incapable. However, that is not the point here. A splendid example of the nearly complete equivalence of these two words, which is the point at issue, appears in *CD* III, 18: "Iam vero Punicis bellis, cum inter utrumque imperium victoria diu anceps atque incerta penderet, populique duo praevalidi impetus in alterutrum fortissimos et opulentissimos

agerent, quot minutiora regna contrita sunt! Quae urbes amplae no-
bilesque deletae, quot adflictae, quot perditae civitates! Quam longe
lateque tot regiones terraeque vastatae sunt! Quotiens victi hinc atque
inde victores. Quid hominum consumptum est vel pugnantium militum
vel ab armis vacantium populorum! Quanta vis navium marinis etiam
proeliis oppressa, et diversarum tempestatum varietate submersa est!
Si ennarrare vel commemorare conemur, nihil aliud quam scriptores
etiam nos erimus historiae. Tunc magno metu perturbata Romana civitas
ad remedia vana et ridenda currebat" (*SAOO* 7, cols. 119–20; Migne
41, col. 98; *CCSL* 47:85). N.B. also the relationship of *populus* and
civitas with *regnum, imperium,* and *urbs.*

29   For a superb presentation of the development and chief meanings of the
term *populus* from the pre-republican period through the third century
A.D., see Theodor Mommsen, *Römisches Staatsrecht,* 1:3–7, 68, 123,
128, 145–49, 607–17, 824–27; 2:1257–61. Mommsen's analysis of this
term is very sensitive to variations in usage, as well as clearly sche-
matized and based on a wide range of sources; nonetheless, *populus* in
his judgment remains consistently ". . . der Staat, insofern er auf der
nationalen Zusammengehörigkeit der Personen ruht, während er als
örtlich unter einer Staatsgewalt begriffen das *imperium,* das Reich ist"
(1:3). *Civitas* he sees as a late-developing term for the *Bürgerschaft*
traditionally designated by *populus,* or as a term referring to "die
Zugehörigkeit zum Populus" (1:140). *Regnum* he almost ignores; it
seems to be a rather poor, pragmatic, general variant for *imperium,* the
relation of which with *populus* he analyzes in 1:824–27. A. J. Carlyle
argues that a *populus* is that body whose consensus is the source of
legitimate political authority in Roman juridical and constitutional theory
from Cicero to the *Corpus Juris Civilis* (*Mediaeval Political Theory* 1:
15–17, 63–70). He considers typical the view of the Flavian jurist
Pomponius (author of a history of Roman law from Romulus to the
emperors) that every law derives in some fashion from the *populus,* of
which the *plebs* was a distinct subdivision, *civitas* a product, etc. The
populus Romanus may in a sense be considered coextensive with the
regnum or *imperium Romanum,* but it is a different kind of entity from
that designated by the latter two (somewhat synonymous) terms.

The language of the texts collected in the *Corpus Juris Civilis* easily
supports Mommsen's and Carlyle's understanding of the relationship
among these terms. Justinian's preface proudly declares: "Et bellicos
quidem sudores nostros barbaricae gentes sub iuga nostra deductae
cognoscunt et tam Africa quam aliae innumerosae provinciae post tanta
temporum spatia nostris victoriis a caelesti numine praestitis iterum
dicioni Romanae nostroque additae imperio protestantur. Omnes vero
populi legibus iam a nobis vel promulgatis vel compositis reguntur."
Book i, title 1, 2 of the *Institutiones* proceeds to a statement of method:
"His generaliter cognitis et incipientibus nobis exponere iura populi

Romani ita maxime videntur posse tradi commodissime, si primo levi ac simplici, post deinde diligentissima atque exactissima interpretatione singula tradantur." These two passages, probably composed between 528 and 533, indicate clearly that the *populus Romanus* was not the same thing as the whole empire in basic, official usage one century after Augustine.

However, if the latter text seems to attribute something like territorial universality to the *populus Romanus,* that possible impression is corrected by a very famous and very traditional theoretical statement, the wording of which depends heavily on the Flavian jurist Gaius: "Omnes populi, qui legibus et moribus reguntur, partim suo proprio, partim communi omnium hominum iure utuntur: nam quod quisque populus ipse sibi ius constituit, id ipsius proprium civitatis est vocaturque ius civile, quasi ius proprium ipsius civitatis: quod vero naturalis ratio inter omnes homines constituit, id apud omnes populos peraeque custoditur vocaturque ius gentium, quasi quo iure omnes gentes utuntur. Et populus itaque Romanus partim suo proprio, partim communi omnium hominum iure utitur. Quae singula qualia sunt, suis locis proponemus" (*Institutiones* i, ii, 1; cf. *Digests* i, 1, 9). If the distinction between *populus* and *gens* is at best ambiguous here, that between *populus* and *civitas* is quite evident. An absolutely clear definition of *plebs* (and of *cives*) within the *populus* follows shortly: "Lex est, quod populus Romanus senatore magistratu interrogante, veluti consule, constituebat. . . . Plebs autem a populo eo differt, quo species a genere: nam appellatione populi universi cives significantur connumeratis etiam patriciis et senatoribus: plebis autem appellatione sine patriciis et senatoribus ceteri cives significantur" (*Institutiones* i, ii, 4). The language of these last two texts accords perfectly with that of the long excerpt from Pomponius's *Enchiridion* (see above) in *Digest* i, ii, 2.

The famous constitutional maxim of the third-century jurist Ulpian, appearing in *Digest* i, iv, 1, depends on a real distinction between *populus* and *imperium:* "Quod principi placuit, legis habet vigorem: utpote cum lege regia, quae de imperio eius lata est, populus ei et in eum omne suum imperium et potestatem conferat." That this understanding of the term *populus* (and for *populi* other than that of Rome, as well) was maintained in the legal language of the Christian empire of the late fourth century, appears clearly from the opening statute of the *Codex Iustinianus* (i, 1, 1; presumably chosen to represent the religious policy characteristic of the *Codex Theodosianus*): "Imppp. Gratianus Valentinianus et Theodosius AAA. ad populum urbis Constantinopolitanae. Cunctos populos, quos clementiae nostrae regit temperantum, in tali volumus religione versari, quam divinum Petrum apostolum tradidisse Romanis religio usque ad nunc ab ipso insinuata declarat quamque pontificem Damasum sequi claret et Petrum Alexandriae episcopum virum apostolicae sanctitatis, . . ." For Augustine's awareness of and cooperation with the antipagan imperial policy best summarized in the *Codex Theodosianus*, xvi, x, see Van der Meer, pp. 34, 37–43. For the texts cited above, see *Corpus Iuris Civilis*, ed. Paul Krueger (*Institutiones* and *Codex Iustinianus*) and Theodor Mommsen (*Digesta*), 2d ed., 2 vols. (Berlin, 1878–80): 1, *Inst.*, 2–4; *Dig.* pp. 1–5, 7; vol. 2, *Cod.*, 5. The last item, *Cunctos populos*, was issued at Thessalonica on 28 April 380. An excellent index for any word in the Code is *Vocabularium Codicis Iustiniani*, ed. R. Mayr, pt. 1: *Latina* (for *civitas, plebs, populus,* and *regnum,* see cols. 618–20, 1833, 1814–42, and 2116).

30 The exact relationship of the terms *populus, civitas,* and *regnum* in Augustine's vocabulary has received some ingenious treatment. McIlwain's claim that Augustine saw justice as a necessary constituent of a *populus,* but not of a *civitas* or *regnum* (*The Growth of Political Thought in the West, from the Greeks to the End of the Middle Ages,* pp. 156–58), tended to suggest other greater affinities between those two latter terms. Cotta, on the other hand, tends to treat all three terms simply as differing aspects of the same entity (pp. 52–53)—the question of synonymity does not arise in his discussion. Marshall observes that "*civitas* commonly is used to refer to the two great socio-religious collectivities [*Civitas Dei* and *Civitas Terrena*]; . . . *populus* seldom is, but is reserved for strictly human collectivities. However, in its definition, the term *populus* is apparently much more inclusive than the term *civitas.*" Later, he asserts (without examples) a traditional closeness between those terms; when he discusses *regnum,* he does so without reference to the other two (pp. 13, 48–49, 75–79). Discussing the ideological significance of *ordo* and *concordia,* del Estal declares: "Desnudo de este vivo y entrañable sentido comunitario, abierto a la arquitectura jerarquizada de la *polis,* el concepto de *civitas* no se distingue gran cosa de este otro más inferior, más pobre y menos fecundo de *populus.* Pero el *populus* latino y el augustiniano, contrariamente a la *civitas,* en que navegan inmersos, miran con frequencia a la sociedad antes que a la comunidad" (p. 388). On p. 398 he describes *populus* as "sujeto o contenido humano de la *civitas* augustiniana, así de la terrena como de la celeste." On p. 416 he asserts: "*Civitas* y *regnum* son vocablos sinónimos en la dialectica activa de San Agustín. El concepto de *civitas* es genérico (no todas las *civitates* son *regna*); la idea de *regnum* es específica (todos los *regna* son *civitates*)." *Ergo,* there must be some societies in Augustine's writings which are at the same time *populus, civitas,* and *regnum.* Unfortunately, that conclusion does not seem to be borne out by the evidence, three representative samples of which follow.

Typical of Augustine's usual establishment of the relationship between these three terms is the third sentence of his notorious definition of a *regnum* in *CD* IV, 4: "Remota itaque iustitia, quid sunt regna, nisi magna latrocinia? quia et ipsa latrocinia quid sunt, nisi parva regna? Manus et ipsa hominum est, imperio principis regitur, pacto societatis astringitur, placiti lege praeda dividitur. Hoc malum si in tantum perditorum hominum accessibus crescit, ut et loca teneat, sedes constituat, civitates occupet, populos subiuget, evidentius regni nomen assumit, . . ." (*SAOO* 7, cols. 142-43; Migne 41, col. 115; *CCSL* 47: 101). Whatever these three terms may have in common here, it is clear that the author is interested in what is specifically different about them, that is, the tangible, physical aspects (probably civic as well as geographical) of the *civitas,* the human membership denoted by the *populus,* the purely titular element conferred on a given power monopoly by *regnum.* The only instance which I have discovered of Augustine's suggesting an equivalence between *civitas* and *regnum* occurs in his attempt to explain why Matthew's Gospel at one point calls Capharnaum "civitas Iesu." "Quae difficultas solveretur, si Matthaeus etiam Nazareth nominaret: nunc vero cum potuerit ipsa Galilaea dici civitas Christi, quia in Galilaea erat Nazareth: sicut universum regnum in tot civitatibus constitutum, dicitur Romana civitas; cumque in tot gentibus constituta civitas sit, de qua scriptum est, 'Gloriosissima dicta sunt de te, civitas Dei'; et cum ipse prior populus Dei in tot civitatibus habitans, etiam una domus dictus sit domus Israel . . ." (*De Consensu Evangelistarum* II, 25: *SAOO* 3, col. 1328; Migne 34, col. 1106). Notice the looseness of this three-part analogy, and the retreat within it from the statement "regnum in civitatibus constitutum dicitur civitas" to the statement "populus in civitatibus habitans dictus est domus." Besides, Augustine is here trying to solve a "contradiction" not of his own making, and to accomplish this is making a statement about the limits of acceptable common usage rather than about the central tendencies of his own. It is true that *civitas* may occasionally seem to correspond to *regnum* when Augustine is being less consciously ingenious, as in his *Enarratio* on Psalm 47: "Manifestum est autem, quod primordia regni Carthaginis navibus floruerunt, et ita floruerunt, ut inter caeteras gentes excellerent negotiationibus et navigationibus. . . . Atque hinc nimium superba facta est civitas illa, ut digne per eius naves intelligatur, superbia gentium, praesumens in incertis tamquam in flatibus ventorum" (*SAOO* 4, col. 595; Migne 36, col. 537). But this example seems representative more of Augustine's love for rich vocabulary-play than of any concern on his part for the ideological nuances of *civitas, regnum,* or even *gens.*

31　Cf. the passages from chaps. 26-28 of *De Vera Religione* cited n. 26 above, and in the passage from the *Tractatus in Ioannis Evangelium* cited in n. 102 below (where Augustine comes close to saying *"populus diaboli"* but does not quite do so).

32　"Nonne ante paucos annos, Arcadio imperatore Constantinopoli (quod dico, audiunt nonnulli forsitan qui noverunt, et sunt in hoc populo qui et illic praesentes fuerunt), volens Deus terrere civitatem, et terrendo emendare, terrendo convertere, terrendo mundare, terrendo mutare, servo cuidam suo fideli, viro, ut dicitur, militari, venit in revelatione, et dixit ei civitatem venturo de coelo igne perituram; eumque admonuit ut episcopo diceret. Dictum est; non contempsit episcopus, et allocutus est populum: conversa est civitas in luctum poenitentiae, quemadmodum quondam illa antiqua Ninive" (*De Urbis Excidio sermo 7: SAOO 6,* col. 1052; Migne 40, col. 722). This section of the sermon refers to an event also mentioned in Prosper of Aquitaine's *Chronicle,* and dated 396 by Baronius. This sermon was printed together with several dubious works by the Maurist editors, although their treatment of it cast no explicit doubt on its authorship. Schanz, Hosius, and Krüger, pp. 459–61, give an account of the research done on that group of *opuscula.* On the basis of that spare set of references, G. McCracken inferred that "Dom Morin did not consider this sermon to be by Augustine . . ." (Loeb *CG,* 1:lxxii, n. 3). However, in his general introductory treatment of the contents of MS. Guelferbytanus 4096, Morin accepts this sermon as a genuine work of Augustine's (Germain Morin, ed., *SI,* p. xxx. Cf. his treatment of the pseudo-Augustinian *De Tempore Barbarico sermo* on p. xxxi.) Otto Seeck assumed the authenticity of Augustine's authorship of the sermon when he cited him as a source for the authenticity of the earthquake, fiery cloud, etc. (*Geschichte des Untergangs der Antiken Welt,* 6 vols., Berlin: Siemenroth & Troschel, 1895–1921, 5:305 ff., 563). Emilienne Demougeot followed him in this particular (*De l'unité à la division de l'Empire romain, 395–410,* p. 194, nn. 408–09). Augustine's authorship now appears definitely established by Sr. Marie Vianney O'Reilly's edition (with translation and commentary) of the sermon, published in 1955 (see n. 28 above); the editors of *CCSL* have accepted her arguments and her text for their edition of the sermon in *CCSL* 46:242–62.

The earthquake and accompanying atmospheric phenomena seem to have occurred in 398. Whether John Chrysostom was the "bishop" involved, and whether or not the seismic events actually served as an occasion for the mass demonstration of spiritual solidarity reported by Augustine about a dozen years later, are questions on which I am presently engaged in research. At any rate, Augustine seems quite confident in his version of the rumor.

33   ". . . ut accedebat super civitatem ita crescebat, donec toti urbi ignis terribiliter imminet. . . . Populus securus paululum factus, iterum audivit omnino esse migrandum, quod civitas esset proximo sabbato peritura. Migravit cum Imperatore tota civitas; . . . Et aliquot millibus tanta illa multitudo progressa, uno tamen loco fundendis ad Deum orationibus congregata. . ." (*SAOO* 6, cols. 1052–53; Migne 40, cols. 721–23; *CCSL* 46:258–60; O'Reilly, ed., pp. 68–70.) Cf. n. 28 above.

34   "Ad communem hanc quasi rem publicam nostram quisque pro modulo nostro exsolvimus quod debemus, et pro possessione virium nostrarum quasi canonem passionum inferimus. . . . Nolite ergo putare, fratres, omnes iustos qui passi sunt persecutionem iniquorum, etiam illos qui venerunt missi ante Domini adventum, non pertinuisse ad membra Christi. Absit ut non pertineat ad membra Christi, qui pertinet ad

civitatem quae regem habet Christum. Illa una est Ierusalem coelestis, civitas sancta: haec una civitas unum habet regem" (*Enarratio in Psalmum* 61, 4: *SAOO* 4, col. 843; Migne 36, col. 731). Henri Rondet has undertaken the valuable project of dating the *Enarrationes,* and so far has gotten through Ps. 54 ("Essais sur la chronologie des 'Enar-rationes in Psalmos' de St. Augustin," *Bulletin de littérature ecclésias-tique,* 61 [1960]:111–27 and 258–86; 65 [1964]:110–36; 68 [1967]: 179–202).

35	"Quid autem illi diversi errores inimici Christi, omnes tantum dicendi sunt? nonne et unus? Plane audeo et unum dicere: quia una civitas et una civitas, unus populus et unus populus, rex et rex. Quid est, una civitas et una civitas? Babylonia una; Ierusalem una. Quibuslibet aliis etiam mysticis nominibus appelletur, una tamen civitas et una civitas: illa rege diabolo; ista rege Christo" (*SAOO* 4, col. 845; Migne 36, col. 733).

36	"De Christo enim dictum est, cum laudaretur excellentia populi primi, et dolerentur fracti rami naturales" (*SAOO* 4, col. 844; Migne 36, cols. 731–32). The reference is to Rom. 11:21.

37	"Respicite ergo populum illum primum, positum etiam ad significandum populum posteriorem; . . ." (*SAOO* 4, col. 848; Migne 36, col. 735). Similar is the reference in col. 847 to the earthly Jerusalem: "Sed si futurus est in populo Dei, destruetur vetus, et aedificabitur novus" (Migne 36, col. 734).

38	"Caput enim vituli corpus erat impiorum, in similitudine vituli mandu-cantis fenum (Ps. 105:20), terrena quaerentium: quia 'omnis caro fenum' (Isa. 40:6). Erat ergo, ut dixi, corpus impiorum. Iratus Moyses in ignem misit, comminuit, in aqua sparsit, bibendum populo dedit; et ira Prophetae administratio facta est prophetiae. Corpus enim illud in ignem mittitur tribulationum et verbo Dei comminuitur. Paulatim enim desistunt ab unitate corporis eius. Sicut enim vestimentum, ita per tempus absumitur. Et unusquisque qui fit christianus, separatur ab illo populo, et quasi a massa comminuitur. . . . Et quid iam evidentius, quam quod in corpus illud civitatis Ierusalem, cuius imago erat populus Israel, per Baptismum traiciendi erant homines? Ideo in aqua sparsum est, ut in potum daretur. Hoc usque in finem sitit iste; currit, et sitit. Multos enim bibit; sed nunquam erit sine siti. Inde est enim, 'Sitio, mulier, da mihi bibere.' (John 4:17) . . . Quid ergo sitis? quid sitis? tantis populis non satiaris?" (*SAOO* 4, cols. 850–51; Migne 36, cols. 736–37).

39	"Ipsa, ut dixi, Troia, mater populi Romani, sacratis in locis deorum suorum munire non potuit cives suos ab ignibus ferroque Graecorum, eosdem ipsos deos colentium: quin etiam,

'. . . Iunonis asylo
custodes lecti, Phoenix et dirus Ulysses
praedam asservabant; . . .'

. . . Compara nunc asylum illud, non cuiuslibet dei gregalis, vel de turba plebis, sed Iovis ipsius sororis et reginae omnium deorum, cum memoriis nostrorum Apostolorum" (*CD* i, 4: *SAOO* 7, col. 7; Migne 41, col. 17; *CCSL* 47:4-5; Loeb *CG* 1:24-25). The internal quotation is from the *Aeneid* II, 761-63. Wolfgang Seyfarth maintains that such distinctions (with which the distinction cited in n. 29 above is entirely consistent) had disappeared by the fourth century; in the majority of the legal, historical, and epigraphic remains of that and the following century, *populus* and *plebs* are synonyms for "das niedere Volk im Gegensatz zu den Senatoren und Dekurionen" (*Soziale Fragen der spätrömischen Kaiserzeit im Spiegel des Theodosianus,* Deutsche Akademie der Wissenschaften zu Berlin, Schriften der Sektion für Altertumswissenschaft, 33:121-27.) If this contention is valid, here is further evidence for the unusually conservative precision of Augustine's social terminology in works of a literary character like *The City of God.* For his usage in more everyday contexts, see nn. 45, 48 below.

40 Van der Meer discusses the incident on pp. 142-43 and 264 of *Augustine the Bishop.* See also Kunzelmann, p. 498, and the brief introduction by C. Lambot in *Sancti Aurelii Augustini Sermones selecti duodeviginti,* Stromata Patristica et Mediaevalia, 1:100. (The text of the sermon appears on pp. 100-11.) According to Peter Brown, the official was commander of the military garrison of Hippo, and his offense was strictly enforced collection of the heavy and unpopular grain-levy (pp. 192, 421). The sermon was well known in the Middle Ages, being alluded to, for example, by Bede in his commentary on Rom. 12 and 13. The Maurist editors interpreted the incident as being primarily an affair of *populares* (*SAOO* 11, col. 1690)—a form which Augustine nowhere uses in this sermon.

41 "Populum quis monet in parte? . . . Quis ducat populum in partem, et nullo sciente moneat populum? . . . Sed parum est, ut dixi, parum est ut doleatis, nisi etiam ea quae ad populi pertinet potestatem pro viribus vestris prohibeatis. Non dico, fratres, quia potest aliquis vestrum exire et populum prohibere: hoc nec nos possumus . . . Fratres mei, iram Dei timeo. Deus non timet turbas. Quam cito dicitur, Quod populus fecit, fecerit; quis est qui vindicet populum? Itane, quis est? nec Deus? Timuit enim Deus universum mundum, quando fecit diluvium? Timuit tot civitates Sodomae et Gomorrhae, quando coelesti delevit igne?" (*Sermo* 302: *SAOO* 5, cols. 1813-14; Migne 38, cols. 1392-93).

42 *Populi* and *popularis* may carry overtones of "the ordinary people" in two passages from the end of Augustine's treatise *Contra Academicos,* composed at Cassiciacum in November 386 (III, xviii, 41): "Nam Epicureorum greges in animis deliciosorum populorum aprica stabula posuerunt." III, xix, 42: "Non enim est ista huius mundi philosophia . . . intelligibilis, . . . nisi summus Deus populari quadam clementia

divini intellectus auctoritatem usque ad ipsum corpus humanum declineret, atque submitteret; . . ." (*SAOO* 1, cols. 486 and 487; Migne 32, col. 956). In the first passage, moral downgrading is at least also present; in any case, this condescending use of *populus* seems to fade out of Augustine's language after the early, rather esoterically Neoplatonic period during and concerning which this treatise was written.

Christine Mohrmann has clarified the significance of the usage of *popularis* which became the central one for Augustine beginning with the years of his priestly ministry in Hippo: "Quand on voulait mettre l'accent sur le caractère pastoral de la prédication, on parlait de *sermo* (ou *tractatus*) *popularis*. Cette expression ne signifie pas, comme on l'explique si souvent, une prédication populaire, au sens d'une prédication simple ou d'un sermon délivré en langue vulgaire. *Popularis* est dérivé ici de *populus* ou *populi* au sens technique de la communauté des fidèles réunie dans l'église" (*"Praedicare-Tractare-Sermo,"* Etudes 2: 71–72). Some examples of this usage may be found in: *Confessions*, VI, 4, 6 (Ambrose's sermons); *CD* XVII, 17; *Enarratio in Ps. 118*, proem.; *Ep.* 224, 2 (equivalence to *homiliae*).

43   "Alloquor itaque uos, unus dies, infantes male nati ex Adam, bene renati in Christo. Videte quia dies estis, uidete quia fecit uos dominus. Fugauit a cordibus uestris tenebras peccatorum, innouauit uitam uestram. Miscendi estis hodie numero populorum: eligite quos imitemini, nolite uobis eligere perditos, eum quibus pereatis. . . . Fideles uocamini, fideliter uiuite: domino uestro in corde et moribus uestris fidem seruate. Nolite uos commiscere moribus malis in turba christianorum malorum" (*Sermo* 18, 2: *SI*, pp. 69–70). For the date, see Kunzelmann, p. 474.

44   Augustine seems to have used it quite strictly when speaking of the historical Roman *plebs*. A good example of this usage is *CD* II, 17 and 18, chapters which deal with the laws and internal intrigues of the kingdom and early republic. These chapters are also a rich source for Augustine's historically strict usage of *populus, civitas, regnum, imperium, res republica, urbs, gens*, and *patria*. These terms are not usually found in such close and frequently repeated association in his works; the influence of Sallust is strong and avowed.

45   For just one example of Augustine's usage of *plebs* for the laity of his own diocese see the salutation of *Ep.* 122, written probably in 410, to reassure his flock during his absence on some business: "Dilectissimis fratribus conclericis et universae plebi, Augustinus, in Domino salutem." The communal totality of the body so addressed is made clear by such sentences as: "In primis peto charitatem vestram, et per Christum obsecro, ne vos mea contristat absentia corporalis," and "Nuntiatum enim est mihi quod morem vestrum de vestiendis pauperibus fueritis obliti; . . ." (*SAOO* 2, cols. 540–41; Migne 33, col. 470).

46   For a particularly effective evocation of this environment and its influence on the adolescent Augustine, see O'Meara's *Young Augustine*, pp.

24–25, 39, 45–46. For the impact of Carthage on him at that stage of his life and his attachment for the metropolis later, see G. G. Lapeyre, "Saint Augustin et Carthage," *MA* 2:91–148, esp. pp. 91–99.

47 Bulla Regia was a favorite residence and perhaps the capital of King Iarbas, who died there early in the first century B.C. It was an *oppidum liberum* before Augustus, and along with two other distinguished repositories of African historical tradition, Utica and Zama, got *ius municipii* (though whether *ius Latii* or *ius Romanorum* is unclear) under Hadrian. Like Hippo Regius, its forum was distinguished by a monumental statue of Vespasian, and under Diocletian and the Tetrarchs several temples were added to its collection of religious monuments, already notable for a temple to Apollo built under Tiberius and one to Diana built shortly after the death of Septimius Severus (and in his honor). In 361–62, the devoutly Christian proconsul Olybrius had collaborated with the legate Attilius Theodotus in repairing Bulla's *tabularium* (public archives). Under the Vandals, Bulla would manage both to become once more a favorite royal residence and to retain a Catholic community strong enough to maintain unbroken episcopal succession. See Pietro Romanelli, *Storia delle province romane dell'Africa*, Istituto Italiano per la Storia Antica, fasc. 14, pp. 83, 95, 213, 245, 298, 346–47, 432, 527, 558; Leo Teutsch, *Das Städtewesen in Nordafrika, in der Zeit von C. Gracchus bis zum Tode des Kaisers Augustus*, p. 10 (excellent summary of recent bibliography), 87, map 1; Christian Courtois, *Les Vandales et l'Afrique*, pp. 126–28 (language patterns among the populace), 190, 306, 314. For road patterns, see Christine Mohrmann and F. Van der Meer, *Atlas of the Early Christian World*, trans. M. F. Hedlund and H. H. Rowley, maps 22 and 33 (the latter on Augustine's travels); *Grosser Historischer Weltatlas*, vol. 1, *Vorgeschichte und Altertum*, ed. Hermann Bengtson and Vladimir Milojčić, maps 31 and 36.

48 "Non plebei solum, non quicumque opifices, non pauperes, non egeni, non mediocres, sed multi etiam magni diuites, senatores, clarissimae etiam feminae ueniente persecutione omnibus suis renuntiauerunt" (*Sermo* Denis 17, 4: *Sancti Augustini Sermones post Maurinos reperti,* ed. G. Morin, *MA* 1:85). For the date, see Kunzelmann, p. 495: Augustine seems to have been passing through on his way from Hippo to Carthage. Representative of his more literary vocabulary for such social distinctions is the comment on 1 Tim. 2:14 in the *Enchiridion,* written for the cultivated Laurentius (brother of the anti-Donatist tribune Dulcitius) in 421 or a little later: ". . . sed ut 'omnes homines' omne genus hominum intelligamus per quascumque differentias distributum, reges, privatos, nobiles, ignobiles, sublimes, humiles, doctos, indoctos, integri corporis, debiles, ingeniosos, tardicordes, fatuos, divites, pauperes, mediocres, mares, feminas, infantes, pueros, adolescentes, iuvenes, seniores, senes; in linguis omnibus, in artibus omnibus, in professionibus omnibus, in voluntatum et conscientiarum varietate innumerabili con-

stitutos, et si quid aliud differentiarum est hominibus" (*Ad Laurentium de fide, spe, et charitate liber unus, sive Enchiridion,* chap. 27, p. 103: (*SAOO* 6, col. 339; Migne 40, col. 280). According to Seyfarth, by Augustine's time "die Grenze zwischen Plebejern und Angehörigen der oberen Stände war durchaus scharf gezogen, keineswegs aber unüberschreitbar." So Augustine's usage of *plebei* in this sermon would seem to be entirely in line with current spoken language and even with the terminology of official documents (Seyfarth cites a famous constitution issued by Honorius and Theodosius II in 412), whereas his use of *pauperes* in the *Enchiridion* is evidence of his literary purism. For a very full analysis of usage on this point (which ignores Augustine for some reason), see Seyfarth, pp. 104–21.

49   "Audeo dicere: uicinam ciuitatem uestram imitamini, uicinam ciuitatem Simittu imitamini. . . . Legatus ibi uoluit agere huiusmodi turpitudines: nullus principalis, nullus plebeius intrauit, nullus Iudaeus intrauit. Ipsi honesti non sunt? Illa ciuitas non est? illa colonia non est, tanto honestior, quanto istis rebus inanior?" *MA* 1:88. Simittu, known today as Chemtou, would seem to have been Bulla Regia's natural rival. An important marble-cutting center from pre-Roman times, it became under Augustus a *colonia Quirina,* entitled Iulia Augusta Numidica Simitthus, and was listed by Pliny as an *oppidum civium Romanorum,* whereas in the same list Bulla was simply *oppidum liberum.* Despite its later reversion to a distinctly non-Latin form of its name (in which it differed markedly from Bulla Regia or Hippo Regius—formerly and natively Ubbone), Simittu seems to have received significant settlement at least by Roman military personnel. Interestingly enough, it would appear that Simittu was better endowed theatrically than Bulla before the fourth century, and in 376 its theater was repaired through the munificence of the proconsul Decimus Hesperius. Perhaps this project is the event to which Augustine refers. See Romanelli, pp. 198–99, 209, 250, 277, 360, 598; Teutsch, pp. 171–72.

50   "Est enim quidam populus natus ad iram Dei, et ad hoc praecognitus" (*In Ioannis Evangelium Tractatus* XIV, 8: *SAOO* 3, col. 1845; Migne 35, col. 1507). This work is now dated ca. 418 (Pope, pp. 347–48).

51   "Eo potissimum ipsarum sollemnitas octauarum, quae toto terrarum orbe quaquauersum gentes Christi nomini salubriter subiugauit, ab omnibus per baptismum eius regeneratis deuotissime celebratur. . . . Cum autem, quod hodierno die sollemniter geritur, ex istis cancellis, quibus uos a ceteris distinguebat, spiritalis infantia, populo permixti fueritis, bonis inhaerete: . . ." *Sermo* Mai 94, *MA* 1:334, 338. Kunzelmann suggests no date.

52   "Ne moras faciamus, acturi multa, regeneratis in baptismo qui hodie miscendi sunt populo, brevis sed gravis sermo reddendus est. Vos qui baptizati estis, et hodie completis sacramentum octavarum vestrarum, breviter accipite et intelligite translatam fuisse figuram circumcisionis

carnis, ad circumcisionem cordis. Dic octavo circumciduntur carne secundum veterem legem: et hoc propter Dominum Christum, qui post diem septimum sabbatorum octavo Dominico resurrexit. Cultellis petrinis iussum est circumcidi: petra erat Christus. Infantes appellamini, quoniam regenerati estis, et novam vitam ingressi estis, et ad vitam aeternam renati estis, si hoc quod in vobis renatum est, male vivendo non suffocetis. Reddendi estis populis, miscendi estis plebi fidelium: cavete ne imitemini malos fideles, imo falso fideles; quasi confitendo fideles, sed male vivendo infideles" (*Sermo* 260: *SAOO* 5, col. 1554; Migne 38, cols. 1201–02). The scene of this sermon was a basilica founded by Bishop Leontius of Hippo, perhaps the same person as the martyr whom both Donatists and Catholics held in emulous reverence (Van der Meer, p. 19; Geoffrey G. Willis, *Saint Augustine and the Donatist Controversy*, pp. 28–29).

53   For the church as *populus*, see pp. 54–59 of this chapter. The conclusion reached here about the relation of the form *populi* and of *plebs* (or *plebes*) to the form *populus* in this ecclesiastical reference does not agree entirely with the conclusion of Josef Ratzinger that *populus* denotes the *Gesamtkirche* in Augustine's sermons, while *populi/plebes* (and *plebs* as well, apparently) denote the "einzelnen Bischofsgemeinden" or "Einzelgemeinde." However, the texts cited here and in section 6 would lend support to his assertion that "Es ist klar: Hier ist populus kein Bildwort mehr, es ist nicht in irgendeiner analogen Weise gemeint, es ist eine praktische, bildlose, sachliche Bezeichnung." The real question in Ratzinger's attention to these terms is "ob es sich bei diesem Sachbegriff noch um einem theologischen Begriff handelt" (*Volk und Haus Gottes*, pp. 159–69, esp. p. 161). His answer is affirmative. My only criticism of the former part of his argument is that, while impressively subtle, it is based on too few examples to be generally valid.

54   Not in connection with *populus*, at any rate. Birth could be linked with *civitas* at times, as in *Sermo* 105, which begins with Luke 11:5–13, but ends up once again discussing the recent sack of Rome: "Manet civitas quae nos carnaliter genuit. Deo gratias. Utinam et spiritualiter genereretur, et nobiscum transeat ad aeternitatem. Si non manet civitas quae nos carnaliter genuit, manet quae nos spiritualiter genuit. 'Aedificans Ierusalem Dominus' . . . Sed non dicat de Roma, dictum est de me: O si taceat de Roma: quasi ego insultator sim, et non potius Domini deprecator, et vester qualiscumque exhortator. Absit a me ut insultem. Avertat Deus a corde meo, et a dolore conscientiae meae. Ibi multos fratres non habuimus? non adhuc habemus? Portio peregrinantis Ierusalem civitatis non ibi magna degit? non ibi temporalia magna? sed aeterna non perdidit" (*SAOO* 5, cols. 782–84; Migne 38, cols 622–24). Once more *civitas* appears to be a word of higher emotional charge and greater empathetic capabilities than *populus*. The theme struck here, with its emphasis on the importance of spiritual rather than of

physical citizenship in the midst of the current calamities, is fairly constant in his sermons and letters on the disaster of 410. See Rudolph Arbesmann, "The Idea of Rome in the Sermons of St. Augustine," *Augustiniana* (special issue for November 1954), pp. 89–108. Augustine's basic attitude is characterized on pp. 91–92, and demonstrated in the rest of the article from several sermons including this one; cf. also, especially for the metaphoric quality of terms like "birth" and "membership" in this context, Johannes Straub, "Augustins Sorge um die *regeneratio imperii," Historisches Jahrbuch* 73 (1954):36–60, passim.

55 "In septimo decimo libro quod dictum est de Samuele, 'Non erat de filiis Aaron', dicendum potius fuit, Non erat filius sacerdotis. Filios quippe sacerdotum defunctis sacerdotibus succedere magis legitimi moris fuit: nam in filiis Aaron reperitur pater Samuelis, sed sacerdos non fuit, nec ita in filiis ut eum ipse genuerit Aaron, sed sicut omnes illius populi dicuntur filii Israel" (trans. from Loeb *CG* 1:4–7. *Retractationes* II, 43: *SAOO* 7, col. lxi; Migne 32, col. 648). As a matter of fact, Augustine was genealogically correct the first time (cf. 1 Par. 6:28), and must have gotten hold of corrupt information in the meantime. The point about birth remains clear, however. The force of this observation is all the greater because it occupies nearly half of Augustine's very brief *Retractatio* on *The City of God,* and thus enjoys nearly equal billing with his statement of the whole work's inspiration and purpose.

56 "Unum cogitate, fratres mei, et videte in ipsa multitudine si delectat, nisi unum. Ecce Deo propitio quam multi estis: quis vos ferret, nisi unum saperetis? Unde in multis quies ista? Da unum, et populus est: tolle unum, et turba est. Quid est enim turba, nisi multitudo turbata?" (*Sermo* 103: *SAOO* 5, col. 772; Migne 38, col. 614). Kunzelmann suggests no date for this sermon.

57 Gilson, pp. 37–38. For a treatment of this traditional connection in the context of the more general philosophical relevance of harmony and order, see Josef Rief, *Der Ordobegriff des jungen Augustinus,* pp. 56–73, 300–02. The relationship of *ordo* to Augustine's early analysis of social cohesion is treated on pp. 350–55. See also the commentary on this passage by R. Jolivet in *BA,* vol. 4 (of which *De Ordine* and the introduction, commentary, and notes are pp. 293–462). Among Augustine's own works, cf. also *De Ordine* II, 4, 12 and *De Libero Arbitrio* I, 5, 6, and 15. A noteworthy variation of this theme which so interested the young Augustine appears much later in *CD* XII, 22, in the quite different context of some of his dominant later interests: predestination, the unique origin and fall of man, etc. "Nec ignorabat Deus hominem peccaturum et morti iam obnoxium morituros propagaturum eoque progressuros peccandi inmanitate mortales, et tutius atque pacatius inter se rationalis voluntatis expertes bestiae sui generis viverent, quarum ex aquis et terris plurium pullulavit exordium, quam homines, quorum

genus ex uno est ad commendandam concordiam propagatum. Neque enim inter se leones aut inter se dracones, qualia homines, bella gesserunt. Sed praevidebat etiam gratia sua populum piorum in adoptionem vocandum remissisque peccatis iustificatum Spiritu sancto sanctis angelis in aeterna pace sociandum, novissima inimica morte destructa; cui populo esset huius rei consideratio profutura, quod ex uno homine Deus ad commendandum hominibus, quam ei grata sit etiam in pluribus unitas, genus instituisset humanum" (*SAOO* 7, cols. 515–16; Migne 41, cols. 372–73; *CCSL* 48:380–81).

58   "Amici quid aliud quam unum esse conantur? Et quanto magis unum, tanto magis amici sunt. Populus una civitas est cui est periculosa dissensio: quid est autem dissensio, nisi non unum sentire? Ex multis militibus fit unus exercitus: nonne quaevis multitudo eo minus vincitur, quo magis in unum coit?" (*De Ordine* II, 18, 48: *SAOO* I, col. 582; Migne 32, col. 1017). Augustine's near-definition of *populus* in this and the previously cited passage as the product of the encounter of *ordo* with a human *multitudo* takes on greater significance if one realizes that there was nothing pejorative about the term *multitudo* for Augustine. One of the most individual of his social attitudes is the notion that the multitudinous character of the Church was a sign of its divine origin, just as the converse sort of membership brought into question the validity of the societies and doctrines of the Academicians and other philosophers (Ratzinger, *Volk und Haus Gottes*, pp. 30–32). *Turba* is the pejorative term, signifying a *multitudo* gone bad through irrationality. Consequently, by virtue of being a more perfect kind of *multitudo*, a *populus* is a very respectable sort of body indeed.

59   "Deus igitur Hebraeorum . . . legem dedit Hebraeo populo suo, hebraeo sermone conscriptam, non obscuram et incognitam, sed omnibus iam gentibus diffamatam, in qua lege scriptum est, 'Sacrificans diis eradicabitur, nisi Domino tantum' " (*CD* XIX, 23: *SAOO* 7, col. 916; Migne 41, col. 654; *CCSL* 48:694; Loeb *CG* 6:228–29).

60   "Quapropter quisquis alienigena, id est, non ex Israel progenitus, nec ab illo populo in canonem sacrarum litterarum receptus, legitur aliquid prophetasse de Christo, si in nostram notitiam venit, aut venerit, ad cumulum a nobis commemorari potest: . . . Nec ipsos Iudaeos existimo audere contendere, neminem pertinuisse ad Deum, praeter Israelitas, ex quo propago Israel esse coepit, reprobato eius fratre maiore. Populus enim revera, qui proprie Dei populus diceretur, nullus alius fuit: homines autem quosdam non terrena, sed coelesti societate ad veros Israelitas supernae cives patriae pertinentes etiam in aliis gentibus fuisse, negare non possunt: quia si negant, facillime convincuntur de sancto et mirabili viro Iob, qui nec indigena, nec proselytus, id est advena populi Israel fuit; sed ex gente Idumea genus ducens, ibi ortus, ibidem mortuus est" (*CD* XVIII, 47: *SAOO* 7, cols. 853–54; Migne 41, col. 609; *CCSL* 48: 645; Loeb *CG* 6:53–55).

61 And of several other group labels, too: "At vero gens illa, ille populus, illa civitas, illa res publica, illi Israelitae, quibus credita sunt eloquia Dei . . ." (*CD* xviii, 41: *SAOO* 7, col. 842; Migne 41, col. 601; *CCSL* 48:637). Augustine is not speaking in definitive terms here, but the participants in this burst of synonymous eloquence would all suit both Israel and his definitions elsewhere with ease.

62 On Moses' relationship with Israel (especially the *populus* thereof), see *CD* xviii, 8 and 11. The usage of *populus* for this relationship seems quite normal in Augustine's context; cf. the pseudo-Augustinian *De Tempore Barbarico sermo*, which Morin tentatively suggests as the work of Bishop Quodvultdeus of Carthage, ca. 439 (*SI*, p. xxxi): "Moyses populum oberrantem, vitulumque fusilem adorantem . . . coercuit . . ." (*SAOO* 6, col. 1052; Migne 40, col. 702).

63 "Quare filii Israel sacrificabant visibiliter pecorum victimas? Quia sunt etiam sacra spiritualia, quorum imagines carnalem populum celebrare oportebat, ut praefiguratio novi populi servitute veteris fieret" (*De Diversis Quaestionibus* 49 [a work begun about 388 in Africa, and completed about 396]; *SAOO* 6, col. 50; Migne 40, col. 31). About three decades later, in *CD* x, 5 and 6, Augustine took up again the question of the animal sacrifices: "Quae nunc Dei populus legit, non facit." Cf. also *CD* xviii, 45, on a misunderstood messianic prophecy: "Sic quippe intelligebat populus ille carnalis, quod praenuntiatum est per Aggaeum prophetam . . ." (*SAOO* 7, col. 848; Migne 41, col. 606; *CCSL* 48:641). On this last citation, cf. pp. 52–53 and n. 90, below.

64 "Christianos, maxime ex Gentibus venientes, iudaizare non oportere Paulus apostolus docet, . . ." (*Ep.* 196: *SAOO* 2, col. 1096; Migne 33, col. 892). The background to this letter is sketched by Bernhard Blumenkranz on pp. 236–37 of his article "Augustin et les juifs; Augustin et le judaisme," *Recherches Augustiniennes,* 1:225–41. This letter is one of the three extant works composed by Augustine exclusively on the relationship between the Church and contemporary Judaism. Asellicus is known only through this letter, but the controversy giving rise to his request for guidance is better known, and was evidently widespread in Africa. Blumenkranz also discusses Augustine's attitude toward Old Testament Judaism and toward the powerful African Jewish communities in less controversial contexts.

65 "Item secundum originem carnis ad Esau, qui dictus est etiam Edom, gentem Idumaeorum; ad Iacob autem, qui dictus est etiam Israel, gentem Iudaeorum: porro secundum mysterium spiritus, ad Esau Iudaeos, ad Israel pertinere Christianos. Ita quippe impletur quod scriptum est, 'Maior serviet minori,' id est prior natus populus Iudaeorum posteriori nato populo Christianorum. Ecce quemadmodum sumus Israel adoptione divina, non humana cognatione gloriantes; nec in manifesto, sed in occulto; nec littera, sed spiritu; nec carnis, sed cordis circumcisione Iudaei" (*SAOO* 2, col. 1103; Migne 33, col. 897).

66 For an evocation of the political and intellectual context within which
    Augustine composed *On Genesis against the Manichees,* his "first ecclesi-
    astical pamphlet", see Peter Brown, pp. 134–35. For the dating of *The
    City of God,* cf. n. 5 to this chapter, above; on the plan of books xi–
    xviii, see the notes by G. Bardy and F.-J. Thonnard in *BA* 36:742–44.

67 "Primordia enim generis humani, in quibus ista luce frui coepit, bene
    comparantur primo diei quo fecit Deus lucem. Haec aetas tanquam
    infantia deputanda est ipsius universi saeculi, quod tanquam unum
    hominem proportione magnitudinis suae cogitare debemus; quia unus-
    quisque homo cum primo nascitur, et exit ad lucem, primam aetatem
    agit infantiam. Haec tenditur ab Adam usque ad Noe generationibus
    decem. Quasi vespera huius diei fit diluvium: quia et infantia nostra
    tanquam oblivionis diluvio deletur" (*SAOO* 1, cols. 1067–68; Migne 34,
    col. 190). Augustine's presentation of this allegory of human develop-
    ment is worth comparing with the more sensitive schema which he pro-
    posed about ten years later in the *Confessions.*

68 "Haec aetas non diluvio deletur, quia et pueritia nostra non oblivione
    tergitur de memoria. Meminimus enim nos fuisse pueros, infantes autem
    non meminimus. Huius vespera est confusio linguarum in eis qui turrem
    faciebant, et fit mane ab Abraham. Sed nec ista aetas secunda generavit
    populum Dei, quia nec pueritia apta est ad generandum" (*SAOO* 1, col.
    1068; Migne 34, cols. 190–91).

69 "Mane ergo fit ab Abraham, et succedit aetas tertia similis adolescentiae.
    Et bene comparatur diei tertio, quo ab aquis terra separata est. Ab
    omnibus enim gentibus, quarum error instabilis et vanis simulacrorum
    doctrinis tanquam ventis omnibus mobilis, maris nomine bene signifi-
    catur; ab hac ergo gentium vanitate et huius saeculi fluctibus separatus
    est populus Dei per Abraham, tanquam terra cum apparuit arida, id
    est, sitiens imbrem coelestem divinorum mandatorum: qui populus
    unum Deum colendo, tanquam irrigata terra, ut fructus utiles posset
    afferre, sanctas Scripturas et Prophetias accepit. Haec enim aetas potuit
    iam generare populum Deo, quia et tertia aetas, id est adolescentia filios
    habere iam potest. Et ideo ad Abraham dictum est: 'Patrem multarum
    gentium posui te, et augeam te nimis valde, et ponam te in gentes, et
    reges de te exient. Et ponam testamentum meum inter me et te, et
    inter semen tuum post te, in generationes eorum in testamentum
    aeternum; ut sim tibi Deus, et semini tuo post te: et dabo tibi et
    semini tuo post te terram in qua habitas, omnem terram Chanaan in
    possessionem aeternam, et ero illis Deus.' Haec aetas porrigitur ab Abra-
    ham usque ad David quatuordecim generationibus. Huius vespera est
    in populi peccatis, quibus divina mandata praeteribant, usque ad
    malitiam pessimi regis Saul" (*SAOO* 1, cols. 1068–69; Migne 34, col.
    110).

70 "Et inde fit mane regnum David. Haec aetas similis iuventutis est. Et
    revera inter omnes aetates regnat iuventus, et ipsa est firmum orna-

mentum omnium aetatum: et ideo bene comparatur quarto diei, quo facta sunt sidera in firmamento coeli. Quid enim evidentius significat splendorem regni, quam solis excellentia? Et plebem obtemperantem regno splendor lunae ostendit, tanquam synagogam ipsam, et stellae principes eius, et omnia tanquam in firmamento in regni stabilitate fundata. Huius quasi vespera est in peccatis regum, quibus illa gens meruit captivari atque servire" (ibid.).

71 "Et fit mane transmigratione in Babyloniam, cum in ea captivitate populus leniter in peregrino otio collocatus est. . . . Et revera sic ista aetas a regni robore inclinata et fracta est in populo Iudaeorum, quemadmodum homo a iuventute fit senior. Et bene comparatur illi diei quinto, quo facta sunt in aquis animalia, et volatilia coeli, postea-quam illi homines inter gentes, tanquam in mari, vivere coeperunt, et habere incertam sedem et instabilem, sicut volantes aves. Sed plane erant ibi etiam ceti magni, id est illi magni homines qui magis dominari fluctibus saeculi, quam servire in illa captivitate potuerunt. . . . revera gens Iudaeorum, ex quo dispersa est per gentes, valde multiplicata est. Huius diei, hoc est huius aetatis, quasi vespera est multiplicatio pec-catorum in populo Iudaeorum, quia sic excaecati sunt, ut etiam Domi-num Iesum Christum non possent agnoscere" (ibid). (Augustine was thirty-five when he wrote this.)

72 "Et sicut in illo die pascitur homo et animalia, quae cum ipso sunt, herbis seminalibus et lignis fructiferis et herbis viridibus; sic ista aetate spiritualis homo quicumque bonus minister est Christi, et eum bene quantum potest imitatur, cum ipso populo spiritualiter pascitur sanc-tarum Scripturarum alimentis et lege divina: partim ad concipiendam fecunditatem rationum atque sermonum, tanquam herbis seminalibus; partim ad utilitatem morum conversationis humanae, tanquam lignis fructiferis; partim ad vigorem fidei, spei et charitatis in vitam aeternam, tanquam herbis viridibus, id est vigentibus, quae nullo aestu tribula-tionum possint arescere" (SAOO 1, cols. 1070-71; Migne 34, cols. 192-93).

73 For general interpretation of books xv-xviii, see the introduction and notes to BA, vol. 36 by G. Bardy and others. For the quantitative data, see Appendix B of this study, esp. pp. 150-55, 157-61. According to my count, populus appears 437 times in The City of God, 376 times in Augustine's own phrasing, 49 times in scriptural citations, and 12 times in citations from classical authors. Books xv-xviii account for 183 of those appearances—147 Augustine's own wording, 34 scriptural, 2 in classical citations—and occupy 262 of the 1115 columns of text in SAOO, vol. 7.

74 "Erigebat ergo cum suis populis turrem contra Dominum, qua est impia significata superbia. Merito autem malus punitur affectus, etiam cui non succedit effectus. Genus vero ipsum poenae quale fuit? Quoniam domi-natio imperantis in lingua est, ibi est damnata superbia, ut non intel-

legeretur iubens homini, qui noluit intellegere ut oboediret Deo iubenti. Sic illa conspiratio dissoluta est, cum quisque ab eo, quem non intellegebat, abscederet nec se nisi ei, cum quo loqui poterat, adgregaret; et per linguas divisae sunt gentes dispersaeque per terras, sicut Deo placuit, qui hoc modis occultis nobisque incomprehensibilibus fecit" (*SAOO* 7, col. 668; Migne 41, col. 483; *CCSL* 48:505; *BA* 36:198–200; Dods *CG* 2:113). The Dods translation has been followed (with frequent revision) for these books of *The City of God* rather than the Loeb McCracken translation because the solemnity of the former seems (despite occasional opacity) to suit the subject matter better. It is also perhaps the most accessible English translation, thanks most recently to its appearance as a one-volume Modern Library Giant (New York, 1950).

75 "Sed talium deorum cultores illud, quod de rege Cretensium diximus [Xanthus's rape of Europa], historicae veritati, hoc autem, quod de Iove poetae cantant, theatra concrepant, populi celebrant, vanitati deputant fabularum, ut esset unde ludi fierent placandis numinibus etiam falsis eorum criminibus" (*SAOO* 7, col. 791; Migne 41, col. 569; *CCSL* 48:603; *BA* 36:514–16; Dods *CG* 2:230).

76 Cf. most of the *populi* of *CD* vi, 1–8, and also those of *CD* ii, 20 and 22 (with some social/moral downgrading implied by the plural form?) discussed on pp. 59–60 and nn. 103, 104, below.

77 ". . . ut intellegamus unde potuerint populi adcrescere, ne in paucis qui commemorantur hominibus occupati pueriliter haesitemus, unde tanta spatia terrarum atque regnorum repleri potuerint de genere Sem, maxime propter Assyriorum regnum, unde Ninus ille Orientalium domitor usquequaque populorum ingenti prosperitate regnavit et latissimum ac fundatissimum regnum, quod diuturno tempore duceretur, suis posteris propagavit" (*SAOO* 7, col. 676; Migne 41, col. 488; *CCSL* 48:511; *BA* 36:216–18; Dods *CG* 2:120 [freely adapted]).

78 "Ne multis morer, condita est civitas Roma velut altera Babylon et velut prioris filia Babylonis, per quam Deo placuit orbem debellare terrarum et in unam societatem rei publicae legumque perductum longe lateque pacare. Erant enim iam populi validi et fortes et armis gentes exercitatae, quae non facile cederent, et quas opus esset ingentibus periculis et vastatione utrimque non parva atque horrendo labore superari. Nam quando regnum Assyriorum totam paene Asiam subiugavit, licet bellando sit factum, non tamen multum asperis et difficilibus bellis fieri potuit, quia rudes adhuc ad resistendum gentes erant nec tam multae vel magnae. Si quidem post illud maximum atque universale diluvium, cum in arca Noe octo soli homines evaserunt, anni non multo amplius quam mille transierant, quando Ninus Asiam totam excepta India subiugavit. Roma vero tot gentes et Orientis et Occidentis, quas imperio Romano subditas cernimus, non ea celeritate ac facilitate perdomuit, quoniam paulatim increscendo robustas eas et bellicosas, quaquaversum

dilatabatur, invenit." And the passage continues immediately: "Tempore igitur, quo Roma condita est, populus Israel habebat in terra promissionis annos septingentos decem et octo" (SAOO 7, cols. 806–07; Migne 41, col. 578; CCSL 48:612; BA 36:550; Dods CG 2:241).

79   "Et cognovit Cain uxorem suam, et concipiens peperit Enoch; et erat aedificans civitatem in nomine filii sui Enoch," in the Old Latin version used by Augustine, who feels called upon to defend the Scripture from the charge of historical absurdity (BA 36:66). Jerome's rendition of this verse was more elegant, but presented the same terminological problem: "Cognovit autem Cain uxorem suam, quae concepit, et peperit Henoch: et aedificavit civitatem, vocavitque nomen eius ex nomine filii sui, Henoch."

80   "Non enim ab re est, ut propter aliquam causam, cum et alios haberet, diligeret eum pater ceteris amplius. Neque enim et Iudas primogenitus fuit, a quo Iudaea cognominata est et Iudaei. Sed etiamsi conditori civitatis illius iste filius primus est natus, non ideo putandum est tunc a patre conditae civitati nomen eius impositum, quando natus est, quia nec constitui tunc ab uno poterat civitas, quae nihil est aliud quam hominum multitudo aliquo societatis vinculo colligata; sed cum illius hominis familia tanta numerositate cresceret, ut haberet iam populi quantitatem, tunc potuit utique fieri, ut et constitueret et nomen primogeniti sui constitutae imponeret civitati. Tam longa quippe vita illorum hominum fuit, ut illic memoratorum, quorum et anni taciti non sunt, qui vixit minimum ante diluvium, ad septingentos quinquaginta tres perveniret" (SAOO 7, col. 618; Migne 41, col. 447; CCSL 48:464; BA 36:66–68; Dods CG 2:63).

81   In citing this massive (and highly improbable) figure, Augustine was adhering faithfully to several texts in Exodus and Numbers, and to standard rabbinical and patristic authority (BA 36:68, n. 2).

82   "Quod ex hoc conici facillime potest, quia ex uno Abraham non multo amplius quadringentis annis numerositas Hebraeae gentis tanta procreata est, ut in exitu eiusdem populi ex Aegypto sescenta hominum milia fuisse referantur bellicae iuventutis; ut omittamus gentem Idumaeorum non pertinentem ad populum Israel, quam genuit frater eius Esau, nepos Abrahae, et alias natas ex semine ipsius Abrahae non per Sarram coniugem procreatas" (SAOO 7, col. 618; Migne 41, col. 447; Dods CG 2:63). CCSL 48:464–65 and BA 36:68 follow the reading "non per Sarram coniugem procreato" for the last phrase.

83   "Propositum quippe scriptoris illius fuit, per quem sanctus Spiritus id agebat, per successiones certarum generationum ex uno homine propagatarum pervenire ad Abraham ac deinde ex eius semine ad populum Dei, in quo distincto a ceteris gentibus praefigurarentur ac praenuntiarentur omnia, quae de civitate, cuius aeternum erit regnum, et de rege eius eodemque conditore Christo in Spiritu praevidebantur esse ventura; ita ut nec de altera societate hominum taceretur, quam terrenam dicimus

civitatem, quantum ei commemorandae satis esset, ut civitas Dei etiam suae adversariae comparatione clarescat" (*SAOO* 7, col. 617; Migne 41, col. 446; *CCSL* 48:463; *BA* 36:64). It seems to me that Augustine is fairly consistent in using *populus* for the group composing one of those *civitates*, and *gens* for the groups making up the other, and that this consistent opposition of terminology is one of the ways in which he expressed his fidelity to his understanding of Genesis in these books of *The City of God;* only he goes further, by discerning different levels of development toward the *civitas Dei* in the internal history of Israel (both *gens* and *populus*).

84   "Defuncto Iacob, defuncto etiam Ioseph per reliquos centum quadraginta quattuor annos, donec exiretur de terra Aegypti, in modum incredibilem illa gens crevit, etiam tantis attrita persecutionibus, ut quodam tempore nati masculi necarentur, cum mirantes Aegyptios nimia populi illius incrementa terrerent. Tunc Moyses . . . in tantum pervenit virum, ut ipse illam gentem mirabiliter multiplicatam ex durissimo et gravissimo, quod ibi ferebat, iugo servitutis extraheret, immo per eum Deus, qui hoc promiserat Abrahae. . . . Tunc per eum Aegyptiis illatae sunt decem memorabiles plagae, cum dimittere populum Dei nollent, . . . Deinde per annos quadraginta duce Moyse Dei populus per desertum actus est, quando tabernaculum testimonii nuncupatum est, ubi Deus sacrificiis futura praenuntiantibus colebatur, cum scilicet iam data lex fuisset in monte multum terribiliter; adtestabatur enim evidentissima mirabilibus signis vocibusque divinitas. Quod factum est, mox ut exitum est de Aegypto et in deserto populus esse coepit, quinquagesimo die post celebratum Pascha per ovis immolationem; . . .

Defuncto Moyse populum rexit Iesus Nave et in terram promissionis introduxit eamque populo divisit. Ab his duobus mirabilibus ducibus bella etiam prosperrime ac mirabiliter gesta sunt, Deo contestante non tam propter merita Hebraei populi quam propter peccata earum, quae debellabantur, gentium illas eis provenisse victorias. Post istos duces iudices fuerunt, iam in terra promissionis populo collocato, ut inciperet interim reddi Abrahae prima promissio de gente una, id est Hebraea, et terra Chanaan, nondum de omnibus gentibus et toto orbe terrarum; quod Christi adventus in carne et non veteris legis observationes, sed evangelii fides fuerat impletura. Cuius rei praefiguratio facta est, quod non Moyses, qui legem populo acceperat in monte Sina, sed Iesus, cui etiam nomen Deo praecipiente mutatum fuerat ut Iesus vocaretur, populum in terram promissionis induxit. Temporibus autem iudicum, sicut se habebant et peccata populi et misericordia Dei, alternaverunt prospera et adversa bellorum.

Inde ventum est ad regum tempora, . . . In quo articulus quidam factus est et exordium quodam modo iuventutis populi Dei; cuius generis quaedam velut adolescentia ducebatur ab ipso Abraham usque ad hunc David. Neque enim frustra Matthaeus evangelista sic generationes commemoravit, ut hoc primum intervallum quattuordecim generationibus commendaret, ab Abraham scilicet usque ad David. Ab adolescentia quippe incipit homo posse generare; propterea generationum ex Abraham sumpsit exordium; qui etiam pater gentium constitutus est, quando mutatum nomen accepit. Ante hunc ergo velut pueritia fuit huius generis populi Dei a Noe usque ad ipsum Abraham; et ideo prima lingua inventa est, id est Hebraea. A pueritia namque homo incipit loqui post infantiam, qua hinc appellata est, quia fari non potest" (*SAOO* 7, cols. 720–22; Migne 41, cols. 521–22; *CCSL* 48:548–50; *BA* 36:328–34).

85 See Appendix B, pp. 151–52. The summary given here does not take account of most of the overlapping applications; in each such case I have made a decision as to precedence. See the Appendix for a fuller presentation of all the figures summarized here. *CD* xvii, 1–2 appear in *SAOO* 7, cols. 723–25; Migne 41, cols. 523–25; *CCSL* 48:550–53; *BA* 36:340–46.

86 Marrou insists that historical materials and modes of thought assumed ever greater importance in Augustine's consciousness and works as his apologetic concerns and pastoral responsibilities increased. Initially familiar with few, if any, Roman historians besides Sallust (thanks to his all-too-typical grammatical education), Augustine came to know the historical tradition of the late republic and early empire better (although usually through intermediaries) so as to acquire the information necessary for the polemical purposes of *The City of God*. During the same period of his life, but for motives of interior contemplation as well as public refutation, he looked more deeply than before into the sacred history of the Church, as set forth both in the Old Testament and in the works of more recent authors like Eusebius. Before either of those complementary lines of "historical research" had gotten under way, the demands of the Donatist controversy had led Augustine to a constantly growing acquaintance with a mass of records, laws, and letters affecting the African churches, which constituted a body of essentially historical documentation. His sympathetic response to all these exposures to historical literature may be discerned, Marrou says, in the favorable role which he allotted the historical discipline in *De Doctrina Christiana* (*Saint Augustin et la fin de la culture antique*, pp. 415–22, 463–66; cf. also *BA* 36:17–22). Nevertheless, Marrou would not (I think) deny that the ordinary historical habits of mind—as opposed both to adroitness in manipulating a dossier of historical data and to transcendental visions of providential change—remained always a little foreign to Augustine.

87 "Cum ergo regnaret Assyriis quartus decimus Saphrus et Sicyoniis duodecimus Orthopolis et Criasus quintus Argivis, natus est in Aegypto Moyses, per quem populus Dei de servitute Aegyptia liberatus est, in qua eum ad desiderandum sui Creatoris auxilium sic exerceri oportebat."

Prometheus and his brother Atlas flourished at the same time, giving rise to many myths. ". . . sed usque ad Cecropem regem Atheniensium, quo regnante eadem civitas etiam tale nomen accepit, et quo regnante Deus per Moysen eduxit ex Aegypto populum suum, relati sunt in deorum numerum aliquot mortui caeca et vana consuetudine ac superstitione Graecorum" (*SAOO* 7, col. 782; Migne 41, col. 565; *CCSL* 48:598-99; *BA* 36:500-02). It is interesting to contrast Augustine's near-reservation of *populus* for orthodox Israel with his incorporation of Varro's and Seneca's use of *gens* for the Jews whom they considered superstitious (*CD* IV, 31 [Varro]; *CD* VI, 11 [Seneca, contrasting the Jewish *gens* with the ritually more rational Roman *populus*]). Augustine seems to match both passages and (even that early in *The City of God*) to reverse their usages of those two nouns in IV, 34 (which announces his intention to demonstrate Jewish superiority to Roman superstition) and VII, 32 (which makes the same promise and sounds the theme of the *sacramentum adventus et remissionis Christi* which unites both ritual sacrifice and oracular utterance in one prophetic purpose).

88 "Regnante vero apud Hebraeos Sedechia et apud Romanos Tarquinio Prisco, qui successerat Anco Martio, ductus est captivus in Babyloniam populus Iudaeorum eversa Hierusalem et templo illo a Salomone constructo. Increpantes enim eos prophetae de iniquitatibus et impietatibus suis haec eis ventura praedixerant, maxime Hieremias, qui etiam numerum definivit annorum. Eo tempore Pittacus Mitylenaeus, alius e septem sapientibus, fuisse perhibetur. Et quinque ceteros, qui, ut septem numerentur, Thaleti, quem supra commemoravimus, et huic Pittaco adduntur, eo tempore fuisse scribit Eusebius, quo captivus Dei populus in Babylonia tenebatur. Hi sunt autem: Solon Atheniensis, Chilon Lacedaemonius, Periandrus Corinthius, Cleobulus Lindius, Bias Prienaeus" (*SAOO* 7, cols, 813-14; Migne 41, col. 582; *CCSL* 48:616; *BA* 36:562-64; Dods *CG* 2:245).

89 ". . . ac per hoc per ea tempora isti velut fontes prophetiae pariter eruperunt, quando regnum defecit Assyrium coepitque Romanum; ut scilicet, quem ad modum regni Assyriorum primo tempore extitit Abraham, cui promissiones apertissimae fierent in eius semine benedictionis omnium gentium, ita occidentalis Babylonis exordio, qua fuerat Christus imperante venturus, in quo implerentur illa promissa, ore prophetarum non solum loquentium, verum etiam scribentium in tantae rei futurae testimonium solverentur. Cum enim prophetae numquam fere defuissent populo Israel, ex quo ibi reges esse coeperunt, in usum tantummodo eorum fuere, non gentium, quando autem scriptura manifestius prophetica condebatur, quae gentibus quandoque prodesset, tunc oportebat inciperet, quando condebatur haec civitas, quae gentibus imperaret" (*SAOO* 7, col. 817; Migne 41, cols. 583-84; *CCSL* 48:618; *BA* 36:568; Dods *CG* 2:247).

90 "Postea quam gens Iudaea coepit non habere prophetas, procul dubio

deterior facta est, eo scilicet tempore, quo se sperabat instaurato templo post captivitatem, quae fuit in Babylonia, futuram esse meliorem. Sic quippe intellegebat populus ille carnalis, quod praenuntiatum est per Aggaeum prophetam dicentem: 'Magna erit gloria domus istius novissimae, plus quam primae'; quod de novo testamento dictum esse paulo superius demonstravit, ubi ait aperte Christum promittens: 'Et movebo omnes gentes, et veniet desideratus cunctis gentibus.' Quo loco Septuaginta interpretes alium sensum magis corpori quam capiti, hoc est magis ecclesiae quam Christo, convenientem prophetica auctoritate dixerunt: 'Venient quae electa sunt Domini de cunctis gentibus,' id est homines, de quibus ipse Iesus in evangelio: 'Multi,' inquit, 'vocati, pauci vero electi.' Talibus enim electis gentium domus aedificatur Dei per testamentum novum lapidibus vivis, longe gloriosior, quam templum illud fuit, quod a rege Salomone constructum est et post captivitatem instauratum. Propter hoc ergo nec prophetas ex illo tempore habuit illa gens et multis cladibus afflicta est ab alienigenis regibus ipsisque Romanis, ne hanc Aggaei prophetiam in illa instauratione templi opinaretur impletam" (*SAOO* 7, cols. 848–49; Migne 41, col. 606; *CCSL* 48:641–42; *BA* 36:642–44; Dods *CG* 2:274–75). The scriptural citations are to Aggeus 2:10; Aggeus 2:8; and Matt. 22:14. Augustine, needless to say, is not always so ready to consider other readings than those of the Septuagint (which as usual he ends up following).

91   "Amicis vero tuis sive in populo christiano se desiderent instrui, sive qualibet superstitione teneantur unde videbuntur per hunc nostrum laborem dei gratia liberari, quomodo impertias ipse videris." Published by Cyrille Lambot in "Lettre inédite de s. Augustin rélative au *De civitate Dei," Revue bénédictine,* 51:109–21 (the letter itself is on pp. 112–13).

92   See n. 10 of this chapter.

93   "Neque enim ob aliud ante adventum Domini scripta sunt omnia quae in sanctis Scripturis legimus, nisi ut illius commendaretur adventus, et futura praesignaretur Ecclesia, id est, populus Dei per omnes gentes, quod est corpus eius; adiunctis atque annumeratis omnibus sanctis, qui etiam ante adventum eius in hoc saeculo vixerunt, ita eum credentes venturum esse, sicut nos venisse" (*De Catechizandis Rudibus,* chap. 36: *SAOO* 6, col. 454; Migne 40, col. 313). For the date and recent editions, see Pope, p. 340.

94   On the authenticity and normality of this title, see A. Wilmart, "La tradition des grands ouvrages de S. Augustin," *MA* 2:295–98.

95   "Cum vero legitur praecipiente auctoritate divina, non reddendum malum pro malo, cum haec tam salubris admonitio congregationibus populorum, tanquam publicis utriusque sexus atque omnium aetatum et dignitatum scholis, de superiore loco personat, accusatur religio tanquam inimica rei publicae!" (*Ep.* 138: *SAOO* 2, col. 617; Migne 33, col. 529). The next sentence indicates clearly Augustine's idea of the

potential contribution of the *populus Dei* to the *populus Romanus:* "Quae si, ut dignum est, audiretur, longe melius Romulo, Numa, Bruto, caeterisque illis Romanae gentis praeclaris viris, constitueret, consecraret, firmaret, augeretque rem publicam." For another appearance of the first sentence's point, cf. *Ep.* 91 to Nectarius, in which Augustine says that the virtues necessary to the health of a *civitas* are now being taught "in Ecclesiis toto orbe crescentibus, tanquam in sanctis auditoriis populorum" (*SAOO* 2, col. 335; Migne 33, col. 317).

Cf. Jean Bayet's assessment of the advantages enjoyed by the Christian Church in its decisive fourth-century struggle with paganism, pp. 269–70. Those peculiar qualities as Bayet described them are nearly congruent with Augustine's definition of a *populus,* especially if that definition is considered in the light of Augustine's application of that noun to the Christian community.

96 "Et omnes, quot erunt? centum quinquaginta tres erunt? Absit, absit a nobis, ut uel in isto populo, qui hic ante me stant, tam paucos dicam esse, qui in regno caelorum futuri sunt, ubi milia, innumerabilia milia, quae uidit Iohannes induta stolis albis" (*Sermo* 15: *SI,* p. 57). Kunzelmann (p. 481) maintains that this sermon was delivered on Easter Friday, 19 April 412.

97 "Scio enim non solus ipse, verum etiam alii fratres et conservi, qui nobiscum tunc intra Hipponensem ecclesiam cum eodem sancto viro vivebant, nobis ad mensam constitutis eum dixisse: 'Advertistis hodie in ecclesia meum sermonem, eiusque initium et finem contra meam consuetudinem processisse, quoniam non eam rem terminatam explicuerim quam proposueram, sed pendentem reliquerim.' Cui respondimus: 'Ita nos in tempore miratos fuisse scimus et recognoscimus.' At ille: 'Credo, sit, forte aliquem errantem in populo Dominus per nostram oblivionem et errorem doceri et curari voluerit: in cuius manu sumus et nos et sermones nostri' " (Possidius, *Sancti Augustini Vita,* ed. H. T. Weiskotten, chap. 15, pp. 72–75). I have altered Weiskotten's translation a little, primarily in order to bring out the unobtrusive but delightful puns on *sermo* and on *errantem-errorem,* which (together with the *quoniam* and *credo . . . forte* constructions) sharply distinguish this alleged quotation from the rest of the surrounding narrative style. These may indicate that the language of this quotation is due simply to Possidius's artfulness, rather than to the accuracy of his memory of Augustine's own habits of speech; however, this *Vita* is practically the only source of anything even purporting to represent Augustine's informal conversation, so the question must remain open. The fact that he was an exceptionally close friend, spiritual son, protégé, etc. of Augustine's, and the further fact that his own style is hardly distinguished for sensitivity or subtle shadings, would lend some plausibility to the argument that this may be a faithful representation of Augustine's general usage.

A cursory examination of the *Vita* (some especially suggestive passages occur in chaps. 1, 4, and 5) leads to the impression that Possidius's terminology is slightly different from Augustine's, in the direction of less varied usage. *Civitas* seems to be reserved for one's home town, or for the city presently under discussion, while any other city (be it small or on the scale of Carthage, Rome, and Milan) is an *urbs*. Somewhat similarly, the Christian laity is usually the *plebs,* and a *populus* most often on those occasions when it is presented as standing before a preaching bishop (perhaps on those occasions the *populus* also includes the lesser clergy). No such simple formula could possibly hold for Augustine's usage of those words. However, in the passage here cited, the usage of *populus* is entirely consistent with the rest of the usage of both men.

According to Peter Brown, that "quidam Firmus nomine, negotiator," who "forte adhuc usque in rebus humanis vivat trans mare constitutus," is the same person as the Carthaginian priest to whom Augustine addressed the letter recently discovered by Lambot (see n. 91 above; Brown, p. 370).

98   "Non longe coeperat Mediolanensis ecclesia genus hoc consolationis et exhortationis celebrare, magno studio fratrum concinentium vocibus et cordibus. Nimirum annus erat, aut non multo amplius, cum Iustina Valentiniani regis pueri mater, hominem tuum Ambrosium persequeretur, haeresis suae causa, qua fuerat seducta ab Arianis. Excubabat pia plebs in ecclesia, mori parata cum episcopo suo, servo tuo. Ibi mater mea, ancilla tua, sollicitudinis et vigiliarum primas tenens, orationibus vivebat. Nos adhuc frigidi a calore Spiritus tui, excitabamur tamen civitate attonita atque turbata. Tunc hymni et psalmi ut canerentur secundum morem orientalium partium, ne populus moeroris taedio contabesceret, institutum est; et ex illo in hodiernum retentum, multis iam ac pene omnibus gregibus tuis, et per caetera orbis imitantibus. . . . verum etiam quidam plures annos caecus civis civitatique notissimus, cum populi tumultuantis laetitiae causam quaesisset atque audisset, exsilivit, eoque se ut duceret, suum ducem rogavit. . . . inde illius inimicae animus etsi ad credendi sanitatem non ampliatus, a persequendi tamen furore compressus est" (*Confessions* ix, 7: *SAOO* i, cols. 277–78; Migne 32, col. 770).

The translation is by Vernon J. Bourke, in *The Confessions of St. Augustine,* The Fathers of the Church, 21:241–43. O'Meara discusses this incident in *Young Augustine,* pp. 123–24, pointing out both that Augustine referred to it frequently (and in less artful language) in the last decade of his life, and that the incident itself occurred at a time when Augustine "was still not greatly interested in Ambrose's personal affairs or the events that loomed large in the life of the Church of Milan." However, by the time he wrote the *Confessions* (probably 396-or 397–400), he was very much interested in the life of other churches.

99   "Canon quippe sacrarum litterarum, quem definitum esse oportebat, illa facit ubique recitari et memoriae cunctorum inhaerere populorum; haec

autem ubicumque fiunt, ibi sciuntur vix a tota ipsa civitate vel quocumque commanentium loco. Nam plerumque etiam ibi paucissimi sciunt ignorantibus ceteris, maxime si magna sit civitas; et quando alibi aliisque narrantur, non tanta ea commendat auctoritas, ut sine difficultate vel dubitatione credantur, quamvis Christianis fidelibus a fidelibus indicentur.

Miraculum, quod Mediolani factum est, cum illic essemus, quando illuminatus est caecus, ad multorum notitiam potuit pervenire, quia et grandis est civitas et ibi erat tunc imperator et immenso populo teste res gesta est concurrente ad corpora martyrum Protasii et Gervasii; . . ." (*SAOO* 7, col. 1058; Migne 41, col. 761; *CCSL* 48:816; Dods *CG* 2:484–85). It is interesting to compare the vocabulary as well as the general narrative or expository presentation of this reference with *Sermo* 286, 5 and *Sermo* 318, 1 (both delivered in 425, and so probably contemporaneous with *CD* XXII); with *Retractationes* 1, 13, 7; and with *Ep.* 22 of Ambrose, as well as with *Confessions* IX, 7, 16.

100 This culminating narrative appears in *SAOO* 7, cols. 1070–72; Migne 41, cols. 769–71; *CCSL* 48:825–27. The following examples represent the full range of the usage of *populus* therein:

"Venit et Pascha, atque ipso die dominico mane, cum iam frequens populus esset et loci sancti cancellos, ubi martyrium erat, idem iuvenis orans teneret. . . ."

"Procedimus ad populum, plena erat ecclesia, personabat vocibus gaudiorum: Deo gratias, Deo laudes! nemine tacente hinc atque inde clamantium. Salutavi populum, et rursus eadem ferventiore voce clamabat."

"Sequenti itaque die post sermonem redditum narrationis eius libellum in crastinum populo recitandum promisi. Quod cum ex dominico Paschae die tertio fieret in gradibus exedrae, in qua de superiore loquebar loco, feci stare ambos fratres, cum eorum legeretur libellus. Intuebatur populus universus . . ."

"Inter haec recitato eorum libello de conspectu populi eos abire praecepi, et de tota ipsa causa aliquanto diligentius coeperam disputare, cum ecce me disputante voces aliae de memoria martyris novae gratulationis audiuntur."

The sermons to which Augustine refers in his narration are *Sermones* 321–24; the incident seems to have taken place in March 425 (*SAOO* 7, col. 1067, n. *b.*), and so hardly more than a year before the completion of *The City of God*.

101 "Miser igitur populus ab isto alienatus Deo. . . . quamdiu permixtae sunt ambae civitates [Dei et diaboli], utimur et nos pace Babylonis, ex qua ita per fidem populus Dei liberatur, ut apud hanc interim peregrinetur" (*SAOO* 7, col. 918; Migne 41, col. 656; *CCSL* 48: 696).

102 "Est quidam populus praeparatus ad iram Dei, damnandus cum diabolo: horum nemo accipit testimonium Christi" (*In Ioannis Evangelium*

Tractatus XIV 8: *SAOO* 3, col. 1845; Migne 35, col. 1507). The reference is to John 3:29–36. Cf. nn. 34 and 53 above.

103 "Populi plaudant, non consultoribus utilitatum suarum, sed largitoribus voluptatum. . . . Illi habentur dii veri, qui hanc adipiscendam populis procuraverint, adeptamque servaverint" (*CD* II, 20: *SAOO* 7, col. 73; Migne 41, col. 65; *CCSL* 47:51–52; Loeb *CG* 1:212–14). Christopher Dawson treats this passage as an epitome of Augustine's attack on what was in fact Christianity's chief rival at the time, a rather vulgarized, hedonistic form of Epicureanism ("St. Augustine and His Age," *A Monument to Saint Augustine,* pp. 11–78, esp. pp. 21–22). Cf. also *Ep.* 138, 3 and 14, as well as most of the *populi* appearing in *CD* VI, 1–8.

104 "Ut ergo non periret, dii custodes eius populo cultori suo dare praecipue vitae ac morum praecepta debuerunt, a quo tot templis, tot sacerdotibus et sacrificiorum generibus, tam multiplicibus variisque sacrificiis, tot festis solemnitatibus, tot tantorumque ludorum celebritatibus colebantur . . ." (*CD* II, 22: *SAOO* 7, col. 78; Migne 41, col. 69; *CCSL* 47:55; Loeb *CG* 1:226–27).

105 *De Libero Arbitrio* I, 5 and 6, passim, esp. such passages as the following:

"*A.* Multo minus ego invenire possum, cur hominibus defensionem quaeras, quos reos nulla lex tenet.

E. Nulla fortasse, sed earum legum quae apparent, et ab hominibus leguntur: nam nescio utrum non aliqua vehementiore ac secretissima lege teneantur, si nihil rerum est quod non administret divina providentia. . . . Videtur ergo mihi et legem istam, quae populo regendo scribitur, recte ista permittere, et divinam providentiam vindicare. . . .

A. . . . Videtur enim tibi lex ista, quae regendis civitatibus fertur, multa concedere atque impunita relinquere, quae per divinam tamen providentiam vindicantur; et recte. . . . Sed dispiciamus diligenter, si placet, quo usque per legem istam quae populos in hac vita cohibet, malefacta ulciscenda sint: deinde quid restet, quod per divinam providentiam inevitabilius secretoque puniatur. . . . Et prius responde mihi, utrum ista lex quae litteris promulgatur, hominibus hanc vitam viventibus opituletur.

E. Manifestum est: nam ex his hominibus utique populi civitatesque consistunt.

A. Quid? ipsi homines et populi, eiusdemne generis rerum sunt, ut interire mutarive non possint, aeternique omnino sint? an vero mutabiles temporibusque subiecti sunt?

E. Mutabile plane atque tempori obnoxium hoc genus esse quis dubitet?

A. Ergo, si populus sit bene moderatus et gravis communisque utilitatis diligentissimus custos, in quo unusquisque minoris rem privatam quam publicam pendat; nonne recte lex fertur, qua huic ipsi populo

liceat creare sibi magistratus, per quos sua res, id est publica, ad-
ministretur?

E. Recte prorsus.

A. Porro si paulatim depravatus idem populus rem privatam rei publicae
praeferat, atque habeat venale suffragium, corruptusque ab eis qui
honores amant, regimen in se flagitiosis committat; nonne item
recte, si quis tunc exstiterit vir bonus, qui plurimum possit, adimat
huic populo potestatem dandi honores, et in paucorum bonorum, vel
etiam unius redigat arbitrium?"

(*SAOO* 1, cols. 935–39; for the passages cited above, see cols. 937–38;
Migne 32, cols. 1228–29). Cf. also *BA* 6:152–63, and the introduction
and notes by F. J. Thonnard, pp. 125–35, 490–93 (for an example
of the misapplication of modern-language definitions to the term
populus, see *note complémentaire* 10, pp. 491–92). Otto Schilling inter-
prets the last two long sentences of Augustine's in the passage cited
above as the epitome of his view on the decline of the republic and
the consequent necessity of the Lex Regia (Ulpian's commentary on
which is cited in n. 29 above) and the autocratic principate for which
it provided. Schilling sees popular sovereignty as an arrangement of
little value in Augustine's mind or in that of Stoic theory in general
(*Die Staats- und Sociallehre des hl. Augustinus,* pp. 76–78, 81–82).

106   The idea that the *populus* exists within a structure of ethical values, to
which it is ultimately either answerable or amenable, is expressed in
other works written by Augustine in this period between his conversion
and his episcopal consecration. For example, *quaestio* 31 of *De Diversis
Quaestionibus,* probably begun a year after *De Libero Arbitrio* and collected a year after its completion, discusses *iustitia* in terms of its relationship to the natural law: "Iustitia est habitus animi, communi utilitate
conservata, suam cuique tribuens dignitatem. Eius initium est ab natura
profectum: deinde quaedam in consuetudinem ex utilitatis ratione
venerunt: postea res et ab natura profectas et a consuetudine probatas,
legum metus et religio sanxit." Elaborating on the modes of *consuetudo,*
he says: "Lege ius est, quod in eo scripto, quod populo expositum est
ut observet, continetur" (*SAOO* 6, col. 37; Migne 40, cols. 20–21).
More contemporary *populi,* within the sphere of the Christian Church's
beneficent influence, appear in a rhetorically heightened passage in
chap. 30 of *De Moribus Ecclesiae Catholicae,* written in 388 and 389.
Augustine says that the maternal Church possesses medicine for every
sin-based ill that afflicts humankind, and particularly for the variety
of disorder which disturbs human relationships; after referring to the
full range of relationships among all ages, sexes, and social ranks, he
says: "Tu cives civibus, gentes gentibus et prorsus homines primorum
parentum recordatione, non societate tantum, sed quadam etiam fra-
ternitate coniungis. Doces reges prospicere populis, mones populos se

subdere regibus" (*SAOO* 1, cols. 1146–47; Migne 32, col. 1336).

107 "Nam et ego tecum credo, et inconcusse credo, omnibusque populis atque gentibus credendum esse clamo, malum esse adulterium . . ." (*SAOO* 1, col. 933; Migne 32, cols. 1224–25).

108 On Evodius, see McNamara, pp. 112–17. It is not clear to what extent Augustine rewrote or even composed outright the remarks of his interlocutors in the dialogues; the point at issue here is not the ideas credited to those personae, but the exact vocabulary in which they ultimately found expression. The clearest hint we have occurs in *De Beata Vita* III, 18: Augustine, struck with admiration at the wisdom of his son Adeodatus's replies to his questions about chastity, seems to have ordered the secretaries recording that session to be sure of getting down Adeodatus's exact words before the dialogue proceeded any further: "Quae verba pueri sicut dicta erant, cum conscribi mihi placuisset: Is ergo, inquam, necesse est ut bene vivat, et qui bene vivit necessario talis est; nisi quid tibi aliud videtur. Concessit cum caeteris" (*SAOO* 1, col. 509; Migne 32, col. 969). What would Augustine's procedure have been in a more formally structured dialogue like *De Libero Arbitrio?* The lapse of seven or eight years between the book's beginning and its final publication would lead one to expect a certain amount of final editing, if not actual revision: even though Evodius was still living in the community which Augustine headed in 395 (shortly thereafter he would accept consecration as bishop of Uzalis), he could hardly be expected to recall details of phrasing uttered so long ago across the sea or over the mountains in Tagaste. Also, there is an economy and logical efficiency in the whole argument of this dialogue which would seem to make direct transcription a less likely medium for its composition than for that of the rather summary *De Beata Vita* (composed in Cassiciacum, probably in November 386).

109 The probability that it is the normal label in Augustine's usage for that sort of society is reinforced by its appearance in the first sentence of book VII, which serves as a summary of the conclusions of books V and VI: "*A.* Age nunc, videamus, homo ipse quomodo in seipso sit ordinatissimus: nam ex hominibus una lege sociatis, populus constat; quae lex, ut dictum est, temporalis est" (*SAOO* 1, col. 939; Migne 32, cols. 1229–30).

110 Cf., besides the evidence of preceding arguments, a sentence from *CD* XVIII, 43: "Septuaginta, . . . tanquam sola esset, sic recepit Ecclesia eaque utuntur Graeci populi christiani, quorum plerique utrum alia sit aliqua ignorant" (*SAOO* 7, cols. 844–45; Migne 41, col. 603; *CCSL* 48:639).

111 At least five or six, really: *Dei, diaboli* or *terrenus, Christianus, Romanus, Hipponensis,* not to mention such special subgroups as *Iudaeus.*

112 Cf. pp. 42–43 and n. 74, above.

113 Cf. Appendix A. On perhaps a lower level of scholarly respectability,

but no less important as a matter of the transmission of general culture, this contention has become a commonplace of American university lecture halls.

114 ". . . quasi alii sint qui susceperunt, alii in quorum medio susceperunt? . . . Nunc quippe populus Dei censentur omnes qui portant sacramenta eius, sed non omnes pertinent ad misericordiam eius. Omnes quippe sacramentum baptismi Christi accipientes, Christiani vocantur; sed non omnes digne illo sacramento vivunt. . . . Tamen propter ipsam speciem pietatis in populo Dei nominantur, quomodo ad aream, quamdiu trituratur, non solum grana, sed etiam palea pertinet. Numquid et ad horreum pertinebit? in hoc medio autem populi mali est populus bonus, qui suscepit misericordiam Dei" (*SAOO* 4, col. 596; Migne 36, col. 538).

115 Or perhaps between *ecclesia* and *civitas Dei,* which may or may not be a different pair of concepts (Marshall, pp. 87–89, and the other opinions discussed therein).

116 I do not think that Augustine was usually supercilious or patronizing to Jerome; on the contrary, he took care to express the greatest admiration for Jerome, who was often a defensively hostile and troublesome correspondent. A good example of this attitude early in their complicated correspondence occurs in the conclusion of a letter which Augustine probably wrote in 397. He expresses concern over the publicly disedifying effect of Jerome's judgments on the sincerity of Peter and Paul in regard to the continuation of Mosaic requirements for Hellenic Christians, but terminates his objections by saying: "Nequaquam vero mihi arrogaverim ut ingenium tuum, divino dono aureum, meis obolis ditare contendam; nec est quisquam te magis idoneus, qui opus illud emendet" (*Ep.* 40: *SAOO* 2, col. 126; Migne 33, col. 155). In the spring of 415, after the exchange of many letters, Augustine wrote even more flatteringly and solicitously to the occasionally still irascible Jerome, "cuius doctrina, in nomine et adiutorio Domini, tantum in latina lingua ecclesiasticae litterae adiutae sunt, quantum nunquam antea potuerunt!" (*Ep.* 167: *SAOO* 2, col. 900; Migne 33, col. 741). Nevertheless, as Hugh Pope says, "The truth is that these twin giants were poles asunder in their outlook on Holy Scripture: Bethlehem wholly occupied with the text, Hippo with its exposition for the needs of souls" (p. 203; for a summary of Augustine's epistolary embroilment with Jerome, see pp. 192–206). Cf. also McNamara, pp. 177–186; Bardy, *Saint Augustin,* pp. 297–99, and the bibliography cited there.

Peter Brown dissents in the main from the general description of the relationship presented here; he feels instead that Augustine usually badgered Jerome, without humor or tact (pp. 208, 274–75). The final word on Augustine's attitude toward the Vulgate when in conflict with the Septuagint or the Septuagint-based *Vetus Latina* seems clearly to be what he stated in *CD* xviii, 43: the translation of no single man, however learned and holy, is to be preferred to that of the Seventy. This chapter was probably written about four years after Jerome's death in September 419. An unmistakable instance of this final intransigence in defense of the Septuagint is the *Quaestiones in Genesim,* clearly written by Augustine in 419 or 420 in order to counter Jerome's attacks on the Septuagint. See Ferdinand Cavallera, "Les 'Quaestiones hebraicae in Genesim' de saint Jérôme et les 'Quaestiones in Genesim' de saint Augustin," *MA* 2:359–72, esp. pp. 359–60, 363, 372.

117   The only "Hebrew" text which might have had any influence on the Gallican Psalter was the transliterated version appearing in one column of the *Hexaplar.* Jerome's main purpose in composing that psalter was to purify the Septuagint-based Latin text of the Psalms then current, and his translation was based only partly on a comparison of the Septuagint with other accepted Greek versions. Consequently, use of the Gallican Psalter would not have been entirely contrary to Augustine's policy as outlined in the previous note. Why did he still not use it? N. 79 above alludes to one instance of his attachment to the old African translations of Scripture despite the greater elegance of Jerome's version—and that instance dates from the early 420s, after Jerome's death and more than a decade after his Pentateuch had become generally available. *Ep.* 261, written a little after 396, about three or four years after Jerome had completed another Psalter directly from the Hebrew text, shows Augustine in a more receptive mood to new versions, and quite concerned about the faulty character of the venerable translations still in liturgical use: "Psalterium a sancto Hieronymo translatum non habeo. Nos autem non interpretati sumus, sed codicum latinorum nonnullas mendositates ex graecis exemplaribus emendavimus. Unde fortassis fecerimus aliquid commodius quam erat, non tamen tale quale esse debebat" (*SAOO* 2, col. 1348; Migne 33, col. 1077). It is also recognized that Augustine was concerned about the exact wording of the Psalms, which he spent so much time trying to explicate. Rondet is disposed to date the *Enarrationes* on Ps. 45–47 before 407, possibly even as early as 403, or between fifteen and twenty years after Augustine might have been expected to have a copy of the Gallican Psalter, which was a product of the sort of revision he describes himself doing in *Ep.* 261. Had he been unable to get a copy? Was he just being polite in the admiration he expressed for Jerome's talents in so many letters?

In any case, Rondet considers the *Enarrationes* on Ps. 45–47 rather plodding exegetical exercises, scarcely worthy to follow the one on Ps. 44. He also discerns a concern with Donatist reaction to scandalous Catholics—a theme relevant to the present discussion—in these three *Enarrationes* (pp. 188–89). For a general treatment of Augustine's handling of current texts of the Psalms, see Donatien De Bruyne, "Saint Augustin reviseur de la Bible," *MA* 2:544–78 (pp. 544–63 deal with the *Enarrationes*).

118 "Venit enim ille sero, et affert quod iussit pater; et invenit fratrem suum benedictum pro se; et non benedicitur altera benedictione. Quia duo illi homines duo populi erant; una benedictio unitatem significat Ecclesiae. Duo autem populi ipsi sunt, qui est et Iacob. Sed alio modo figurati duo populi pertinentes ad Iacob. Etenim Dominus noster Iesus Christus, qui ad Iudaeos et Gentes venerat, repudiatus est a Iudaeis, qui pertinebant ad filium maiorem: elegit tamen quosdam, qui pertinebant ad filium minorem, qui spiritualiter coeperant desiderare et intelligere promissa Domini, non carnaliter illam terram quam desiderabant accipientes; sed spiritualem illam civitatem desiderantes, ubi nemo nascitur carnaliter; quia nemo ibi carnaliter, nemo spiritualiter moritur. . . . Ipsi duo populi tanquam de diverso venientes, etiam duobus parietibus significantur. Venit enim Ecclesia Iudaeorum de circumcisione, venit Ecclesia Gentium de praeputio . . . Duo ergo haedi, ipsi sunt duo populi, ipsi sunt duo ovilia, ipsi sunt duo parietes; ipsi sunt duo caeci qui sedebant in via; ipsi sunt duae naves in quas levati sunt pisces. Multis in locis Scripturarum intelliguntur duo populi: sed unum sunt in Iacob" (*Sermo* 4: *SAOO* 5, cols. 29–30; Migne 38, cols. 42–43). The whole sermon is rich in instances of Augustine's use of *populus* for the Church and for the two historical and mystical groups involved in her composition and inheritance.

119 "Sed forte dicitis: Nos Carthagini similes sumus. Quomodo apud Carthaginem est plebs sancta et religiosa, sic tanta turba est in magna ciuitate, ut se excusent omnes de aliis. Pagani faciunt, Iudaei faciunt, potest dici Carthagine; hic, quicumque faciunt, Christiani faciunt. . . . Dicimus caritati uestrae, nouimus in nomine dei ciuitatem et uestram, et uicinae uobis, quanta est hic multitudo, quantus populus: potestis nisi noti omnes ei, qui uobis dispensator est constitutus uerbi et sacramenti? Quis excuset ab hac turpitudine? . . . Dicitis fortasse: Bene uos ab istis abstinetis, qui clerici estis, qui episcopi estis, non autem nos laici. Itane uero haec uox iusta uobis uidetur? Quid enim sumus nos, si peritis uos? Aliud est, quod sumus propter nos; aliud, quod sumus propter uos. Christiani sumus propter nos, clerici et episcopi non nisi propter uos. Apostolus non clericis, non episcopis et presbyteris loquebatur, quando dicebat: 'Vos autem estis membra Christi.' Plebibus dicebat, fidelibus dicebat, christianis dicebat. . . . Valde timeo, ne dicat nobis Christus in iudicio suo: Mali serui, laudes populi mei libenter accipiebatis, et mortem ipsorum eis tacebatis" (*Sermo* Denis 17, 7, 8, 9: *MA* 1:88–89). See nn. 45–49, above.

120 Cf. nn. 45, 53, 98 above for other examples of such usage.

121 Two papers read at the convention of the American Historical Association in Washington, D.C., on 29 December 1964, argued strongly that Roman citizenship remained a sign of distinct status as well as a minority phenomenon in Attica and Lower Egypt (the two areas among the eastern provinces for which we have the best evidence), as long as a

century after Caracalla's edict. The authors, Elias Kapetanopoulos ("The Evidence of Greece") and John F. Oates ("The Evidence of Egypt"), did not, however, go far into the fourth century, and did see a gradual widening even of this publicly declared sense of Roman citizenship as the period under discussion advanced. Besides, Attica and Lower Egypt could hardly be called regions typical of the empire either in social structure or in self-conscious cultural tradition. Consequently, it would not seem unreasonable to expect a more homogeneous picture of citizenship-awareness in North Africa ca. 400 than in either of those districts in the course of the third century. Despite Augustine's acute awareness of the continuing division between Latin-speaking and Punic-speaking members of his flock (cf. Van der Meer, pp. 26–28, 81, 111, 116, 228, 230, 258, 345), which might be supposed to have produced in the latter group some feeling of alienation from the dominant elements, one looks in vain among the relevant documents for any evidence that that awareness affected his use of *populus*.

122 *Ep.* 91 to Nectarius, treated previously, was one result of the riots at Calama in answer to such regulations. It is far from the only evidence of Augustine's attitude on that issue. Cf. n. 27 above, and Van der Meer, pp. 34, 37–43.

123 Opposition in principle (if not always in tactic) to imperial civil authority, and not only on the question of official imperial ecclesiastical policy, was a mainstay of Donatist apologetics in Augustine's time. This tendency derived in a nearly canonical tradition from Donatus's famous question, "Quid imperatori cum ecclesia?", and expressed itself internally as well in what G. G. Willis characterizes as a peculiarly Donatist "fissiparous tendency" (pp. 31–35). Willis asserts that even in his appeal to civil power against the Donatists, Augustine avoided the question of jurisdiction in principle, and made the core of his own apologetic an appeal to *pax* and *caritas* (ibid., pp. 133–35, 172–74). See also Bonner, pp. 237–51, and, for a treatment of the factors of social division which Augustine tried to counteract in his campaign against Donatism, Hans-Joachim Diesner, *Studien zur Gesellschaftslehre und sozialen Haltung Augustins,* pp. 66–73. On these and other related aspects of Augustine's reaction to the Donatists, see the finely nuanced judgments of Peter Brown, pp. 226–43 (two chapters entitled "Instantia" and "Disciplina"), 331–39.

124 Brown has discerned a comparable—perhaps parallel—balance between grammatical fidelity and dialectical flexibility in Augustine's exegetical technique for use in sermons: that is, a complete mastery of the exact words of the text combined with endless subtlety in their interpretation (p. 254). Cf. Marrou's remarks about Augustine's purist attitude toward choice of vocabulary, *even* in the genre of the popular sermon—an attitude representative of the whole of his literary culture (n. 23, above),

Chapter 3

1 Jean Steinmann, the most enthusiastic recent biographer of Jerome (and a voice deserving attention thanks to his own great expertise as translator of Jeremias for the Bible de Jerusalem and to his studies on that prophet) declares: "Certes, cet incomparable épistolier, ce polémiste brillant n'était pas un philosophe, ni un théologien. On dit que le P. Cavallera a renoncé à écrire son second volume qui devait analyser la pensée de saint Jérôme, parce que cette pensée, il ne l'a point trouvée, elle n'existe pas" (*Saint Jérôme*, p. 370). This judgment is quite in accord with the point of view that minimizes Jerome's scholarship, deplores his personality, and generally considers him a baneful influence on the Latin Church; Hans von Campenhausen perhaps epitomizes this estimate in his chapter on Jerome (pp. 129–82) in *The Fathers of the Latin Church*, trans. M. Hoffmann. In the same work (p. 183), on the other hand, he asserts: "Augustine is the only church father who even today remains an intellectual power. Irrespective of school and denomination he attracts pagans and Christians, philosophers and theologians alike by his writings and makes them come to terms with his intentions and his person." This study follows the more positive but still cautious estimate of Jerome's contribution conveyed by the work of Ferdinand Cavallera. In pt. 1, pp. 11–12 of his two-volume *Saint Jérôme, sa vie et son oeuvre*, he asserts: "Entre tous les écrivains chrétiens de ce siècle et du suivant, Jérôme se distinguera par l'art du style, la richesse et la variété de sa langue, le caractère personnel des compositions, la souplesse du talent. Plus qu'aucun d'eux il reste sensible à la louange pour une phrase artistement travaillée ou à la critique blâmant un terme mal choisi, une locution impropre, une tournure de phrase mal venu . . . Ami du pittoresque et du concret, curieux de tout ce qui pouvait lui offrir un détail réaliste, une donnée inédite, une précision savante, c'était, avant la lettre, l'humaniste aussi féru d'érudition encyclopédique qu'amoureux du beau langage."

2 Jean Leclercq, *The Love of Learning and the Desire for God*, trans. C. Misrahi, p. 123. The edition of Jerome's letters used in this study is that of Isidore Hilberg in *Sancti Eusebii Hieronymi Epistulae*, vols. 54–56 of *CSEL*. For chronology and attributions, I have relied on Cavallera, *Saint Jérôme*, vol. 2, comparing the conclusions of that work with those of Steinmann, *Saint Jérôme*, J. Labourt, trans., *Saint Jérôme: Lettres*, and T. C. Lawler, intro. and notes to *The Letters of St. Jerome*, trans. C. C. Mierow, vol. 1. For English translation I have followed the last book for letters 1–22, and F. A. Wright's translation of certain others in *Select Letters of St. Jerome*. Where the translator is not cited, the translation is mine. For *De Viris Illustribus* I have used the text edited by E. C. Richardson in Texte und Untersuchungen zur Geschichte

der altchristlichen Literatur, 14:ix–56. For evaluation and another text, I have relied upon S. von Sychowski's *Hieronymus als Litterarhistoriker*. On the question of medieval influence, see pp. 7–14 of von Sychowski.

3   "Nec hoc dicimus, quo rennuamus regnum dei intra nos esse et sanctos uiros etiam in ceteris esse regionibus, sed quo hoc adseramus uel maxime, eos, qui in toto orbe sunt primi, huc pariter congregari. ad quae nos loca non ut primae, sed ut extremae uenimus, ut primos in eis omnium gentium cerneremus . . . quicumque in Gallia fuerit primus, huc properat. diuisus ab orbe nostro Britannus, si in religione processerit, occiduo sole dimisso quaerit locum fama sibi tantum et scripturarum relatione cognitum. quid referamus Armenios, quid Persas, quid Indiae et Aethiopum populos ipsamque iuxta Aegyptum fertilem monachorum, Pontum et Cappadociam, Syriam Coelen et Mesopotamiam cunctaque orientis examina?" (*Ep.* 46, 10: *CSEL* 54:339–40). Despite his long comradeship with Paula and close affection for Eustochium (and indeed all that family), Marcella had probably been the member of the Aventine circle intellectually closest to Jerome. Until her death shortly after the sack of Rome, she remained his chief adviser in Rome and one of his chief defenders there. The style of this letter, not surprisingly, is considerably more ornate than was normal for him; consequently, concern for richness of vocabulary is entirely to be expected.

4   "Ubi tunc totius orbis homines ab India usque ad Britanniam, a rigida septentrionis plaga usque ad feruores Atlantici oceani, tam innumerabiles populi et tantarum gentium multitudines

            quam variae linguis, habitu tam vestis et armis?

piscium ritu ac lucustarum et uelut muscae et culices conterebantur; absque notitia enim creatoris sui omnis homo pecus est. nunc uero passionem Christi et resurrectionem eius cunctarum gentium uoces et litterae sonant. taceo de Hebraeis, Graecis, et Latinis, quas nationes fidei suae in crucis titulo dominus dedicauit. . . . Bessorum feritas et pellitorum turba populorum, qui mortuorum quondam inferiis homines immolabant, stridorem suum in dulce crucis fregerunt melos et totius mundi una uox Christus est" (*Ep.* 60, 4: *CSEL* 54:552–53; translation: Wright, pp. 271–73). The uncle was Heliodorus, so that a major literary effort was obviously in order. Consequently, an effort toward varied vocabulary is once again to be expected. The line of verse is from the *Aeneid* VIII, 723.

5   "In mea enim patria rusticitatis uernacula deus uenter est et de die uiuitur: sanctior est ille, qui ditior est. accessit huic patellae iuxta tritum populi sermone prouerbium dignum operculum, Lupicinus sacerdos—" (*Ep.* 7, 5: *CSEL* 54:29–30; translation: Wright, p. 25).

6   "Baias peterent, unguenta eligerent, diuitias et uiduitatem haberent, materias luxuriae et libertatis, domnae uocarentur et sanctae: nunc in sacco et cinere formosae uolunt uideri et in gehennae ignis cum ieiuniis et pedore descendere. uidelicet non eis licet adplaudente populo

perire cum turbis" (*Ep.* 45, 4: *CSEL* 54:326; translation: Wright, pp. 183–85). Jerome goes so far as to call Rome Babylon in this letter. Cf. Cavallera, *Saint Jérôme,* 2:86–88 (n. G).

7 "Nulla eo tempore nobilium feminarum nouerat Romae propositum monachorum nec audebat propter rei nouitatem ignominiosum, ut tunc putabatur, et uile in populis nomen adsumere" (*Ep.* 127, 5: *CSEL* 56: 149). By contrast to the previous letter above, this one (also addressed to a lady of the "Aventine circle") is full of sorrowing love for the city, rising in paragraph 12 to the well-known threnody ("capitur urbs, quae totum cepit orbem," etc.) in which Jerome associates Isaias and Vergil with his own lament.

8 "Scio ego sanctas uirgines, quae diebus festis propter populorum frequentiam pedem domi cohibent nec tunc egrediuntur, quando maior est adhibenda custodia et publicum penitus deuitandum" (*Ep.* 130, 19: *CSEL* 56:199). This extremely ornate letter to a young woman whom he had never met probably represents the culmination of his social snobbery as well as of his tendency to rhetorical artificiality. Daughter of the consul Olybrius Probus, paternal granddaughter of the celebrated grande dame Juliana, Demetrias had caused considerable enthusiasm in elegant and pious circles by her decision to embrace the religious life just after the sack of Rome (L. Duchesne, *Histoire ancienne de l'Eglise,* 3:199–201).

9 ". . . et solitudinem, in qua multa populorum milia paucis saturata sunt panibus et de reliquiis uescentium repleti sunt cophini duodecim tribuum Israhel" (*Ep.* 108, 13: *CSEL* 55:323). Written (according to his own account) in great haste and in a state of acute grief, this long letter may be an unusually good sample of his usage reflexes.

10 "Philosophus, gloriae animal et popularis aurae uile mancipium, totam semel sarcinam, et tu te putas in uirtutum culmine constitutum, si partem ex toto offeras?" (*Ep.* 118, 5: *CSEL* 55:441).

11 ". . . fuerit illa affectata seueritas et gloriam quaerens auramque popularem" (*Ep.* 130, 13: *CSEL* 56:193).

12 ". . . quidam Alexandrinus monachus, qui ad Aegyptios confessores et uoluntate iam martyres pio plebis fuerat transmissus obsequio . . ." *Ep.* 3, 2: *CSEL* 54:13; translation: Mierow, p. 30).

13 *Ep.* 52, 8. For text and fuller treatment, see below, n. 19.

14 "Quantus beatitudinis rumor diversa populorum ora compleuerit, hinc poteris aestimare, quod ego te ante incipio amare, quam nosse" (*Ep.* 4, 1: *CSEL* 54:19; translation: Mierow, p. 35).

15 "Quoniam uetusto oriens inter se populorum furore conlisus indiscissam domini tunicam et desuper textam minutatim per frusta discerpit et Christi uineam exterminant uulpes, ut inter lacus contritos, qui aquam non habent, difficile, ubi fons signatus et hortus ille conclusus sit, possit intellegi, ideo mihi cathedram Petri et fidem apostolico ore laudatam censui consulendam inde nunc meae animae postulans cibum, unde olim

Christi uestimenta suscepi" (*Ep.* 15, 1: *CSEL* 54:62–63; translation:
Mierow, p. 70). The chauvinism of this letter is not entirely due to
the solemnity of the rhetorical occasion, and it undoubtedly has a lot
to do with entirely secular regional sentiment. However, the context of
this dispute is presented in entirely ecclesiastical/sacred terms, and
hence the units involved (i.e., the *populi*) are seen in their ecclesiastical
aspect. Cf. the following passage, beginning two sentences further:
"profligato a subole male patrimonio apud uos solos incorrupta patrum
seruatur hereditas. ibi caespite terra fecundo dominici seminis puritatem
centeno fructu refert; hic obruta sulcis frumenta in lolium auenasque
degenerant. nunc in occidente sol iustitiae oritur; in oriente autem lucifer
ille, qui ceciderat, super sidera posuit thronum suum."

16   "Absit hoc a Romana fide: sacrilegium tantum religiosa populorum
corda non hauriant" (*Ep.* 15, 4: *CSEL* 54:66; translation: Mierow, p.
72).

17   "Plane times, ne eloquentissimus homo in Syro sermone uel Graeco
ecclesias circumeam, populos seducam, scisma conficiam" (*Ep.* 17, 2:
CSEL 54:72; translation: Mierow, p. 77). Jerome is unquestionably
being ironic about his command of Greek (which he had studied in
school but did not really master until his stay in Constantinople from
379 to 382) and Syriac (which he never pretended to know at all well).

18   "Dionysius, Corinthiorum ecclesiae episcopus, tantae eloquentiae et in-
dustriae fuit, ut non solum suae civitatis et provinciae populos, sed et
aliarum urbium et provinciarum epistulis erudiret." "Pinytus Cretensis,
Gnosiae urbis episcopus, scripsit ad Dionysium Corinthiorum valde
elegantem epistolam, in qua docet, non semper lacte populos enutriendos,
ne quasi parvuli ab ultimo occupentur die, sed et solido vesci debere
cibo, ut in spiritalem proficiant senectutem" (*DVI*, chaps. 27 and 28,
Altchristlichen Literatur, 14:23). Stanislaus von Sychowski gives a
slightly different version of these chapters (pp. 117–18), and makes the
startling assertion that the first sentence of the former chapter comes
"Fast wörtlich aus" Eusebius's *Historia ecclesiastica* IV, 31. I have not
been able to locate the Lämmer edition of Eusebius which von Sychowski used, but the most recent edition by Gustave Bardy (Eusèbe de Cé-
sarée, *Histoire Ecclésiastique,* Greek text, trans. and annotation by
Bardy) raises two doubts about von Sychowski's accuracy in this case.
First of all, the relevant chapter seems to be 21 or 23, not 31—elsewhere the chapter numbers cited for the Lämmer edition agree with
the Bardy edition; secondly, Jerome's Latin sentence seems very different indeed from any sentence of Eusebius's Greek in those chapters—
Jerome clearly condensed and paraphrased quite freely in this case. The
first objection undoubtedly arises from a mere typographical error, but
the second would seem to cast suspicion on the fundamental soundness
of the author's judgments in what he has entitled *Quellenkritische
Untersuchung.* If this lapse is at all typical, Jerome emerges as much

more original or (at least) freely adaptive than von Sychowski claims.

19 "Dicente te in ecclesia non clamor populi, sed gemitus suscitetur; lacrimae auditorum laudes tuae sint; sermo presbyteri scripturarum lectione conditus sit. nolo te declamatorem esse et rabulam garrulamque, sed mysterii peritum et sacramentorum dei tui eruditissimum. uerba uoluere et celeritate dicendi apud inperitum uulgus admirationem sui facere indoctorum hominum est. adtrita frons interpretatur saepe, quod nescit, et, cum aliis suaserit, sibi quoque usurpat scientiam. praeceptor quondam meus Gregorius Nazianzenus rogatus a me, ut exponeret, quid sibi uellet in Luca sabbatum δευτερόπρωτον, id est 'secundoprimum' eleganter lusit: 'docebo te' inquiens 'super hac re in ecclesia, in qua omni mihi populo adclamante cogeris inuitus scire, quod nescis, aut certe, si solus tacueris, solus ab omnibus stultitiae condemnaberis.' nihil tam facile, quam uilem plebiculam et indoctam contionem linguae uolubilitate decipere, quae, quidquid non intellegit, plus miratur. Marcus Tullius, . . ." (Ep. 52, 8: CSEL 54:428–29; translation: Wright, pp. 211–13).

20 However, this sort of transfer may be exemplified in a passage from Ep. 20, 4, written in 383 in reply to Pope Damasus's question about the meaning of the word Hosanna: Jerome refers to Ps. 172, "qui manifeste de Christo prophetat et in synagogis Iudaeorum celeberrime legebatur, unde et populis notior erat . . ." Should populis be taken as strictly appositive to synagogis, or simply as denoting the "populace"? A little further, Jerome continues (still on the subject of the psalm's popularity): ". . . unde et euangelistarum scriptura commemorat pharisaeos et scribas haec indignatos, quod uiderunt populum psalmi prophetiam super Christo intellegere conpletam . . ." (CSEL 54:107–08). Should this populum be interpreted as meaning the "people of Israel" (in the grips of an opinion sacred in nature), or as meaning the "common people" as distinct from the Pharisees and Scribes? If the latter interpretation is correct, it would agree better with previous usage than would the former with the usage now under discussion in the Letters. It would also run counter to Jerome's tendency in the Vulgate to use plebs for the body politic considered separately from specific elements of its leadership (see above, pp. 100–03). But then it might be a sign of a minor disparity in usage between his commentaries on the Scripture and his translation of it, a disparity of particular interest since the date of this commentary is also the generally accepted date of his publication of the Vulgate Gospels, his first major translation effort.

This discussion has been included in the notes partly as a sample of some of the problems of method involved in this study but, more importantly, to indicate how unusual it is to find usages of equal ambiguity in Jerome's writing. The passages quoted in nn. 14–19 are much more typical as far as clarity is concerned. It should also be noted that each of them represents a progressive crystallization and clarification of the usage as well as a progression in time over the twenty years between 374 and 394.

21 ". . . rudes illi Italiae homines, quos cascos Ennius appellat" *Ep.* 8, 1: *CSEL* 54:31–32. The reference is to Ennius's *Annales,* 24. It is not improbable that Jerome had that book with him, since his renunciation of property in Chalcis did not include his considerable library. His tendency simply to insert the wording of other authors has been thoroughly and constantly attacked ever since the Reformation. However, see n. 18, above, for an examination of one instance of this charge. Jerome has also (and with equal frequency) been accused of careless paraphrasing. In any case, this reference is clearly a paraphrase of some degree of independence.

22 Von Campenhausen, p. 147, asserts with typical vigor, "Jerome was at all times a naive Roman patriot." Duchesne's judgment on 410 remains the classic statement of a more balanced position: "Les saints gens qui, dès avant les dernières catastrophes, avaient pris le monde en dégoût, se trouvaient moins disposés que les autres à s'apitoyer sur sa débacle. Mais ce qu'ils voyaient disparaître sans regret, c'était plutôt la futilité du siècle en général, que le prestige de la vieille Rome. La *res Romana* tenait toujours à coeur aux Jérôme, aux Augustin, aux Paulin. Ils l'auraient mieux aimée dans l'austerité des vertus antiques, gouvernée par les Fabricius et les Cincinnatus. Telle qu'ils la voyaient, avec son pauvre sénat, sa cour tout en clinquant, sa hiérarchie vermoulue, ils l'aimaient encore. Ils en étaient trop, et par leur éducation et par toutes leurs fibres, pour avoir l'idée de s'en détacher" *Histoire ancienne de l'Eglise,* 3:197. For a treatment of Augustine's complex and ambivalent attitude toward Rome, see P. Gerosa, "S. Agostino e l'imperialismo romano," *MA* 2:976–1040. A useful summary of the bibliography appears on pp. 977–90; Rome as the second Babylon in Augustine's writings is considered on pp. 1025–27.

23 Cavallera treats the question of Jerome's ethnic origins, native language, and so on, as well as the question of the location of Stridon, in *Saint Jérôme,* 2:67–71 (*note complémentaire* A). His conclusions lead to the following judgment, with which the research done for this study has produced only agreement: "En dehors du patriotisme local, comme d'autres, nombreux en ce temps-là, il n'a point connu le patriotisme provincial, mais seulement le patriotisme impérial. Rome était le centre de sa vie de citoyen, comme elle l'était de sa vie religieuse." For a classic example of scholarly regional consciousness, which in the final analysis does not really detract from Cavallera's estimate, see Francesco Bulic, "Stridone luogo natale di S. Girolamo," *Miscellanea Geronimiana,* pp. 253–30. A good example of the extent to which the experiences of his student days affected his whole outlook appears in his *Commentary on Ezechiel* XII, 40, 5: ed. F. Glorie, *CCSL* 75:556–57; for the Antiochene divisions see F. Cavallera, *Le schisme d'Antioche (IVᵉ–Vᵉ siècle).* The

conflict with John of Jerusalem reached its riotous head in 416 or 417; Jerome owed papal assistance to the intervention of Eustochium, who took it upon herself to write Innocent. The degree of Melanie and Rufinus's integration into the episcopal community of Jerusalem can be surmised from the fact that Rufinus served as John's secretary (just as Jerome had served Damasus).

24   "Cum in Babylone versarer et purpuratae meretricis essem colonus, et iure Quiritium viverem, volui garrire aliquid de Spiritu Sancto, et coeptum opusculum eiusdem urbis pontifici dedicare. Et ecce olla illa, quae in Jeremia post baculum cernitur a facie aquilonis, coepit ardere; et Pharisaeorum conclamavit senatus et nullus scriba vel fictus sed omnis quasi indicto sibi proelio doctrinam, adversum me imperitiae factio coniuravit. Illic ergo, velut postliminio, Ierosolymam sum reversus: et post Romuli casam, et ludorum Lupercalia, diversorium Mariae et Salvatoris speluncam aspexi. . . . canticum quod cantare non potui in terra aliena, hic a vobis in Judaea provocatus immurmuro; angustiorem multo locum existimans, qui Salvatorem mundi quam qui fratris genuit parricidam." This is from the preface dedicated to his brother Paulinianus. (Migne, 25, cols. 107–08.) Compare with this the prologue to the *Commentary on Ezechiel*, written in 410: "Postquam uero clarissimum terrarum omnium lumen exstinctum est, immo romani imperii truncatum caput et, ut uerius dicam, in una urbe totus orbis interiit, 'obmutui et humiliatus sum et silui de bonis, et dolor meus renouatus est; concaluit intra me cor meum, et in meditatione mea exardescet ignis' (Ps. 38:3–4), nec putaui illam sententiam neglegendam: 'Musica in luctu importuna narratio' (Eccles. 22:6)." Cf. also the opening of book III: "Quis crederet ut totius urbis exstructa uictoriis Roma corrueret, ut ipsa suis populis et mater fieret et sepulcrum, ut tota Orientis, Aegypti, Africae littora olim dominatricis urbis, seruorum et ancillarum numero complerentur, ut cotidie sancta Bethleem, nobiles quondam utriusque sexus atque omnibus diuitiis affluentes, susciperet mendicantes?" (*CCSL* 75:3, 91).

25   For example (in addition to the passages quoted in the previous footnote), *Ep.* 127, written in 411: 1, ". . . Romanae urbis inclitum decus . . ."; 3, "Difficile est in maledicta ciuitate et in urbe, in qua orbis quondam populus fuit palmaque uitiorum, si honestis detraherent et pura et munda macularent, non aliquam sinistri rumoris fabulam trahere" (*CSEL* 56:145, 147).

26   ". . . alter toto orbe fugituus tandem Bithyniae mortem ueneno repperit, alter reuersus in patriam in suo regno occubuit; et utriusque prouinciae Romani populi uectigales sunt" (*Ep.* 123, 16: *CSEL* 56:93–94).

27   "Urbs tua, quondam orbis caput, Romani populi sepulchrum est, et tu in Libyco litore, exulem uirum ipsa exul accipies? . . . non sic post Trebiam, Trasummenum et Cannas, in quibus locis Romanorum exercitum caesa sunt milia, Marcelli primum apud Nolam proelio se

populus Romanus erexit. minori prius gaudio strata Gallorum agmina auro redempta nobilitas et seminarium Romani generis in arce cognouit" (*Ep.* 130, 5 and 6: *CSEL* 56:180–82).

28   "Iosephus antiquitatem adprobans Iudaici populi duos libros scribit contra Apionem, Alexandrinum grammaticum, . . ." (*Ep.* 70, 3: *CSEL* 54:704).

29   ". . . dum Pharao uixit, populus Israhel ex luti et lateris palearumque opere non suspirauit ad dominum; . . ." (*Ep.* 18, 2: *CSEL* 54:76; translation: Mierow, p. 81). Cf. *Ep.* 128, 2: *CSEL* 56:157.

30   ". . . in lege mense septimo post clangorem tubarum, decima die mensis totius gentis Hebraeae ieiunium et exterminatur anima illa de populo suo, quae saturitatem praetulerit continentiae" (*Ep.* 130, 10: *CSEL* 56: 190). The clause "exterminatur . . . de populo" derives from an Exodus formula (30:33, 38, for example), and is not original with Jerome; on the other hand, it is quite consistent with his nonbiblical usage.

31   *Ep.* 18, 15. The implication that Israel is the people is present in some sections of a letter written about 412 to Dardanus, although the *gentes* are not present to provide explicit contrast. See *Ep.* 129, 4 and 5; *CSEL* 56:169, 172, for example.

32   ". . . et Iudaicus populus primas sibi cathedras et salutationes in foro uindicans deputato antea in stillam situlae gentili populo succedente deletus est" (*Ep.* 12, 2: *CSEL* 54:41; translation: Mierow, p. 55).

33   ". . . ut Iudaeorum superbiam reprobet et in commune omnium peccatorum, siue gentilium siue Israhel, paenitentiam probet, quod autem ait 'duos filios,' omnes paene scripturae de duorum uocatione populorum plenae sunt sacramentis" (*Ep.* 21, 4: *CSEL* 54:117; translation: Mierow, p. 113).

34   *Ep.* 40: *CSEL* 54:140. Cf. also *Ep.* 3, in which Jerome argues against Tertullian's position that (in Jerome's words) "publicanos Iudaeos non fuisse, ut in persona eorum gentilium tantum populus potest intelligi" (*CSEL* 54:116).

35   ". . . dicamus duo sacerdotia inter se ab apostolo comparata, prioris populi et posterioris, . . . "(*Ep.* 73, 4: *CSEL* 55:17).

36   ". . . et iuxta uiam caecorum loca, qui receptis luminibus utriusque populi credentis in dominum sacramenta praemiserant" (*Ep.* 108, 12: *CSEL* 55:321).

37   "Et tam diu in te Dauitici generis origo permansit, donec uirgo pareret, et reliquiae populi credentis in Christum conuerteretur ad filios Israhel et libere praedicarent: 'uobis oportebat primum loqui uerbum dei, sed, quoniam repellitis et indignos uos iudicastis aeternae uitae, conuertimur ad gentes' " (*CSEL* 55:317).

38   "Statimque concito gradu coepit per uiam ueterem pergere, quae ducit Gazam, ad potentias uel diuitias dei, et tacita secum uoluere, quomodo eunuchus Aethiops gentium populos praefigurans mutauerit pellem suam

et, dum uetus relegit instrumentum, fontem repperit euangelii" (*CSEL* 55:318–19).

39 "Totus ad spectaculum populus effunditur et, prorsus quasi migrare ciuitas putaretur, stipatis proruens portis turba densatur. . . . Tandem ergo ad feminam uindicandam populus armatur. omnis aetas, omnis sexus carnificem fugat et coetu in circulum coeunte non credit paene unusquisque, quod uidit. turbatur tali nuntio urbs propinqua et tota lictorum caterua glomeratur. e quibus medius, ad quem damnatorum cura pertinebat, erumpens et 'canitiem inmundam perfuso puluere turpans': 'meum,' inquit, 'o ciues, petitis caput, me illi uicarium datis! si misericordes, si clementes estis, si uultis seruare damnatam, innocens certe perire non debeo.' quo fletu uulgi consussus est animus maestusque se per omnes torpor insinuat et mirum in modum uoluntate mutata, cum pietatis fuisset, quod ante defenderant, pietatis uisum est genus, ut paterentur occidi" (*Ep.* 1, 7, 10: *CSEL* 54:4, 6–7; translation: Mierow, pp. 4, 6–7). The quotation before the old man's appeal is from the *Aeneid* XII, 611 (King Latinus distraught at the victorious Trojans' approach to the walls of his city).

40 "Ueniet, ueniet, illa dies, qua corruptiuum hoc et mortale incorruptionem induat et inmortalitatem. beatus seruus, quem dominus inuenerit uigilantem. tunc ad uocem tubae pauebit terra cum populis, tu gaudebis. iudicaturo domino lugubre mundus inmugiet; tribus ad tribum ferient pectora; potentissimi quondam reges nudo latere palpitabunt; exhibebitur cum prole sua uere tunc ignitus Iuppiter; adducetur et cum suis stultus Plato discipulis; Aristoteli argumenta non proderunt. tunc tu rusticanus et pauper exultabis, . . . "(*Ep.* 14, 11: *CSEL* 54:61).

41 "Ozias, rex Iuda, postquam lepra percussus est, habitarit in domo separata et filius eius Ioatham imperium rexerit iudicaueritque populum terrae usque ad diem mortis patris sui et tamen post mortem fllius, . . . Ex quo intellegi uoluit non statim post patris mortem filium imperio subrogatum, sed uel seditionibus populi uel quibusdam interregnis aut certe prementibus malis et hic inde consurgentibus bellis regnum eius fuisse dilatum" (*Ep.* 72, 4: *CSEL* 55:11–12). For one specific significance of the term *populus terrae*, see pp. 91–92 of this chapter and n. 55.

42 ". . . ingrediebatur templum et fixis genibus pro populo deprecabatur . . . Tradit autem Josephus tantae eum sanctitatis fuisse et celebritatis in populo, ut propter eius necem creditum sit subuersam Hierosolymam" (*DVI*, chap. 2: Altchristlichen Literatur, 14:7, 8).

43 "Postea vero . . . Smyrnae sedente proconsule et universo populo in amphitheatro adversus eum personante, igni traditus est" (Ibid., chap. 17, p. 18).

44 ". . . dum interpretationis κακοζηλίαν sequimur, omnem decorem translationis, amittimus; et hanc esse regulam boni interpretis, ut ἰδιώματα linguae alterius suae linguae exprimat proprietate. . . . nec ex eo quis latinam linguam angustissimam putet, quod non possit

uerbum transferre de uerbo cum etiam Graeci pleraque nostra circuitu transferant et uerba Hebraica non interpretationis fide, sed linguae suae proprietatibus nitantur exprimere" (*Ep.* 106, 3: *CSEL* 55:250). Some of the other passages consistent with this point of view are the preface to Jerome's translation of Eusebius's *Chronology* (ca. 380); *Ep.* 57: "ad Pammachium, de optimo genere interpretandi" (ca. 389); a reference to that letter in *Ep.* 12, 20; and the *Commentary on Amos* III, 11 (composed in 406). Angelo Penna, in *Principi e carattere dell'esegesi di San Gerolamo,* pp. 77–79, discusses Jerome's attitude toward the translation of metaphor and metonymy, in the course of an extended treatment of the "literal sense."

45   "Iuvencus, nobilissimi generis Hispanus presbyter, quattuor Evangelia hexametris versibus paene ad verbum transferens, . . ." (*DVI,* chap. 84: Altchristlichen Literatur, 14:44). Von Sychowski vouches for the originality of Jerome's opinion in this case (pp. 174–75). To test the *ad verbum* quality of this work, compare the forty lines (book IV, lines 586–625) dealing with the trial of Christ before Pilate, with the accounts of the same event given by the Synoptic Gospels, discussed above on pp. 105–08. Juvencus's version begins (typically, too): "Sidera iam luci concedunt et rapidus sol Progreditur radiis terras trepidantibus inplens. Iamque e concilio Christum post terga reuinctum Praesidis ad gremium magno clamore trahebant" (*Gai Vetti Aquilini Iuuenci Euangeliorum libri quattuor,* ed. J. Huemer, *CSEL* 24:136–38). A cursory examination of the work seems to indicate that Juvencus's use of *populus* is much less clear and consistent than Jerome's and Augustine's, but that there is less difference in regard to *gens* and *natio,* and little if any in regard to *patria.* Prosodic and metrical requirements may be one reason for this disparity in usage.

46   See Appendix C for a discussion of the texts and some of the secondary authorities utilized in this study's examination of scriptural passages.

47   The Hebrew for the first locus is גּוֹיִם

48   "Nam Latinorum interpretum, qui de Graeco in nostrum eloquium transtulerunt (ut meminit sanctus Augustinus) infinitus numerus. Sicut enim (inquit) primis fidei temporibus ad manus venit codex Graecus, atque aliquantulum sibi utriusque linguae peritiam sumpsit, ausus est statim interpretari, atque inde accidit tam innumerabiles apud Latinos exstitisse interpretes.

De Hebraeo autem in Latinum eloquium tantummodo Hieronymus presbyter sacras scripturas convertit. Cujus editione generaliter omnes ecclesiae usquequaque utuntur, pro eo quod veracior sit in sententiis et clarior in verbis": *De Ecclesiasticis Officiis,* I, 12: *Sancti Isidori, Hispalensis episcopi, opera omnia,* ed. F. Arévalo, vol. 6 (Migne, 83, cols. 748–49). *Codex Toletanus,* written in Seville in the eighth or ninth century, is generally held to represent Isidore's copy of the Vulgate; its reading of this verse agrees with his citation of it in *Etymologiae* VII, 29 on these points.

The reference to Augustine is a paraphrase of the last part of *De doctrina Christiana* II, 11. A little further on, in II, 15, Augustine asserts strongly the Septuagint's claim to final authority. It has been suggested that the "Itala" praised in that latter passage was the Vulgate; but that suggestion seems to have been effectively and finally refuted: see the excellent summary of this question in *Le magistère chrétien,* ed. Combès et Farges, *BA* 11:574–75 (*notes complémentaires*). Consequently, Isidore's reverence for the authority of both Augustine and Jerome in the passage cited above represents a definite stage in the Latin churches' reconciliation of the dispute which divided those two Fathers.

49 No Old Latin versions of this text have been located by editors of the Benediktbeuron *Vetus Latina.*

50 Roland de Vaux, "Israel—People of God," *The Critic* 24, no. 1:57–63. The central thesis of the article relevant to this inquiry is "Israel does not owe its character as the people of God to any of the human factors which constitute a nation: a common race, language, or dwelling-place. It became the people of Yahweh by a free choice on the part of God . . . a choice . . . inspired by love, which is directed toward a mission and which imposes certain obligations. This theology of election is elaborated by Deuteronomy and forms the central doctrine of the book" (p. 58). See also De Vaux's *Ancient Israel, Its Life and Institutions,* trans. J. McHugh, chap. 4, pp. 91–99; M. Noth, "Gott, König, Volk im Alten Testament," *Zeitschrift für Theologie und Kirche,* 47:157–91.

51 Although Sabatier reports no Old Latin readings for these verses, some are available in *Pentateuchi versio latina antiquissima e codice Lugdunensi,* ed. Ulysse Robert. They are:

    a. plebs

    b. gentes

    c. populus praecipuus

    d. gentes (non quia magna turba sitis inter ceteras gentes)

    e. (—) (et elegit vos)

The Vulgate text of *d* and *e,* verse 7, reads: "Non quia cunctas gentes numero vincebatis, vobis iunctus est Dominus et elegit vos, cum omnibus sitis populis pauciores." The divergence should indicate how improbable it would be to suggest any influence of Lugdunensis on the Vulgate. Robert argues that this codex is a sixth-century copy of a version composed in Africa perhaps as early as the late third century, and based on a Greek text different from that represented by Vaticanus and Alexandrinus (but not exactly the so-called "Western" text). Its language is extremely popular; Augustine seems to have known it, but tended to use other African versions of the Pentateuch. However, numerous Hellenisms are present in the text, and the existing copy shows signs of corrections which seek to conform to the Vulgate. Consequently, although not too relevant to this inquiry's concerns, Lugdunensis is a good example of the sort of text Jerome set out to replace: aside from crudities of style, verse 7 simply makes no sense. Lugdunensis' version of the important doublet of this passage in Deut. 14:2 is less distant from the Septuagint *textus receptus*, although far from Jerome's preferred Latin usages, "For you are a *people* [a] sacred to the Lord, your God, who has chosen you from all the *nations* [b] on the face of the earth to be a *people* [c] peculiarly his own."

			(*Septuagint*)	(*Old Latin*)	(*Vulgate*)
a.	עַם	ām	λαός	plebs	populus
b.	הָעַמִּים	(haāmim)	ἐθνῶν	gentibus	gentibus
c.	לְעַם־סְגֻלָּה	(l'ām	λαὸς	plebem	populum
		s'gulah)	περιούσιος	exuperantem	peculiarem

52 Jerome says, in *Ep.* 125, 12 (*CSEL* 56:131), that he began studying Hebrew while still a monk in Chalcis, at least partly in order to discipline his sensuality. *Ep.* 36, 1, written in answer to three of Damasus's questions on Genesis, begins by explaining Jerome's delay: "interim iam et ego linguam et ille articulum mouebamus, cum subito Hebraeus interuenit deferens non pauca uolumina, quae de synagoga quasi lecturus acceperat. et ilico 'habes,' inquit, 'quod postulaueras' meque dubium et, quid facerem, nescientem ita festinus exterruit, ut omnibus praetermissis ad scribendum transuolarem; quod quidem usque ad praesens facio" (*CSEL* 54:268). The clandestine atmosphere of this incident (if it is not simply literary artifice useful in an apology for tardiness) would seem to suggest that neither Jerome's study of the language nor his transcription of texts was undertaken with systematic care while he lived in Rome. On the question of his familiarity with rabbinical wisdom (as well as this specific issue), see Moritz Rahmer, *Die Hebräischen Traditionen in den Werken des Hieronymus* (pp. 4–16 discuss his Jewish teachers; the rest deals with the *Quaestiones hebraicae in Genesim*); Gustave Bardy, "St. Jérôme et ses maîtres hébreux," *Revue bénédictine* 46:145–64, for discussion of later views. Cf. also Penna, *Esegesi di S. Gerolamo*, pp. 5–10.

53 Jerome's concern to make this distinction is put into especially clear relief by a comparison with the vocabulary of Hilary of Poitiers's commentary on that verse. While at Trier (Oct. 367–ca. 370), Jerome copied Hilary's commentary on the Psalms with his own hand, as either a present or a special favor for Rufinus (*Ep.* 5, 2: *CSEL* 54:22). In book II of his *Commentarium in Galatas*, written about 390—and so only one or two years at most before the *Psalterium iuxta Hebraeos*—Jerome reminisces about his stay in Gaul and reasserts (in effect) his admiration for Hilary, whom he calls "the Rhone of Latin eloquence." Consequently, it is quite interesting to note that Hilary shows none of Jerome's concern for semantic precision when his commentary explains the meaning of the words *gentes* and *populi* in this verse: "'Populi' autem 'inania meditati sunt' id est inani in doctrinis dei uersati, cum per meditationem legis non intellexerint, qui praedicabatur in lege. iam

enim tum non tantum ex illa secundum carnem Abrahae generatione synagogae populus abundabat, sed ex multis populis; in uno Israhel populi nomine multorum populorum diuersitas continebatur, et hoc in Actorum libro ita scribitur: 'erant autem in Hierusalem habitantes Iudaei, uiri timentes deum, ab omni gente, quae sub caelo est.' populi itaque isti meditati inania sunt ex multis populis in unum populum congregati" (S. Hilarii episcopi Pictauensis Tractatus super Psalmos, ed. A. Zingerle, CSEL 22:41.)

54 Menahem Kasher, ed., Genesis, vol. 2 of Torah Shelemah, Talmudic-Midrashic Interpretation of the Pentateuch, p. 506, indicates that Gen. 10:32 is treated only in Mordecai Margulies, ed., Genesis, vol. 1 of Midrash Haggadol on the Pentateuch, pp. 196–97. The questions of authorship and sources are discussed thoroughly in S. Fisch's edition of Numbers (in English) in the Midrash. Haggadol on the Pentateuch (pp. 6–96). Fisch argues that Maimonides' son was the author, but Margulies inclines to al-Adeni (pp. 7–9 of his edition). The Targum of Jonathan ben-Uziel, frequently, if rather vaguely, suggested as a repository of rabbinical readings influential on Jerome, uses the word לְיִחוּסֵיהוֹן (l'yihuseyhon: a grouping more like a populus than like a generatio) in its Aramaic paraphrase of Gen. 10:32, but is not otherwise enlightening חמשה חומשי תורה (New York, 1951).

55 See de Vaux, Ancient Israel, pp. 70–72, and bibliographical summary on p. 524. One work which should be included for the rabbinic period is Adolf Büchler's Der galiläische 'Am-ha 'Ares des zweiten Jahrhunderts. Although this book is mostly a detailed treatment of complicated socio-economic and liturgical developments two centuries before Jerome came to Palestine and of which he may or may not have been aware, pp. 157–212 deal with their impact on the opinions of rabbinical traditions with which he was certainly in some contact.

56 The Hethites are called עַם־הָאָרֶץ (ām-haarets); in this context the word means something like "native Gentiles," quite a different meaning from the one it carries in 4 Kings according to any interpretation. The fact that Jerome translates it quite literally, treating it differently than he did in that latter context, is further indication of his conscious interpretation of 4 Kings 25:19.

57 Cf. 24:3, a doublet for 19:25; 19:25: "Descenditque Moyses ad populum et omnia narravit eis." 24:3: "Venit ergo Moyses et narravit plebi omnia verba Domini et iudicia; responditque omnis populus una voce: Omnia verba Domini, quae locutus est, faciemus." Here the distinction between activity and passivity of the עַם (ām) seems to be drawn within the confines of one verse.

58 See above, p. 87; cf. also 19:18, for which Sabatier reports a widespread interpolation, "et mente confusus est omnis populus vehementer," the existence of which emphasizes yet further Jerome's individuality in using plebs anywhere in this section of Exodus.

59 Albert Condamin has indicated the extent to which synonym variation

is normal in the Vulgate, in his brief but trenchant "Un procédé littéraire de St. Jérôme dans sa traduction de la Bible," *Miscellanea Geronimiana,* pp. 89-96. P. 92 mentions several instances in which Jerome apparently confused a substantive difference between two Hebrew words with mere vocabulary variety, and so varied his Latin rendering of them by the same standards, thus gravely confusing the meaning of the original. Albert Roehrich presents further evidence that "Jérôme s'appliquait . . . à varier les termes de sa traduction" (for conjunctions as well as stock formulas) (*Essai sur Saint Jérôme exégète,* pp. 42-43).

60 Cf. the article "Λαός in LXX," in *Theologisches Wörterbuch zum Neuen Testament,* ed. Gerhard Kittel, 4:32-37.

61 The Septuagint has γένους and the Old Latin versions *genus* for the original עם of this verse.

62 For example, 1 Kings 10:17, 23-25: eight appearances (in the case of one—verse 24—Jerome rejected a Septuagint variation—ἐν πᾶσιν ὑμῖν); 12:19-22: four appearances.

63 For example, 25:11, 19, 22, 26. This heavy run of *populi* is well prepared for by such verses as 23:2, 3 ("omnis populus a parvo usque ad magnum," the grand assembly which reratifies the Covenant in the reign of Josias), 23:21 (an account of Josias's legislation on the observance of the law), and 23:30, 35 and 24:14, which also contain the expression *populus terrae.*

64 "Et dixit Dominus ad Osee: Vade, sume tibi uxorem fornicationum et fac tibi filios fornicationum, quia fornicans fornicabitur terra a Domino./ Et abiit et accepit Gomer filiam Debelaim, et concepit et peperit ei filium./ [1:2, 3] . . . et concepit et peperit filium./ Et dixit: Voca nomen eius 'Non-populus-meus,' quia vos non populus meus, et ego non ero vester./ [1:9] . . . Et erit in die illa, ait Dominus, vocabit me: Vir meus, et non me vocabit ultra: Baali./ . . . et sponsabo te mihi in fide, et scies quia ego Dominus./ . . . et dicam 'Non-populo-meo'; Populus meus es tu; et ipse dicet: Deus meus es tu [2:16, 20, 24]."

65 See Appendix C for a discussion of the texts and some of the secondary authorities utilized in this study's examination of passages from books of the New Testament other than the Acts of the Apostles.

66 See Appendix D for a discussion of the texts and secondary authorities considered in this study's treatment of the Acts of the Apostles. After a discussion similar to that of Appendix C, Appendix D goes on to consider the suggestion that Jerome did not translate Acts, and continues with a description of the Old Latin translations and their relationship to the Vulgate text.

67 Jerome states flatly in chap. 7 of *De Viris Illustribus* that Luke wrote Acts. Is it necessary to interpret as less positive the remark made two years later (394) to Paulinus of Nola: "Actus apostolorum nudam

quidem sonare uidentur historiam et nascentis ecclesiae infantiam texere, sed, si nouerimus scriptorem eorum Lucam esse medicum, cuius laus est in euangelio, animaduertimus pariter omnis uerba illius languentis animae esse medicamina" (*Ep.* 53, 9: *CSEL* 54:463)? The whole point of the letter seems to be that one cannot get full profit from the books of Scripture (or of pagan literature) without the instruction of a guide. Jerome's constraint in the case of more commented books may be discernible in the fact that when Ambrose began to publish a commentary on Luke's Gospel, Jerome hastened to translate Origen's commentary rather than to write his own. But haste to counteract Ambrose's baneful influence may have been the cause rather than modesty (the incident occurred in 390; cf. his entry on Ambrose in *De Viris Illustribus* [392]: "Ambrosius, Mediolanensis episcopus, usque in praesentem diem scribit, de quo, quia superest, meum iudicium subtraham, ne in alterutram partem aut adulatio in me reprehendatur aut veritas" [chap. 124: Altchristlichen Literatur, 14:53]). The relative paucity of patristic use of Acts before 300 is indicated in Hermann von Soden, *Schriften des Neuen Testaments*, vol. 1, pt. 3, pp. 1836–40.

68 In three other loci within the same chapter, ὄχλος becomes some form of *turba* quite regularly in the Vulgate and in most Old Latin versions (*h* is the exception since it follows the *turba*-translation of ὄχλος in verses 11 and 19, but quite solitarily translates it by *plebs* in verses 13 and 14. The Vulgate seems more consistently subtle in turning only verse 13's ὄχλοις into *populis*, but keeping *turbae* as the label for the same group before and after its brief formation into a liturgically active entity. The *turbis* of verse 19 really belongs to another incident.

69 But notice that Jerome is stricter than *e*, which has *plebem* rather than *populum* in verse 28: " 'Men of Israel, help! This is the man who teaches all men everywhere against the *people* and the law and this place, and moreover he has brought Gentiles also into the temple and has desecrated this holy place.' " It is interesting to note that *d* has *populum* along with the Vulgate, while *gig* simply omits the word (reading: ". . . qui adversus legem et locum hunc ubique omnes docet."). One might expect the unimaginative, Greek-dominated *d* to render the λαοῦ of D by *populum* without recourse to specifically Latin alternatives like *plebem*, but it is a little surprising to see that the two native-Latin relatives of the Vulgate differ from it so loosely: the context leaves little doubt that the "people" of this verse is all Israel.

70 The same terminal formula appears in Exod. 30:33, 38; Gen. 17:14; Lev. 7:20, 21, 25, 27, and 17:4, 9, 10, etc., with the following variations of the prepositional phrase: *de populo suo, de populis suis, de* or *in medio populi sui* (in descending order of frequency), and the following (much freer) variations of the verb (in no particular order): *peribit, interibit, delebitur, exterminabitur, disperdam.* This formula seems to be another instance of Jerome's refusal to follow the free synonym-varia-

tion normal to his style when *populus* is involved: the only variations in the object of the prepositional phrase are among the inflected forms of that one rather special noun.

71 See Appendix E for a collation of the non-Acts citations from the New Testament that have been of chief relevance to this study; the Vulgate vocabulary is compared with that of several Old Latin mss.

72 See above, p. 93.

73 The Vulgate version of those five New Testament texts is Titus 2:14: "qui dedit semet ipsum pro nobis, ut nos redimeret ab omni iniquitate, et mundaret sibi populum acceptabilem, sectatorem bonorum operum." 1 Pet. 2:10: "qui aliquando non populus, nunc autem populus Dei: qui non consecuti misericordiam, nunc autem misericordiam consecuti." 2 Cor. 6:16: "Qui autem consensus templo Dei cum idolis? Vos enim estis templum Dei vivi, sicut dicit Deus: Quoniam inhabitabo in illis, et inambulabo: et ero illorum Deus, et ipsi erunt mihi populus." Matt. 1:21: "pariet autem filium et vocabis nomen eius Iesum: ipse enim salvum faciet populum suum a peccatis eorum." Heb. 4:9: "Itaque relinquitur sabbatismus populo Dei."

This study's conclusions about the meanings of *populus* and *plebs* and the relationship between them contradict to a certain extent and in several important ways the standard statements about those words in the standard literature on Jerome's latinity—for example, C. Paucker, *De latinitate B. Hieronymi* (1880), and the much more sophisticated work of Henri Goelzer, *Etude lexicographique et grammaticale de la latinité de Saint Jérôme* (1884). (see Goelzer, pp. 10–28, for an excellent treatment of Jerome's individual contribution toward expanding the resources of the Latin language). Paucker's entire treatment of these two terms occurs as follows (p. 84): *"plebs* eccl. Gemeinde (Cypr. ep. 45, clero et plebi) c. Joan II 'quis hoc umquam presbytero suo coram plebe imperavit episcopus?'; in Gal. II ad 4, 17 sq: itemque populus; adv. Lucif. 4 'aut episcopum cum populo recipimus, . . . aut, si episcopum non recipimus, scimus etiam nobis populum reiciendum.' adv. Vigil 5 'omnium ecclesiarum populi.' " This sort of treatment suggests clearly enough the recklessness of establishing a meaning by scatter-shot selections, which may on deeper investigation turn out to be at best only partly typical. More serious is the author's apparent failure to look closely at the fragments selected: the ones offered above, suggest strongly, even in their truncated state, that there is an important shade of difference between *plebs* and *populus* which is ill expressed by the word *itemque.* As a matter of fact, those examples could be used quite effectively to establish the differences noted in the present study. Goelzer's treatment of this question begins by arousing hope, but quickly becomes disappointing (p. 232): "Si nous examinons maintenant les termes consacrés à designer l'Eglise chrétienne et les membres qui la composent, nous aurons à noter le sens spécial que prennent dans saint Jérôme les mots *plebs* et *populus;* ils signifient la masse des fidèles par opposition à *clerus,* le clergé, comme on le voit clairement dans saint Cyprien: Ep. 45.2: 'clero et plebi . . .' " The four examples which follow are from "c. Joann. II. . . . In Gal. II ad. 4:17, . . . Adv. Lucif. 4, . . . Adv. Vigil. 5." At least Goelzer has the grace to dedicate much of his preface to acknowledging his debt to Paucker!

74 The two exceptions are Veronensis and Ambrose's commentary on Luke (to which, as has been remarked in n. 67, Jerome was hardly very partial, and which almost certainly came out six years after Jerome published his version of the Gospels). The presentation of the relationship between the Old Latin versions and the Vulgate in regard to the Synoptic accounts of this incident has been simplified for purposes of economical exposition, and should be checked with Appendix E. It should be stressed that the purpose of this study is not to assert the unique and consciously individual style of Jerome; far from it. The chief significance of the Vulgate to Jerome's and subsequent generations is the fact that it brought internally consistent order to the scattered and often contradictory diversity of the Old Latin biblical texts. It could hardly have gained its ultimate victory over those texts if its characteristic usages had been entirely at variance with theirs.

75 Cf. Apoc. 5:9, 13:7, and 17:15, among which the formula φυλή καὶ γλῶσσα καὶ λαὸς καὶ ἔθνος varies only slightly. The Old Latin renderings are quite unimaginatively forthright and literal, with the exception of Cyprian's version of 17:15: "aquae, quas vidisti, super quas sedet meretrix illa, populi et turbae et gentes ethnicorum sunt et linguae." Not only does this wording seem to present an interesting interpretation of the always slippery term *gentes,* it represents one of the few instances in which the old African version is closer to the Greek *textus receptus* than the Vulgate is; the fourth-century European recension represented by *gig* is closest of all:

Gk. Text. Receptus	Cyprian	Gigas	Vulgate
καὶ λέγει μοι·	—	Et ait mihi:	et dixit mihi:
τὰ ὕδατα ἅ εἶδες,	aquae, quas vidisti	Aquae quas uidisti,	Aquas quas vidisti
οὗ ἡ πόρνη	super quas sedet	ubi sedet	ubi meretrix
κάθηται,	meretrix illa,	meretrix	sedet,
λαοὶ καὶ ὄχλοι	populi et turbae	populi sunt	populi sunt,
εἰσὶν	et gentes	et turbae	et gentes
καὶ ἔθνη	ethnicorum sunt	et gentes	
καὶ γλῶσσαι.	et linguae.	et linguae.	et linguae.

Atypical in regard to textual lineage, this verse is a fairly good example of the stylistic relationships among these four major versions of the New Testament circulating in the urban centers of the West when Rome (still the *meretrix* in some eyes) was sacked by Alaric's Visigoths.

Chapter 4

1   André Piganiol, *L'Empire chrétien, 325–395*, pp. 411–22.

2   One useful and accessible introduction to the immense bibliography on this aspect of the Investiture Controversy is available in Brian Tierney, *The Crisis of Church & State, 1050–1300*, pp. 9–10, 46–47, 56–57.

3   Most of the chief current positions on this issue have been perceptively noted in Theodor E. Mommsen's essay, "St. Augustine and the Christian Idea of Progress: the Background of the *City of God*," *Journal of the History of Ideas* 12 (1951):346–74; reprinted in Mommsen, *Medieval and Renaissance Studies*, ed. Eugene F. Rice, pp. 265–98. In Mommsen's own view, Augustine rejected the optimistic notions of Christian and Roman progress dear to Eusebius, Prudentius, and other spokesmen of the intellectual tendency which Jean Bayet and Gerhart Ladner (among others) have called the Constantinian-Theodosian Renaissance, as well as several less simplistic but comparable opinions of Orosius and Jerome. He proposed instead a more nuanced, temporally pessimistic explanation of the often paradoxical operation of providence in human affairs. This view would later be subjected to much caricaturing, but ultimately exert a decisive influence on Western thought. (See also Mommsen's "Orosius and Augustine" in *Medieval and Renaissance Studies*, pp. 325–48).

In *L'ambivalence du temps de l'histoire chez Saint Augustin* H.-I. Marrou argued that three attitudes toward the directional movement of history can be discerned in Augustine's works. Like many pagan thinkers of late antiquity as well as the deeply antisecular Fathers of the African Church, Augustine was keenly aware that much of the record of human experience was a dark *series huius calamitatis*, which might even be getting worse as time went on. On the other hand, Augustine was aware of "le progrès technique des connaissances, des institutions, et des industries humaines" (p. 28). This awareness remained unsystematic, however, and was never confused in Augustine's mind with his adherence to the revealed Christian idea of the spiritual progress of mankind toward the second Parousia of the Lord, an evolution which he compared vividly to the spiritual advance of the individual man "qui ad populum Dei pertinet" (*CD* x, 14; cf. the end of Appendix A). A more abstract but reconcilable subsequent approach to the problem is ably represented by the article of Michele Sciacca, "Il concetto di storia in S. Agostino," *San Agustín, Estudios y coloquios* pp. 11–25. Denying as does Marrou any valid connection with the various optimistic "historicisms" promulgated by modern thinkers from Vico and Gentile through Kant, Hegel, and Marx, Sciacca sees Augustine nevertheless as the father of the most specifically modern conception of history (p. 11). By this Sciacca means the fundamental awareness that history operates in the realm of contingency, within the framework of a dialectic between time and eternity (and between the two loves of *The City of God*), through a progressive process to which creation and finality are always contemporaneous. Not that the reader will easily locate this "concept" in Augustine's treatment of "il tempo esteriore," in which history is understood, as for most of the classical tradition, "come erudizione, esempio, conoscenza utile di cose accadite, ecc." (p. 16). It is rather in Augustine's analysis of "il tempo interiore" —and primarily in the *Confessions* rather than *The City of God*—that his true "concept of history" (and hence of progress) emerges.

In collecting data primarily related to other questions, the present study has had occasion to discern: (a) a fairly steady awareness on Augustine's part of instances of *progrès technique,* which appear (b) in fairly close relation to the providentially managed, onward movement of the *populus Dei,* (c) which is the chief referent of a particularly striking organic metaphor which Augustine uses to express and elaborate the doctrine of collective spiritual progress. Might that evidence, seen in the light of those relationships, lead to a useful, systematically synthetic analysis of Augustine's thought on the notion of progress which we moderns find so congenial? I think that such an approach might be worth exploring. In view of Augustine's predilection for antithetical argument (see Marrou, *Saint Augustin et la fin de la culture antique,* pp. 80, 659, and Appendix A of this study, p. 132), it might be a doomed effort, but I offer the suggestion for what it is worth.

Bibliography

Primary Sources

BIBLICAL TEXTS

Belsheim, Johannes, ed. *Acta Apostolorum ante Hieronymum latine translata ex codice latino-graeco Laudiano Oxoniensi.* Forhandlinger i Videnskals-Selskabet i Christiania 19. Christiania, 1893.

————. *Die Apostelgeschichte und die Offenbarung Johannis, in einer alten lateinischen Uebersetzung aus dem "Gigas librorum" auf der königlichen Bibliothek zu Stockholm.* Christiania, 1879.

————. *Codex Colbertinus Parisiensis. Quatuor evangelia ante Hieronymum latine translata post editionem Petri Sabatier cum ipso codice collatam.* Christiania, 1888.

————. *Codex f² Corbeiensis, sive Quatuor Evangelia ante Hieronymum latine translata.* Christiania, 1887.

————. *Codex Vercellensis. Quatuor evangelia ante Hieronymum latine translata ex reliquiis codicis Vercellensis . . . et ex editione Iriciana principe.* Christiania, 1894.

————. *Codex Veronensis: Quattuor evangelia ante Hieronymum latine translata.* Prague: Grégr, 1904.

————. *Codex Vindobonensis . . . antiquissimae Evangeliorum Lucae et Marci translationis latinae fragmenta.* Leipzig, 1885.

————. *Evangelium Palatinum. Reliquias IV evangeliorum ante Hieronymum latine translatorum, . . ex codice Palatino purpureo Vindobonensi . . . et ex editione Tischendorfiana principe.* Christiania, 1896.

Beuron, Archabbey of. *Vetus Latina: Die Reste der altlateinischen Bibel nach Petrus Sabatier neu gesammelt und herausgegeben.* Vol. 2, *Genesis.* Edited by Bonifatius Fischer. Freiburg-im-Breisgau: Herder, 1951–54.

Buchanan, E. S., ed. *The Four Gospels from the Codex Corbeiensis, . . together with fragments of the Catholic Epistles, of the Acts and of the Apocalypse from the Fleury Palimpsest.* Old-Latin Biblical Texts 5. Oxford: Oxford University Press, 1907.

———. *The Four Gospels from the Codex Veronensis (b).* Old-Latin Biblical Texts 6. Oxford: Oxford University Press, 1911.

Clark, Albert C., ed. *The Acts of the Apostles, a critical edition, with introduction and notes.* Oxford: Oxford University Press, 1933.

Coleman, A. M., ed. *The Biblical Text of Lucifer of Cagliari (Acts).* Welwyn, Herts.: Lawrence, 1927.

Confraternity of Christian Doctrine, Episcopal Committee, tr. *The New Testament . . . translated from the Latin Vulgate.* Paterson, N.J.: Guild, 1947.

———. *The Old Testament.* Notes by Joseph A. Grispino. New York: Guild, 1965.

Corssen, Peter, ed. *Der Cyprianische Text der Acta apostolorum.* Berlin, 1892.

Fisch, S., ed. *Midrash Haggadol on the Pentateuch: Numbers.* Manchester, 1940.

Gasquet, A., genl. ed. *Biblia Sacra iuxta latinam vulgatam versionem ad codicum fidem.* Vol. 1, *Genesis,* edited by H. Quentin, Rome, 1926. Vol. 2, *Exodus & Leviticus,* edited by H. Quentin, Rome, 1929. Vol. 3, *Numeri & Deuteronomium,* edited by H. Quentin and others, Rome: S. Gerolamo, 1936.

Gramatica, Aloisius, ed. *Bibliorum Sacrorum iuxta vulgatam Clementinam nova editio.* Rome: Tipografia poliglotta Vaticana, 1951.

Kasher, Menahem, ed. *Genesis,* vol. 2 of *Torah Shelemah, Talmudic-Midrashic Interpretation of the Pentateuch.* New York: A.B.E.S., 1951.

Kittel, R., ed. *Biblia Hebraica.* 2 vols. 3d ed. Stuttgart: Priv. Württ. Bibelanstalt, 1929–35.

Margulies, Mordecai, ed. *Midrash Haggadol on the Pentateuch.* Vol. 1, *Genesis.* Jerusalem: Kook, 1947.

Rahlfs, Alfred, ed. *Septuaginta, id est, Vetus Testamentum graece iuxta LXX interpretes.* 2 vols. 6th ed. Stuttgart: Priv. Württ. Bibelanstalt, n.d.

Robert, Ulysse, ed. *Heptateuchi partis posterioris versio latina antiquissima, e codice Lugdunensi.* Lyons: Rey, 1900.

———. *Pentateuchi versio latina antiquissima, e codice Lugdunensi.* Paris, 1881.

Ropes, James Hardy. *The Text of Acts.* Vol. 3 of pt. 1 (*The Acts of the Apostles*) of *The Beginnings of Christianity,* edited by F. J. Foakes Jackson and Kirsopp Lake. London: Macmillan, 1926.

Sabatier, Pierre, ed. *Bibliorum Sacrorum latinae versiones antiquae, seu Vetus Italica.* 3 vols. Paris, 1743–51.

Ste.-Marie, Henri de, ed. *S. Hieronymi Psalterium. iuxta Hebraeos.* Rome: S. Gerolamo, 1954.

Scrivener, Frederick, ed. *Bezae Codex Cantabrigiensis.* Cambridge, 1864.

Soden, Hans von, ed. *Das lateinische Neue Testament in Afrika zur Zeit Cyprians.* Texte und Untersuchungen zur Geschichte der altchristlichen Literatur, vol. 33. Leipzig: Hinrichs, 1909.

חמשה חומשי תורה: (*Chamishah Chumshey: Torah*). New York: Schulsinger, 1951.

Vogels, Heinrich Josef, ed. *Evangelium Colbertinum.* Vol. 1, *Text.* Bonner Biblische Beiträge, no. 4. Bonn: Hanstein, 1953.

————. *Evangelium Palatinum: Studien zur ältesten Geschichte der lateinischen Evangelienübersetzung.* Münster-i-W.: Aschendorff, 1926.

————. *Vulgatastudien, die Evangelien der Vulgata untersucht auf ihre lateinische und griechische Vorlage.* Münster-i-W.: Aschendorff, 1928.

Weber, Robert, ed. *Le Psautier Romain et les autres anciens psautiers latins.* Rome: S. Gerolamo, 1953.

Wordsworth, John, Sanday, W., and White, H. J., eds. *Portions of the Gospels according to St. Mark and St. Matthew from the Bobbio Ms.* (*k*). Old-Latin Biblical Texts 2. Oxford, 1886.

Wordsworth, John, and White, Henry Julian, eds. *Nouum Testamentum Domini Nostri Iesu Christi latine, secundum editionem Sancti Hieronymi.* 3 vols. Oxford: Oxford University Press, 1889–1954.

PATRISTIC AUTHORS

Augustine. *Sancti Aurelii Augustini, Hipponensis episcopi, opera omnia.* Edited by Benedictine monks of the congregation of St. Maur. 11 vols. 2d ed. Paris, 1836–39. Cited herein as *SAOO.*

————. *Sancti Aurelii Augustini . . . opera omnia.* The Maurist edition, reprinted. *Patrologiae Cursus Completus* (or *Patrologia Latina*). General editor J.-P. Migne. Vols. 32–47. Paris, 1841–45. Cited herein as Migne.

————. Bibliothèque Augustinienne.*Oeuvres de Saint Augustin.* Edited, translated, with introductions and notes by various authors. 71 vols. projected. Paris-Brussels, 1947–. Cited herein as *BA.*

————. *De Beata Vita: SAOO* 1, cols. 497–520; Migne 32, cols. 959–76.

———. *De Catechizandis Rudibus: SAOO* 6, cols. 449–496; Migne 40, cols. 309–48.

———. *De Civitate Dei: SAOO* 7; Migne 41; *CCSL,* vols. 47, 48 (Turnhout, 1955); *BA* vols. 33–37, edited by Gustave Bardy and others, translated by Gustave Combès and others, Paris, 1960.

———. *Confessiones: SAOO* 1, cols. 133–410; Migne 32, cols. 659–868.

———. *De Consensu Evangelistarum: SAOO* 3, cols. 1243–1486; Migne 34, cols. 1041–1230.

———. *Contra Academicos: SAOO* 1, cols. 421–90; Migne 32, cols. 905–58.

———. *De Diversis Quaestionibus: SAOO* 6, cols. 25–138; Migne 40, cols. 11–100.

———. *De Doctrina Christiana: SAOO* 3, cols. 13–152; Migne 34, cols. 15–122; *BA* 11; 181–544.

———. *Enarrationes in Psalmos: SAOO* 4; Migne 36, 37.

———. *Enchiridion ad Laurentium, sive de fide, spe, et charitate: SAOO* 6, cols. 341–410; Migne 40, cols. 231–90.

———. *Epistolae: SAOO* 2; Migne 33.

———. *De Genesi contra Manichaeos: SAOO* 1, cols. 1045–1106; Migne 34, cols. 173–220.

———. *In Ioannis Evangelium Tractatus: SAOO* 3, cols. 1677–2474; Migne 35, cols. 1379–1976.

———. *De Libero Arbitrio: SAOO* 1, cols. 929–1040; Migne 32, cols. 1221–1310; *BA* 6; 125–474.

———. *De Moribus Ecclesiae Catholicae: SAOO* 1, cols. 1115–56; Migne 32, cols. 1309–44.

———. *De Ordine: SAOO* 1, cols. 529–86; Migne 32, cols. 977–1020; *BA* 4: 303–462.

———. *Retractationes: SAOO* 1, cols. 21–122, and in sections with the relevant works; Migne 32, cols. 583–656.

———. *Sermones ad populum: SAOO* 5; Migne 38, 39.

———. *De Urbis Excidio Sermo: SAOO* 6, cols. 1045–54; Migne 40, cols. 715–24; *CCSL* 46 (Turnhout, 1969), pp. 242–62.

———. *De Vera Religione: SAOO* 1, cols. 1207–68; Migne 34, cols. 121–72.

———. *Sancti Augustini Sermones post Maurinos reperti.* Edited by Germain Morin. *MA* 1. Rome: Tipografia poliglotta Vaticana, 1930.

———. *Sancti Aureli Augustini Tractatus siue Sermones inediti, ex codice Guelferbytano 4096.* Edited by Germain Morin. Mons: Koesel, 1917.

———. *The City of God*. Translated by Marcus Dods. 2 vols. 9th ed. Edinburgh, 1949.

———. *The City of God*. Translated and with an introduction by George E. McCracken. 7 vols. The Loeb Classical Library. Cambridge, Mass.: Harvard University Press, 1957.

———. *The Confessions of St. Augustine*. Translated by Vernon J. Bourke. The Fathers of the Church, vol. 21. New York, 1953.

———. Cyrille Lambot, "Lettre inédite de s. Augustin rélative au *De civitate Dei*." *Revue bénédictine* 51 (1939): 109-21.

Pseudo-Augustine (Quodvultdeus of Carthage?). *De Tempore Barbarico Sermo: SAOO* 6, cols. 1019-30.

Cicero. M. *Tulli Ciceronis Laelius de amicitia dialogus*. Edited by Morris Seyffert. 2d. ed. Leipzig, 1876.

———. *De Re Publica*. Edited by K. Ziegler. 3d ed. Leipzig, 1955.

Corpus Iuris Civilis. Edited by Paul Krueger and Theodor Mommsen. 2 vols. 2d ed. Berlin, 1878-80.

Eusebius of Caesarea. *Histoire ecclésiastique*. Greek text, with translation and notes by Gustave Bardy. 4 vols. Paris: Editions du Cerf, 1952.

Hilary of Poitiers. *S. Hilarii episcopi Pictauensis Tractatus super Psalmos*. Edited by Anton Zingerle. *CSEL*, vol. 22. Vienna, 1891.

Isidore of Seville. *Sancti Isidori, Hispalensis episcopi, opera omnia*. Edited by Faustino Arévalo. Rome, 1797. Reprinted in Migne, vols. 81-84. Paris, 1850.

———. *Differentiae, sive de proprietate sermonum:* Migne 83, cols. 9-98.

———. *De Ecclesiasticis Officiis:* Migne 83, cols. 737-826.

———. *Etymologiae:* Migne, vol. 82.

———. *Isidori, Hispalensis episcopi, Etymologiae sive Origines*. Edited by W. M. Lindsay. 2 vols. Oxford: Oxford University Press, 1911.

Jerome. *S. Hieronymi Presbyteri opera*. Pt. 1, vol. 4: *Commentarii in Hiezechielem*. Edited by F. Glorie. *CCSL*, vol. 75. Turnhout: Brepols, 1964.

———. *Sancti Eusebii Hieronymi Epistulae*. Edited by Isidor Hilberg. 3 vols. *CSEL*, vols. 54-56. Vienna: Tempsky, 1910-18.

———. *SS. Eusebii Hieronymi et Aurelii Augustini Epistulae mutuae*. Edited by Josef Schmid. Florilegium Patristicum, fasc. 22. Bonn: Hanstein, 1930.

———. *Interpretatio libri Didymi de Spiritu sancto: Praefatio ad Paulinianum*. Migne 23, cols. 107-10.

———. *De Viris Illustribus*. Edited by E. C. Richardson. Texte und

Untersuchungen zur Geschichte der altchristlichen Literatur 14:ix–56. Leipzig, 1896.

———. *De Viris Illustribus.* Edited by Stanislaus von Sychowski in *Hieronymus als Litterarhistoriker.* Münster-i-W., 1894.

———. *Saint Jérôme: Lettres.* Translated by J. Labourt. 8 vols. Paris: Belles Lettres, 1949–64.

———. *The Letters of Saint Jerome.* Translated by Charles C. Mierow. Introduction and notes by Thomas C. Lawler. One vol. to date. Ancient Christian Writers, vol. 33. Westminster, Md.: Newman, 1963.

———. *Select Letters of St. Jerome.* Translated by F. A. Wright. Loeb Classical Library. London–New York: Harvard University Press, 1933.

Juvencus. *Gai Vetti Aquilini Iuuenci Euangeliorum libri quattuor.* Edited by Johann Huemer. *CSEL,* vol. 24. Vienna, 1891.

Possidius. *Sancti Augustini Vita.* Edited, translated, and with notes by Herbert T. Weiskotten. Princeton: Princeton University Press, 1919.

Secondary Sources

Adams, Jeremy. "The Political Grammar of Isidore of Seville." *Actes du quatrième Congrès International de la Philosophie Médiévale,* Montreal, Aug.–Sept. 1967: *Arts libéraux et philosophie au moyen âge.* Montreal–Paris: Vrin, 1969, pp. 763–75.

Alfaric, Prosper. *L'évolution intellectuelle de Saint Augustin (Du Manichéisme au Néoplatonisme).* Paris: Nourry, 1918.

Altaner, Berthold. *Patrology.* Translated by Hilda Graef. New York: Herder, 1960.

Andresen, Carl, ed. *Bibliographia Augustiniana.* Darmstadt: Wissenschaftliche Buchgesellschaft, 1962.

Angus, S. *The Sources of the First Ten Books of Augustine's "De Civitate Dei."* Princeton: Princeton University Press, 1906.

Arbesmann, Rudolph, "The Idea of Rome in the Sermons of St. Augustine." *Augustiniana* (special issue for Nov. 1954) (separate publication of vol. 4, fasc. 3–4, pp. 221–542): 89–108.

Arndt, W. F., and Gingrich, F. W. *A Greek-English Lexicon of the New Testament.* 4th ed. Chicago: University of Chicago Press, 1952.

Arquillière, H.-X. *L'augustinisme politique.* 2d ed. Paris: Vrin, 1955.

———. "L'essence de l'augustinisme politique," *AM* pp. 991–1002.

Auerbach, Erich. *Literary Language and Its Public in Late Latin Antiquity and in the Middle Ages.* Translated by Ralph Manheim. Bollingen Series, vol. 74. New York: Pantheon, 1965.

Augustinus Magister. Congrès International Augustinien, 21–24 September 1954: Communications. Etudes Augustiniennes. Paris, 1954.

Bardy, Gustave. *Saint Augustin, l'homme et l'oeuvre.* Bibliothèque Augustinienne. 7th ed. Paris, 1948.

———. "St. Jérôme et ses maîtres hébreux." *Revue bénédictine* 46 (1934): 145–64.

Bardy, Gustave; Thonnard, F.-J; and others. Introduction and notes to *De Civitate Dei,* books xv–xxii. *BA,* vols. 36–37. Paris, 1960.

Bayet, Jean. *Histoire politique et psychologique de la religion romaine.* 2d ed. Paris: Payot, 1969.

Baynes, Norman H. *The Political Ideas of St. Augustine's "De Civitate Dei."* Historical Association Pamphlet no. 104. London: Bell, 1936. Reprinted in *Byzantine Studies and Other Essays,* London: Univ. of London, 1955, pp. 288–306.

Becker, Hans. *Augustin: Studien zu seiner geistigen Entwicklung.* Leipzig: Hinrichs, 1908.

Bellissima, Giuseppina. "Sant'Agostino grammatico." *AM* pp. 35–42.

Berlinger, Rudolph. *Augustins dialogische Metaphysik.* Frankfurt-am-Main:Klostermann, 1962.

Blumenkranz, Bernhard. "Augustin et les juifs; Augustin et le judaisme." *Recherches Augustiniennes* 1 (1958): 225–41.

———. *Juifs et Chrétiens dans le monde occidental, 430–1096.* Paris: Mouton, 1960.

Bonner, Gerald. *St. Augustine of Hippo, Life and Controversies.* The Library of History and Doctrine. London: Westminster Press, 1963.

Brezzi, Paolo. *Analisi ed interpretazione del "De Civitate Dei" di sant'Agostino.* Quaderni della Cattedra Agostiniana, 2. Tolentino: Edizioni agostiniane, 1960.

Brown, Peter R. L. *Augustine of Hippo: a Biography.* Berkeley and Los Angeles: University of California Press, 1967.

Büchler, Adolf. *Der galiläische 'Am-ha 'Ares des zweiten Jahrhunderts.* Vienna: Holder, 1906.

Bulic, Francesco, "Stridone luogo natale di S. Girolamo." *Miscellanea Geronimiana,* pp. 253–330.

Campenhausen, Hans von. *The Fathers of the Latin Church.* Translated by M. Hoffmann. London: Black, 1964.

Capelle, Paul. *Le texte du psautier latin en Afrique.* Collectanea Biblica Latina, vol. 4. Rome: Pustet, 1913.

Carlyle, A. J. *A History of Mediaeval Political Theory in the West.* Vol. 1, *The Second Century to the Ninth.* 2d ed. Edinburgh–London: Blackwood, 1927.

———. "St. Augustine and the City of God." *The Social and Political*

Ideas of Some Great Mediaeval Thinkers, edited by F. J. C. Hearnshaw. London: Harrap, 1928, pp. 34–52.

Cavallera, Ferdinand. "Les 'Quaestiones hebraicae in Genesim' de saint Jérôme et les 'Quaestiones in Genesim' de saint Augustin." *MA* 2: 359–72.

——. *Saint Jérôme, sa vie et son oeuvre.* Pt. 1, 2 vols. Spicilegium sacrum Lovaniense. Louvain: Champion, 1922.

——. *Le schisme d'Antioche (IVe–Ve siècle).* Paris: Picard, 1905.

Chevalier, Irénée. *S. Augustin et la pensée grecque: Les relations trinitaires.* Iubilaria Friburgensia, 1889–1939: Collectanea Friburgensia, fasc. 33 (n.s. 24). Fribourg-en-Suisse, 1940.

Cochrane, Charles Norris. *Christianity and Classical Culture: A Study of Thought and Action from Augustus to Augustine.* New York: Oxford University Press, 1944 (2d ed., 1957).

Colbert, Mary Columkille. *The Syntax of the De Civitate Dei of St. Augustine.* Patristic Studies, vol. 4. Washington, D.C.: Catholic University of America Press, 1923.

Combès, Gustave. *La doctrine politique de Saint Augustin.* Paris: Plon, 1927.

Combès, Gustave, and Farges, J. Translation, introduction, and notes to *De Doctrina Christiana. BA,* 11:151–596. Paris, 1949.

Condamin, Albert. "Un procédé littéraire de St. Jérôme dans sa traduction de la Bible." *Miscellanea Geronimiana,* pp. 89–96.

Cotta, Sergio, *La città politica di sant'Agostino.* Milan: Comunità, 1960.

Cottineau, L. H. "Chronologie des versions bibliques de St. Jérôme." *Miscellanea Geronimiana,* pp. 43–68.

Courcelle, Pierre. *Les lettres grecques en Occident, de Macrobe à Cassiodore.* Bibliothèque des Ecoles Françaises d'Athènes et de Rome, fasc. 159. Paris: de Boccard, 1948.

——. "Litiges sur la lecture des 'Libri Platonicorum' par saint Augustin." *Augustiniana* (special issue for Nov. 1954) (separate publication of vol. 4, fasc. 3–4, pp. 221–542), pp. 9–23.

Courtois, Christian. *Les Vandales et l'Afrique.* Paris: Arts & métiers graphiques, 1955.

Dawson, Christopher. "St. Augustine and His Age." *A Monument to Saint Augustine.* London: Sheed & Ward, 1930, pp. 11–78.

Deane, Herbert A. *The Political and Social Ideas of St. Augustine.* New York: Columbia University Press, 1963.

De Bruyne, Donatien. "Saint Augustin reviseur de la Bible." *MA* 2: 521–606.

Demougeot, Emilienne. *De l'unité à la division de l'Empire romain, 395–410: Essai sur le gouvernement impérial.* Paris: Adrien-Maisonneuve, 1951.

Diesner, Hans-Joachim. *Studien zur Gesellschaftslehre und sozialen Haltung Augustins.* Halle: Niemeyer, 1954.

Duchesne, Louis-Marie-Olivier. *Histoire ancienne de l'Eglise,* vol. 3. Paris: Fontemoing, 1910.

Duchrow, Ulrich. *Sprachverständnis und biblisches Hören bei Augustin.* Tübingen: Mohr, 1965.

Empson, William. *The Structure of Complex Words.* Norfolk, Conn.: New Directions, 1951.

Ernout, A., and Meillet, A. *Dictionnaire étymologique de la langue latine.* 4th ed. Paris: Klincksieck, 1959–60.

Estal, Gabriel del, and Rosado, Juan José R. "Equivalencia de 'civitas' en el 'De Civitate Dei.'" *Estudios sobre la "Ciudad de Dios"* (*La Ciudad de Dios,* vol. 167), 2:367–454. El Escorial, 1954.

Figgis, John Neville. *The Political Aspects of S. Augustine's 'City of God.'* London: Longmans, 1921.

Finaert, Joseph. *L'évolution littéraire de Saint Augustin.* Collection d'Etudes Latines, 17. Paris: Belles Lettres, 1939.

———. *Saint Augustin rhéteur.* Paris: Belles Lettres, 1939.

Fischer, David Hackett. *Historians' Fallacies: Toward a Logic of Historical Thought.* New York: Harper & Row, 1970.

Gagé, Jean. "La *plebs* et le *populus* et leurs encadrements respectifs dans la Rome de la première moitié du Ve siècle avant J.-C." *Revue historique,* no. 493 (Jan.–Mar. 1970), pp. 5–30.

Gerosa, P. "S. Agostino e l'imperialismo romano." *MA* 2:976–1040.

Gesenius, Wilhelm. *Hebräisches und Aramäisches Handwörterbuch über das Alte Testament.* 17th ed., rev. Frantz Buhl. Leipzig: Vogel, 1915.

Gilson, Etienne. *Les métamorphoses de la Cité de Dieu.* Louvain–Paris: Vrin, 1952.

Goelzer, Henri. *Etude lexicographique et grammaticale de la latinité de Saint Jérôme.* Paris, 1884.

Grandgeorge, L. *Saint Augustin et le néo-platonisme.* Bibliothèque de l'Ecole des Hautes Etudes, Sciences Religieuses, vol. 8. Paris, 1896.

Grosser Historischer Weltatlas. Vol. 1, *Vorgeschichte und Altertum.* Edited by Hermann Bengtson and Vladimir Milojčić. 4th ed. Munich: Bayerischer Schulbuch Verlag, 1963.

Harnack, Adolf. *The Acts of the Apostles.* Translated by J. R. Wilkinson. New Testament Studies, vol. 3. New York–London: Putnam, 1909.

Hendrikx, Ephraem. "Platonisches und biblisches Denken bei Augustinus." *AM*, pp. 285–92.

Henry, Paul. *Plotin et l'Occident: Firmicus Maternus, Marius Victorinus, Saint Augustin et Macrobe.* Spicilegium sacrum Lovaniense, fasc. 15. Louvain: Champion, 1934.

Hohensee, H. *The Augustinian Concept of Authority.* Folia, supp. 2. New York: Paulist Press, 1954.

Horn, Carl-Victor von. *Beiträge zur Staatslehre St. Augustins nach "De Civitate Dei."* Breslau, 1934.

Jolivet, Regis. Translation, introduction, and notes to *De Ordine. BA* 4: 293–466.

Jülicher, Adolf. *Einleitung in das Neue Testament.* 6th ed. *Grundriss der Theologischen Wissenschaften,* pt. 3, vol. 1. Tübingen: Mohr, 1913.

———. "Kritische Analyse der lateinischen Übersetzungen der Apostelgeschichte." *Zeitschrift für die neutestamentliche Wissenschaft* 15 (1914): 168–88.

Kedar-Kopfstein, Benjamin. "Divergent Hebrew Readings in Jerome's Isaiah." *Textus* 4 (1964): 176–210.

Kittel, Gerhard, ed. *Theologisches Wörterbuch zum Neuen Testament.* 7 vols. to date. Stuttgart: Kohlhammer, 1933–1964.

Kunzelmann, A. "Die Chronologie der Sermones des hl. Augustinus," *MA* 2:417–520.

Ladner, Gerhart B. *The Idea of Reform; Its Impact on Christian Thought and Action in the Age of the Fathers.* Cambridge, Mass.: Harvard University Press, 1959.

Lagrange, Marie-Joseph. *Introduction à l'étude du Nouveau Testament.* Pt. 2, *Critique textuelle,* vol. 2, *La critique rationelle.* Paris: Gabalda, 1935.

Lambot, Cyrille, ed. *Sancti Aurelii Augustini Sermones selecti duodeviginti.* Stromata Patristica et Mediaevalia, 1. Utrecht-Brussels, 1950.

Lapeyre, G. G. "Saint Augustin et Carthage," *MA* 2:91–148.

Leclercq, Jean. *The Love of Learning and the Desire for God.* Translated by C. Misrahi. New York: Fordham University Press, 1961.

Liddell, H. G., and Scott, R. *A Greek-English Lexicon.* 2 vols. Rev. ed., H. S. Jones. Oxford: Oxford University Press, 1933.

Lisowsky, Gerhard. *Konkordanz zum hebräischen Alten Testament.* Stuttgart: Priv. Württ. Bibelanstalt, 1958.

Marrou, Henri-Irénée. *L'ambivalence du temps de l'histoire chez Saint Augustin.* Conférence Albert-le-Grand, 1950. Montreal–Paris: Vrin, 1950.

Marrou, Henri-Irénée. "La division en chapitres de *La Cité de Dieu*." *Mélanges Joseph de Ghellinck, S. J.* Gembloux: Duculot, 1951, 1:235–49.

———. *Saint Augustin et l'augustinisme.* Maîtres spirituels. Paris: Editions du Seuil, 1956.

———. *Saint Augustin et la fin de la culture antique.* 4th ed. Bibliothèque des Ecoles Françaises d'Athènes et de Rome, fasc. 145 and 145 *bis*. Paris: De Boccard, 1938, 1949.

Marshall, R. T. *Studies in the Political and Socio-Religious Terminology of the "De Civitate Dei."* Patristic Studies, vol. 86. Washington, D.C.: Catholic University of America Press, 1952.

Martínez Morán, Felipe. "El espiritu virgiliano en la 'Ciudad de Dios,' " *Estudios sobre la "Ciudad de Dios"* (*La Ciudad de Dios*, vol. 167), 1:433–58. El Escorial, 1954.

Mayr, Robert, ed. *Vocabularium Codicis Iustiniani.* Pt. 1, *Latina.* Prague: Česká Grafická Unic, 1923.

McIlwain, Charles Howard. *The Growth of Political Thought in the West, from the Greeks to the End of the Middle Ages.* New York: Macmillan, 1932.

McNamara, Marie Aquinas. *Friendship in St. Augustine.* Studia Friburgensia, n.s. 20. Fribourg-en-Suisse, 1958.

Merguet, Hugo. *Lexikon zu den philosophischen Schriften Cicero's,* vol. 3. Jena, 1894. Reprinted, Hildesheim: Olms, 1961.

———. *Lexikon zu den Reden des Cicero,* vol. 3. Jena, 1882.

Millar, Moorhouse F. X. "The Significance of St. Augustine's Criticism of Cicero's Definition of the State." *Philosophia Perennis,* edited by F.-J. von Rintelen. Vol. 1 (*Abhandlungen zu ihrer Vergangenheit und Gegenwart; Festgabe Josef Geyser*): 99–109. Regensburg: Habbel, 1930.

Miscellanea Agostiniana (cited herein as *MA*). Vol. 2, *Studi Agostiniani.* Rome: Tipografia poliglotta Vaticana, 1931.

Miscellanea Geronimiana. Introduction by Vincenzo Vannutelli. Rome: Tipografia poliglotta Vaticana, 1920.

Mohrmann, Christine. *Etudes sur le latin des chrétiens.* 2 vols. Vol. 1, Rome: Storia e letteratura, 1958. Vol. 2 (*Latin chrétien et médiéval*), Rome: Storia e letteratura, 1961.

Mohrmann, Christine, and Van der Meer, F. *Atlas of the Early Christian World.* Translated and edited by Mary F. Hedlund and H. H. Rowley. London: Nelson, 1958.

Mommsen, Theodor. *Römisches Staatsrecht.* 2 vols. Handbuch der römischen Altertümer, vol. 3 pts. 1 and 2. 3d ed. Leipzig, 1887–88. Photoprint, Graz: Akademische D.u.V., 1952.

Mommsen, Theodor E. *Medieval and Renaissance Studies,* edited by Eugene F. Rice. Ithaca, N.Y.: Cornell University Press, 1959.

———. "St. Augustine and the Christian Idea of Progress: The Background of the *City of God." Journal of the History of Ideas* 12 (1951): 346–74. Reprinted in *Medieval and Renaissance Studies,* pp. 265–98.

Noth, M. "Gott, König, Volk im Alten Testament." *Zeitschrift für Theologie und Kirche* 47 (1950): 157–91.

O'Meara, John J. "Augustine the Artist and the *Aeneid." Mélanges offerts à Mademoiselle Christine Mohrmann,* pp. 252–61. Utrecht–Antwerp: Spectrum, 1963.

———. *Charter of Christendom: The Significance of the "City of God."* Saint Augustine and the Augustinian Tradition, 1961 lecture. New York: Macmillan, 1961.

———. *Porphyry's Philosophy from Oracles in Augustine.* Etudes Augustiniennes. Paris, 1959.

———. *The Young Augustine.* London: Longmans, Green, 1954.

O'Reilly, Marie Vianney. *Sancti Aurelii Augustini De excidio urbis Romae: A Critical Text and Translation, with Introduction and Commentary.* Patristic Studies, vol. 89. Washington, D.C.: Catholic University of America Press, 1955.

Paucker, C. *De latinitate B. Hieronymi: observationes ad nominum verborumque usum pertinentes.* Berlin, 1888.

Pellegrino, Michele. *Le Confessioni di s. Agostino.* Rome: Studium, 1956.

———. "Osservazione sullo stile delle Lettere di S. Agostino," *Mélanges offerts à Mademoiselle Christine Mohrmann,* pp. 240–51. Utrecht–Antwerp: Spectrum, 1963.

Penna, Angelo. *Principi e carattere dell'esegesi di S. Gerolamo.* Scripta Pontificii Instituti Biblici, 102. Rome: Pontificio Istituto Biblico, 1950.

Pesce, Domenico. *Città terrena e città celeste nel pensiero antico: Platone, Cicerone, S. Agostino.* Biblioteca del Leonardo, 57. Florence: Sansoni, 1957.

Piganiol, André. *L'Empire chrétien, 325–395.* Vol. 4, pt. 2 of *Histoire romaine.* Paris: Presses Universitaires de France, 1947. In the series *Histoire générale,* ed. Gustave Glotz.

Pope, Hugh. *St. Augustine of Hippo.* Garden City, N.Y.: Doubleday, 1961.

Poschl, Viktor. "Augustinus und die römische Geschichtsauffassung." *AM,* pp. 957–63.

Rahmer, Moritz. *Die Hebräische Traditionen in den Werken des Hieronymus.* Breslau, 1861.

Ratzinger, Josef. "Herkunft und Sinn der *Civitas*-Lehre Augustins." *AM,* pp. 965–80.

———. *Volk und Haus Gottes in Augustins Lehre von der Kirche.* Münchener Theologische Studien, 2 (Systematische) Abteilung, vol. 7. Munich: Zink, 1954.

Regnier, A. *De la latinité des sermons de Saint Augustin.* Paris, 1886.

Reuschenbach, Felix. *Hieronymus als Übersetzer der Genesis,* pt. 1. Limburg: Lahn, 1948.

Rief, Josef. *Der Ordobegriff des jungen Augustinus.* Paderborn: Schöningh, 1962.

Roehrich, Albert. *Essai sur Saint Jérôme exégète.* Geneva, 1891.

Roger, Maurice. *L'enseignement des lettres classiques d'Ausone à Alcuin.* Paris: Picard, 1905.

Rollero, Piero. "L'influsso della *Expositio in Lucam* di Ambrogio nell'esegesi agostiniana." *AM,* pp. 211–20.

Romanelli, Pietro. *Storia delle province romane dell'Africa.* Studi pubblicati dall'Istituto Italiano per la Storia Antica, fasc. 14. Rome: L'Erma, 1959.

Rondet, H. "Essai sur la chronologie des 'Enarrationes in Psalmos' de St. Augustin." *Bulletin de littérature ecclésiastique* 61 (1960): 111–27 and 258–86; 65 (1964): 110–36; 68 (1967): 179–202.

Rönsch, Hermann. *Itala und Vulgata, das Sprachidiom der urchristlichen Itala und der katholischen Vulgata: unter Berücksichtigung der römischen Volkssprache.* Marburg-Leipzig, 1869.

Salin, Edgar. *Civitas Dei.* Tübingen: Mohr, 1926.

Schanz, Martin; Hosius, Carl; and Krüger, Gustav. *Geschichte der römischen Litteratur.* Vol. 4, *Die römische Litteratur von Constantin bis zum Gesetzgebungswerk Justinians,* pt. 2, "Die Litteratur des fünften und sechsten Jahrhunderts." Munich: Beck, 1920.

Schelkle, Karl Hermann. *Virgil in der Deutung Augustins.* Tübinger Beiträge zur Altertumswissenschaft, no. 32. Stuttgart–Berlin: Kohlhammer, 1939.

Schilling, Otto. *Die Staats- und Soziallehre des hl. Augustinus.* Freiburg-im-Breisgau: Herder, 1910.

Schmidt, Roderich. "Aetates Mundi: Die Weltalter als Gliederungsprinzip der Geschichte." *Zeitschrift für Kirchengeschichte* 67 (1955–56): 288–317.

Schmoller, Alfred. *Concordantiae Novi Testamenti Graeci.* Published with Nestle edition of *Novum Testamentum Graece.* Stuttgart: Privileg. Württ. Bibelanstalt, [1953].

Scholz, Heinrich. *Glaube und Unglaube in der Weltgeschichte: ein Kommentar zu Augustins "De Civitate Dei."* Leipzig: Hinrichs, 1911.

Schrijnen, Josef. *Charakteristik des altchristlichen Latein.* Latinitas Christianorum Primaeva, fasc. 1. Nijmegen, 1932.

Sciacca, Michele Federico. "Il concetto di storia in S. Agostino." *San Agustín, Estudios y coloquios,* pp. 11–25. Saragossa: Consejo Superior de Investigaciones Científicas, 1960.

———. *S. Agostino.* Vol. 1, *La vita e l'opera; l'itinerario della mente.* Brescia: Morcelliana, 1949.

———. *Saint Augustin et le Néoplatonisme.* Louvain–Paris: Pub. univ. de Louvain, 1956.

Scrivener, Frederick. *A Plain Introduction to the Criticism of the New Testament,* vol. 2. 4th ed., rev. Edward Miller. London, 1894.

Seyfarth, Wolfgang. *Soziale Fragen der spätrömischen Kaiserzeit im Spiegel des Theodosianus.* Deutsche Akademie der Wissenschaften zu Berlin, Schriften der Sektion für Altertumswissenschaft, 33. Berlin: Akademie–Verlag, 1963.

Soden, Hermann von. *Die Schriften des Neuen Testaments.* Vol. 1, *Untersuchungen,* pts. 2 and 3, "Die Textformen." 2d ed. Göttingen: Vandenhoeck & Ruprecht, 1911.

Stakemeier, Eduard. *Civitas Dei; Die Geschichtstheologie des heiligen Augustinus als Apologie der Kirche.* Paderborn: Schöningh, 1955.

Stegemann, Viktor. *Augustins Gottesstaat.* Heidelberger Abhandlungen zur Philosophie und ihrer Geschichte, no. 15. Tübingen: Mohr, 1928.

Steinmann, Jean. *Saint Jérôme.* Paris: Editions du Cerf, 1958.

Straub, Johannes. "Augustins Sorge um die *regeneratio imperii.*" *Historisches Jahrbuch* 73 (1954): 36–60.

Sutcliffe, E. F. "St. Jerome's Hebrew Manuscripts." *Biblica* 29 (1948): 112–25.

Testard, Maurice. *Saint Augustin et Cicéron.* 2 vols. Vol. 1, *Cicéron dans la formation et dans l'oeuvre de Saint Augustin;* vol. 2, *Répertoire des textes.* Etudes Augustiniennes. Paris, 1958.

Teutsch, Leo. *Das Städtewesen in Nordafrika, in der Zeit von C. Gracchus bis zum Tode des Kaisers Augustus.* Berlin: De Gruyter, 1962.

Thonnard, F. J. Translation, introduction, and notes to *De Libero Arbitrio. BA,* 6:125–474, 490–524. Paris, 1941.

Tierney, Brian. *The Crisis of Church & State, 1050–1300.* Englewood Cliffs, N.J.: Prentice-Hall, 1964.

Troeltsch, Ernst. *Augustin, die christliche Antike und das Mittelalter: Im Anschluss an die Schrift "De Civitate Dei."* Munich–Berlin: Oldenbourg, 1915.

Troeltsch, Ernst. *The Social Teaching of the Christian Churches,* vol.
    1. Translated by Olive Wyon. New York: Harper & Row, 1960.
Van der Meer, Frederik. *Augustine the Bishop.* Translated by Brian
    Battershaw and G. R. Lamb. London: Sheed & Ward, 1961.
Vaux, Roland de. *Ancient Israel: Its Life and Institutions.* Translated
    by John McHugh. New York: McGraw-Hill, 1961.
————. "Israel—People of God." *The Critic* 24, no. 1 (Aug.–Sept.
    1965): 57–63.
Verheijen, Melchior. *Eloquentia pedisequa: Observations sur le style
    des Confessions de saint Augustin.* Latinitas Christianorum Primaeva,
    10. Nijmegen: Dekker & van de Vegt, 1949.
Vogels, Heinrich. *Handbuch der Textkritik des Neuen Testaments.* 2d
    ed. Bonn: Hanstein, 1955.
Wikenhauser, Alfred. *New Testament Introduction.* Translated by
    Joseph Cunningham. Freiburg-im-Breisgau: Herder, 1958.
Willis, Geoffrey Grimshaw. *Saint Augustine and the Donatist Contro-
    versy.* London: S.P.C.K., 1950.
Wilmart, André. "La tradition des grands ouvrages de S. Augustin."
    MA, 2:257–316.
Ziegler, L. *Die lateinischen Bibelübersetzungen vor Hieronymus und
    die Itala des Augustins.* Munich, 1879.

Index

This index is intended to serve as a guide to the topical synthesization of this study's data, and as a selective (but not exhaustive) *index rerum, verborum, et locorum citatorum*. Page references to the notes are given only when the notes in question cite substantially some work, person, place, word, or topic not easily inferred from the main text.

Selective *Index Verborum*